Pipeline

To my friends Lula, Paolo, Gian, Souzy,
Jürgen, Raniero, Romano, Mario, Alberto, Italo,
Massimo, Sergio, Guido, Francesco,
Luciano, Franco, Christian, Yann, Nanni,
Félix, Sylvie and so many, many others

Pipeline

Letters from Prison

Antonio Negri

Translated by Ed Emery

polity

Copyright © Antonio Negri 2014

The right of Antonio Negri to be identified as Author of this Work has been asserted in accordance with the UK Copyright, Designs and Patents Act 1988.

First published in 2014 by Polity Press

Polity Press
65 Bridge Street
Cambridge CB2 1UR, UK

Polity Press
350 Main Street
Malden, MA 02148, USA

All rights reserved. Except for the quotation of short passages for the purpose of criticism and review, no part of this publication may be reproduced, stored in a retrieval system, or transmitted, in any form or by any means, electronic, mechanical, photocopying, recording or otherwise, without the prior permission of the publisher.

ISBN-13: 978-0-7456-5564-2
ISBN-13: 978-0-7456-5565-9 (pb)

A catalogue record for this book is available from the British Library.

Typeset in 10.5 on 12 pt Plantin by
Servis Filmsetting Ltd, Stockport, Cheshire
Printed and bound in the United Kingdom by
T.J. International Ltd, Padstow, Cornwall

The publisher has used its best endeavours to ensure that the URLs for external websites referred to in this book are correct and active at the time of going to press. However, the publisher has no responsibility for the websites and can make no guarantee that a site will remain live or that the content is or will remain appropriate.

Every effort has been made to trace all copyright holders, but if any have been inadvertently overlooked the publisher will be pleased to include any necessary credits in any subsequent reprint or edition.

For further information on Polity, visit our website: politybooks.com

Contents

Translator's Preface	xi
Introduction by Timothy S. Murphy	1
Letter One: The Dry Veneto	13
Letter Two: The Labour Movement	24
Letter Three: Souzy	34
Letter Four: *Admiratio*	44
Letter Five: Jürgen	56
Letter Six: Turin	67
Letter Seven: July 1960	76
Letter Eight: Piazza Statuto	87
Letter Nine: Autonomy	97
Letter Ten: New Year's Eve 1968	107
Letter Eleven: Golem 1968–70	118
Letter Twelve: *Civill Warre*	129
Letter Thirteen: Separation	141
Letter Fourteen: A Leap of Joy	152
Letter Fifteen: Carnival	162
Letter Sixteen: 1977 as a Turning Point	173
Letter Seventeen: Manhattan	183
Letter Eighteen: Moro	193
Letter Nineteen: Ferocious Alphabets	203
Letter Twenty: Renaissance	213
Index	223

The 'remembrance' is complementary to the 'lived experience'. In it is deposited the growing self-alienation of man, who catalogues his past like a dead possession . . . the relic derives from the corpse, the 'remembrance' from the dead experience, which is defined euphemistically as 'lived experience'.

Walter Benjamin

An image is an idea through which the mind considers a thing as being present; however it indicates more the present state of the human body, rather than the nature of the external thing.

Baruch Spinoza

Pygmalion himself would not succeed in making his work believe that it possessed a life, despite all his efforts; it is only when he puts down his sculptor's chisel and falls to his knees like a poor man that divinity descends upon him.

Franz Rosenzweig

Desire, which arises out of Reason, cannot have excess.

Baruch Spinoza

The dates of these letters (10 October 1981 to 7 April 1982) and the place (a special section of Rebibbia prison) are real. The text contains political and literary references and references to everyday life which are to be understood in this framework and in this time. The existence or nonexistence of references does not change the fact that the genre is one of imagination.

Translator's Preface

The letters in this book were composed in prison, under trying circumstances. The text is very dense – 'shorthand' and 'baroque', as Negri himself admits; take for example the phrase *lo stuzzichino è giapponese* in Letter 19, translated here 'Like Japanese soldiers from a war long since over.' I have paraphrased where necessary and have kept explanatory notes to a minimum.

The editorial process of writing this book was somewhat unusual. As Negri explained in an interview that I did with him in 2013, in Rebibbia there were four of them in the cell – Negri, Franco Tommei, and two other comrades (varying according to the vagaries of prisoners being moved between cells). Negri would write the text by hand, to provide the basic manuscript; Tommei would then type the text on a manual typewriter, chapter by chapter; and then it would be sent to the outside world.

Inevitably there were scribal errors – some we have discovered only today, others perhaps will never be discovered – but the book was eventually completed for publication. It emerged wreathed in tobacco smoke. As the author recalls: 'In the cells we were all of us smokers. We smoked all the time. That was what destroyed my lungs, with the effects that I feel today.'

In accordance with my previous practice, in places where the sense suggests the French contrast between *pouvoir* and *puissance*, I have translated *potere* as 'Power' (capitalised) and have generally rendered *potenza* as *potenza*, occasionally opting for 'potentiality' where that helps the meaning.

Special thanks to Manuela Tecusan (Cambridge) and Tim Murphy (Oklahoma) for help with sourcing citations. Many of the citations were unsourced in the original letters, often taken from books that arrived in Negri's cell more or less by happenstance. As the author explains: 'The Hofmannsthal play. Which one was it? Maybe it was *Elektra*. How do you expect me to remember? This was thirty years ago, and I was in prison, and I don't have the manuscript. You can tell them that in the preface.'

Cambridge, 5.viii.2014

Introduction

Timothy S. Murphy

In order to understand what value Antonio Negri's *Pipeline* has today, the reader needs to understand the significance of the book's original appearance, its place in his critical development. This book was first published in Italy by Giulio Einaudi in 1983, under the title *Pipe-Line: Lettere da Rebibbia* (*Pipeline: Letters from Rebibbia*). Rebibbia will be explained shortly, but first things first: why '*Pipeline*'? The term appears several times in the text, perhaps most notably in the concluding lines of the fourth letter: 'There is energy in what I am expressing. But is my writing up to it? Energy – flow – a gas pipeline – an oil pipeline – a pipeline – it is moving forward, but it's filthy' (Letter Four, p. 54). But *Pipeline* is more than an industrial or hydrodynamic metaphor, as the opening lines of the twentieth letter reveal: 'These conversations that I'm having with myself are elemental, even in the strong sense – rather than having the fragmented rhythm of philosophy, they are more like music in their flowingness. Pipeline' (Letter Twenty, p. 213). This emergent complexity is no more than what Negri had promised in the second paragraph of the first letter: 'A real flow. Pipeline' (Letter One, p. 14). Negri intends his letters to act as a conduit, then, not only between himself and his reader but between individual and collective, between autobiography and art, between philosophy and militancy, between past and future, and between Italy and the world.

Today Negri is well known around the world as a provocative theorist of capitalist globalisation and of the novel forms of resistance that the phenomenon has inspired. His books written in collaboration with Michael Hardt – *Empire, Multitude, Commonwealth* and *Declaration* – have been translated into dozens of languages and their concepts and strategies have been taken up, both for prolonged debate and for immediate use, by subversive movements in many nations. At the time these letters were written, in the early eighties, Negri was already prominent and controversial in Italy for his organising activities in workplaces and as a radical political theorist to the left of both the Communist and the Socialist Party. As he explains at the start of the sixth letter, he became actively involved in Italian left politics upon completing his formal education at home and abroad in 1959. As a professor of the philosophy of law at the University of Padua's Institute for Political Science, he was uniquely well situated to construct links between the students, who became increasingly politically active as the sixties progressed, and the industrial workers of the Veneto, who were losing patience with their political representatives in the left-wing parties. By working with his colleagues to create situations in which those groups could come together, Negri helped to cross-pollinate a counterculture that would be unmatched by any other for size, inventiveness and dedication to practical militancy. These letters tell the story of that counterculture as much as they tell Negri's own story.

Along with colleagues from the university and comrades from the factories, Negri co-founded the radical group Workers' Power (Potere Operaio, Potop) in 1969, in the hope of consolidating the many local victories that workers were winning throughout Italy despite opposition from their own unions and from the left parties that claimed to speak for them. Potop openly organised wildcat strikes, work slowdowns, occupations and workers' seminars in defiance of the unions. At the dawn of the seventies, the Italian radical movements diversified as feminists, unemployed, gays and lesbians, and other subjects ignored by the existing political party structure began to make demands as aggressive as those of the students and factory workers. Their challenges to the exclusionary composition of Workers' Power led Negri and his comrades to dissolve the group and begin constituting a more open-ended organisation, or rather a network of organisations, which came to be called Workers' Autonomy (Autonomia Operaia). In most western nations the radical rupture of 'politics as usual' that defined 1968 was soon absorbed back into conventional political structures; but in Italy it persisted for another decade, taking on increasingly dramatic and outrageous forms that ranged from the wildly theatrical Metropolitan Indians to the underground cells of the Red Brigades and Armed Proletarian Nuclei. At the height of the movements in 1977–8, millions of Italians of all ages were involved to some degree in organised dissent, and the state was increasingly unable to preserve the kind of order required for capitalist management of the economy. It was a pivotal time of widespread social instability, when small events could have gigantic ramifications. At that moment the Red Brigades kidnapped former Italian Prime Minister Aldo Moro and, after holding him for weeks and subjecting him to a 'people's trial' for the crime of trying to build an alliance between the centre-right Christian Democratic Party and the Italian Communist Party, murdered him. Their overall aim was to shatter the Italian state's legitimacy and cause it to collapse, whereupon some version of the 'dictatorship of the proletariat' could take charge.[1] Unsurprisingly, this did not happen; on the contrary, Moro's murder heightened public fears of the more chaotic aspects of the radical movements and gave the state the support it needed to finally strike back at them. One of the first such strikes was launched against Negri on 7 April 1979, when he and a number of his colleagues were arrested on charges of involvement in Moro's kidnapping and murder and of 'armed insurrection against the powers of the state' (see Letter Nineteen, p. 204).

Pipeline was written while Negri was incarcerated in Rebibbia Prison, a penal complex consisting of three separate men's facilities and one women's facility, which was built in the northeast quarter of Rome in 1972. Negri was held there for several years pending trial, originally on the Moro and armed insurrection charges; by the time this book was written, however, the Moro charges had been dropped and replaced by a continually mutating set of accusations involving terrorism. The sole purpose of these accusations was to allow the Italian state to lock him up for as long as possible *before* trial. In addition to the crimes listed above, Negri was accused of being the mastermind behind not only Workers' Power but also the clandestine terrorist organisation of the Red Brigades, with which he had never been involved and which he had regularly criticised and denounced in his writings and speeches over many years. As a result of the many warrants issued in other jurisdictions following his original arrest, he had been held at other prisons too before being brought to Rebibbia: Rovigo (outside Padua), Fossombrone (east of Florence), Palmi (northeast of Messina at the southern tip of Italy) and Trani (on the Adriatic coast in Puglia). Negri describes the different atmospheres of those prisons in the opening paragraphs of the nineteenth letter (p. 204). By mid-1981 his transfers from prison to prison had come to an end and he remained in Rome, incarcerated under terrorism and armed insurrection charges until his release from prison in late June 1983. The release came as a result of his election to the Chamber of Deputies, the lower house in the Italian parliament.

Although *Pipeline* was published in February 1983, the letters that comprise it were composed between 10 October 1981 and 7 April 1982, during Negri's third year in custody, as he awaited trial. In his first year of imprisonment he had managed to write his influential study of Spinoza, *The Savage Anomaly*, despite the constant interruptions of interrogations, preliminary court hearings, meetings with legal counsel, and transfers from one high-security prison to another; indeed at the conclusion to that book's preface he insists: 'I do not believe that prison has given a different quality, either better or worse', to *Savage Anomaly* than freedom had to his earlier works. He concludes the preface with the hope that 'the solitude of this damned cell has proved as fertile as the Spinozan solitude of the optical laboratory', and signs it 'From the prisons of Rovigo, Rebibbia, Fossombrone, Palmi and Trani: April 7, 1979 to April 7, 1980'.[2] Part of the reason why Negri was able to write not only *The Savage Anomaly* but also many other, shorter texts while imprisoned was the fact that, although confined, he was not wholly isolated in prison. 7 April 1979 marks not only the date of Negri's arrest but also the start of a vast effort on the part of the Italian state to criminalise the radical movements, including Workers' Power and Workers' Autonomy, that had been convulsing the country's political landscape since the late sixties. This effort began with the arrest of thousands of militants in all parts of Italy – many of whom, like Negri, would be tried collectively only after many lengthy postponements. In a late 1980 interview Negri admitted:

> My life in prison isn't bad. There are about 3,000 comrades currently held in the Special Prisons (for 'terrorists'). There is therefore a very rich level of political discussion. Our strength, even in prison, is indubitable. So, our conditions of imprisonment are not of the worst. They are without doubt better than those that the common prisoner had to undergo before the influx of comrades into the prisons.[3]

Conditions in the prisons would soon become worse. During Negri's second year of incarceration, 1980 to 1981, he continued to write prolifically, as the many essays that make up his 1982 book *Macchina tempo: Rompicapi, liberazione, costituzione* (*Time Machine: New Problems, Liberation, Constitution*) demonstrate.[4] The strength of the radical comrades within the Italian prison system undergirded his ongoing work, but that strength also led to confrontations with and retribution from the prison authorities. Not long after the interview cited above, Negri and his colleagues got caught up in a prison revolt led by Red Brigades prisoners who were being held in the same unit of Trani Prison. On 28 December 1980, the Red Brigaders took a guard prisoner after wounding him with an improvised knife, and used his keys to release other prisoners and then take other guards hostage. At sunset the next day, while negotiations between the Red Brigaders and the prison governor were breaking down, a military assault squad descended upon Trani in helicopters. Gunfire and grenade explosions announced their entrance. In their rush to retake the prison building, the soldiers made no distinctions between the Red Brigade prisoners, who were the instigators and the only active participants in the revolt, and the other prisoners, like Negri and his Padua colleague Emilio Vesce, who were nonparticipant bystanders. Vesce had two ribs broken and Negri was kicked in the head before both were driven by the soldiers into the arms of a platoon of masked prison guards, who beat them further. Once the prison building had been secured by the military, the guards systematically destroyed the prisoners' belongings, including their personal letters and defence documents. Negri writes briefly about this revolt in Letter Nineteen (p. 208), but a more detailed account of the event is given in *Revolution Retrieved*.[5]

By the middle of his third year of imprisonment, when Negri began to write *Pipeline*, his earlier confidence in the strength of the militant movements and in their ultimate victory over the state's forces had begun to weaken as a result of the endless changes in the charges against him, concomitant deferrals of his trial, and ongoing torments and indignities of prison life. (See the opening lines of Letter Ten, p. 107) As he notes in Letter Eighteen, by kidnapping, 'prosecuting' and then murdering Moro, the Red Brigades had not really attacked the Italian state, as they claimed; on the contrary, they had strengthened the state – in that Moro's murder served as a pretext for the state's criminalisation and suppression of the militant movements that it viewed as the greatest threat to its stability. This should come as no surprise, since the hierarchical structure and vanguardist ideology of the Red Brigades constituted a mirror image of the state's administrative form and legal logic. So did the sham trial to which the Red Brigades subjected Moro before killing him. The proof of this gift that the Red Brigades gave to the state lay not only in the mass arrests of 7 April 1979 and in the brutal treatment of political prisoners, but also in the passage of legislation extending the maximum period of preventive detention prior to trial from six to eleven years in cases of alleged terrorism and granting leniency to 'repentant' terrorists (the *pentiti*) who implicated others in terrorist acts. By mid-1981, after even more comrades were crammed into the special prisons, Negri knew that he might be facing up to nine more years of incarceration before his trial began; and a deluge of new charges was brought against him on the basis of the claims of *pentiti* anxious to reduce their own sentences.[6] In writing his letters against this backdrop, Negri was trying to set the power of militant desire, both his own and that of his comrades, flowing again, so as to build a pipeline that could serve at least as an affective and conceptual – if not physical or legal – line of flight from the prison's and the state's rigid walls, which had closed around all of them.

The letters themselves may seem confusing or even offputting to readers who expect either a concerted legalistic self-defence, complete with exculpatory evidence, or a glimpse of the everyday life of a notorious 'wicked teacher' (in Italian *cattivo maestro*, as Negri and his fellow militant professors were labelled in the Italian press – see his tribute to Raniero Panzieri in Letter Seven). Although he writes movingly of his childhood (Letters One and Two), first love (Letter Three), his wife and children (Letters Six and Ten), his mother's death (Letter Eleven), and his arrest and revulsion at prison life (Letter Nineteen), his main purpose is not to chronicle the details of his individual experience. The letters do not constitute an autobiography or memoir, at least not a full one. At most they offer a narrative of those experiences, whether intellectual or somatic, individual or collective, that made Negri into the militant theorist he was at that moment. This book is really an attempt at a philosophical definition and defence of militant practice, both his own and that of the radical movements more broadly. It is also an implicit political self-criticism, in the tradition of Georg Lukács' *Defence of History and Class Consciousness*.[7] As Negri puts it at the start of the first letter, 'Tell me your name, claim what you are' (Letter One, p. 13). His method here is not so different from the 'biographical materialism' that he deployed in his studies of Descartes and Spinoza, though the tone of this book is quite different from the tone of those earlier ones.[8] In the postscript to Letter Fifteen, he acknowledges that

> what I'm writing is unnecessarily convoluted. Or maybe convoluted is not the right word: overloaded, rather, with content added to the basic theme – baroque, because it seems that I can't avoid alternatives, variants and derivations. Bombastic. This redundancy conceals, it does not clarify. Please forgive this limitation of mine – and also its complement, which is that sometimes I am clumsy, irritated, inattentive, late, dreamy, writing in shorthand – and this happens each time that some involuntary memory pushes itself forward in me and brings to the

surface that other aspect of life that is my ego, my history, my private things, my memories, my loves, and all that. (Letter Fifteen, pp. 171–2)

The book's distance from conventional autobiography or memoir becomes even clearer when we examine the author's note that immediately precedes the first letter. In that note, Negri insists upon the accuracy of the site and dates of the letters' composition and the actuality of its references to literature, political events and events of everyday life, but he also tells the reader frankly that the book's genre is imaginative rather than historical. What does he mean by this? First and foremost, he is alerting the reader to the fact that his addressee throughout the book, the young French philosopher and militant David, is a fiction or, more precisely, a composite of the many comrades with whom Negri worked, intimately and passionately, to construct a viable radical political organisation over the course of the sixties and seventies.[9] From this fact it follows that the letter form Negri adopts is also part of the fiction, in the sense that these letters were never really sent to anyone – as for example Antonio Gramsci's and later George Jackson's prison letters were – but instead are addressed to the book's general readers, over David's head as it were.[10] The regular recurrence of references to the book's title further confirms this. Thus, while Negri is implicitly and self-consciously referring to the tradition of earlier prison letters, particularly those of incarcerated radicals like Gramsci and Jackson, his book adopts the documentary mode of that tradition as a formal device that allows him to address an unknown, potentially international readership in familiar terms.

In the self-conscious fictional artifice of this book, as in its unique mixture of artistic, philosophical and political references, we can see one of the earliest substantive flowerings of Negri's own aesthetic impulse, which has recently given rise to his series of stage dramas, the *Trilogy of Resistance*[11] (to be followed by a *Trilogy of Critique* and a *Trilogy of Love*). Negri's pantheon has always included James Joyce, Bertolt Brecht, Giacomo Leopardi and other poets, playwrights and novelists – along with philosophers like Spinoza and militant thinkers like Machiavelli, Marx and Lenin, all of whom influence his craft in *Pipeline* (see especially Letters Ten and Fifteen). Even science fiction, in the form of Isaac Asimov's Foundation books, provides Negri with both inspiration and consolation (in Letter Seventeen). This aesthetic impulse will later lead him in surprising directions, some of which are first signalled in these letters. For example, at the beginning of Letter Eighteen Negri pens a tribute, couched in explicitly literary terms, to the man he was accused of murdering:

He, Moro, with incredible skill and an intelligence born of despair, strove to make the whole story even more far-reaching and enriched it with true substance, through his letters during the two months of his captivity. The disclosure of a politician's humanity, as we know, is a topos of classical tragedy. The pity elicited could be profound. (Letter Eighteen, p. 194)

The first play of Negri's *Trilogy of Critique*, still in progress, endeavours to stage Moro's 'classical tragedy', but also to go beyond it in order to honour the prime minister's daring candour; its title is *L'uomo che ride: Critica della politica* (*The Laughing Man: Critique of Politics*).[12]

Pipeline is the only one of Negri's more than sixty books to be published by Giulio Einaudi Editore of Turin, which at that time was perhaps the most prestigious publishing house in Italy. Einaudi had published the first edition of Antonio Gramsci's *Letters from Prison* in 1947, and went on to become a major left-leaning publisher while remaining independent of both the Italian Communist Party and the Italian Socialist Party.[13] Many of the best-known and best-loved names in postwar Italian literature were published by Einaudi, for example Cesare Pavese, Italo Calvino and Giorgio Agamben. According to the back cover of the original edition, Giulio Einaudi himself invited Negri to write *Pipeline* because he felt that Negri's story amounted to a 'central testimony of our time'.[14] It is difficult to overstate the significance of this gesture of Einaudi's at that moment in Negri's judicial predicament – a moment when Negri and his co-defendants had been thoroughly demonised in the eyes of the Italian public as a result of the mainstream media's shamefully uncritical parroting of prosecution claims (even the Communist Party-controlled paper *L'Unità* endorsed those claims). The fledgling independent left media, such as the newspaper *Il Manifesto*, and the more specialised journals of the academic left had consistently been more supportive of Negri and his comrades, though sometimes only on the basis of their commitment to civil liberties and due process; but their influence was comparatively small. Against this backdrop, Einaudi's invitation can only have been understood as a gesture of solidarity, since Negri's writings had never been bestsellers and *Pipeline* itself is too unusual and demanding in style to appeal to a broad popular audience. Given all this, the publication of *Pipeline* inaugurated a period, corresponding to the fourth year of Negri's incarceration, in which prominent figures in Italian cultural life who were not involved with the militant movements expressed public support for the demonised prisoners. For Negri, ultimately the most important (though not unproblematic) of these figures would be Marco Panella, the leader of the small but inventive Radical Party, which would nominate Negri for a seat in the Italian parliament in the 1983 elections. Negri's election as a deputy for Rome, Milan and Naples forced the state to release him from prison and later allowed him to flee to France when parliament voted to strip him of his immunity from prosecution.[15] Soon thereafter he was found guilty of the freshest charges against him and sentenced to 30 years of imprisonment; but the French government, which interpreted his prosecution as political, refused to extradite him in response to Italian requests. He remained in exile for 14 years, during which a series of appeals reduced his sentence to 13 years, before returning to Italy in 1997 to serve out his sentence. All told, Negri served six and a half years of full-time detention plus another three years of half-time house arrest before being released on parole in 2003.

The letters that make up this book are important as a participant's account of how the radical social movements of the sixties and seventies emerged, fragmented and were ultimately destroyed in Italy, as well as of how the movements' innovations in theory and practice survived that defeat to influence struggle in the new millennium. Hence their significance is largely retrospective. However, they also have a prospective relevance, although it is much less readily apparent than their historical value. The letters occupy a key position in the evolution of Negri's later work, which proved so influential, on collective resistance to the new paradigm of capitalist power – that is, on the multitude against Empire. Many of the observations, proposals and themes in these letters constitute the embryos from which later analyses and concepts would grow. The first letter evokes the poor as the fundamental category of future resistance – 'The poor is the sign of the collective' (Letter One, p. 23) – just as Hardt and Negri would in *Multitude*,[16] and the third letter links that collective subject to the project of a materialist utopia, defined as 'the collective desire to go beyond the limit set up by enemies in order to guarantee of their power' (Letter Three, p. 42). The thirteenth and fourteenth letters acknowledge the increasing significance of feminist thought and struggle for Negri's conception of a subversive subjectivity, which would ultimately lead to the definition of affective, immaterial or cyborg labour in Hardt and Negri's *Labor of Dionysus*[17] and to the emphasis on the 'living flesh' of the multitude in their *Multitude*.[18] Moreover, Negri's prison experience as a whole made his and Hardt's extension of Michel

Foucault's analysis of the expanding 'carceral' dimension of contemporary biopolitics, as well as their adoption of Gilles Deleuze's concept of the society of control, frighteningly concrete.[19] To put it bluntly, the techniques pioneered by the Italian legislature, judiciary and prison system to suppress the radical movements of the sixties and seventies – techniques that were first tested on Negri and his comrades – are among the clearest and most direct sources for the generalised state of exception from the rule of law that defines Empire's global rule today.

Despite this firsthand experience with the new forms of repression that now make militancy so risky, Negri's ultimate assessment of his prison experience is affirmative, indeed hopeful. As he writes near the end of the nineteenth letter:

> I was living in prison the first concrete dimensions of a long-term project, the realisation of the new dislocation of proletarian composition. A major effort that nevertheless enabled us, within the continuing struggle, to be participants again, but now transformed, in the resumption of the movement. (Letter Nineteen, p. 211)

And the very last words of the book take this notion a step further: 'We are in the future – our present reflects some features of that future ... The future has a relationship of reciprocity with the past – but it is ontologically prior to the past, even though in logical terms it comes after' (Letter Twenty, pp. 221–2). In other words, the future already exists in the past and in the present, in the form of real tendencies that, although minor and difficult to discern, will grow and intensify to the point where they transform the world. Such was the destiny facing industrial labour in the eighteenth century, colonial emancipation in the nineteenth century, and self-organising social and technical systems in the mid-twentieth century. The art of subversive politics lies in recognising and nurturing those tendencies until they mature, in affirming their difference and all the unanticipated differences to which they will give rise in the fullness of time. This is what Negri describes – but also enacts – in *Pipeline*: the affirmation of difference, both individual and collective, as the active constitution of new political subjects, and ultimately the invention of a new, fluid social order that will not divide, reduce and conquer the inclusive diversity of the multitude but rather extend and intensify it. This is the future toward which Negri's pipeline carries us.

Notes

1 This is Negri's own interpretation of Red Brigades strategy, for example throughout his pamphlet 'Domination and Sabotage', in his *Books for Burning: Between Civil War and Democracy in 1970s Italy*, trans. T. Murphy, A. Bove, E. Emery and F. Novello, New York: Verso, 2005, especially at pp. 231–4, 257–8, 264–7 and 274–8. As David Moss notes in his *Politics of Left-Wing Violence in Italy 1969–1985*, London: Macmillan, 1989, the Red Brigades' most specific aims in kidnapping, trying and killing Moro were to demonstrate their own military capacity and to secure their own hegemony over the extra-parliamentary left by increasing state repression against non-clandestine radical movements like Workers' Autonomy and by encouraging rival clandestine groups to ally themselves with the Red Brigades; see pp. 72, 74, 151–2, 230–1.
2 Antonio Negri, *The Savage Anomaly: The Power of Spinoza's Metaphysics and Politics*, trans. Michael Hardt, Minneapolis: University of Minnesota Press, 1991, p. xxiii (translation modified).
3 'Interview with Toni Negri (1980)', in Antonio Negri, *Revolution Retrieved: Selected Writings on Marx, Keynes, Capitalist Crisis and New Social Subjects 1967–1983*, trans. Ed Emery and John Merrington, London: Red Notes, 1988, p. 247.
4 The most substantive and forward-looking piece in *Macchina tempo*, has been translated into English by Matteo Mandarini as 'The Constitution of Time: The Timepieces of Capital and Communist Liberation' and published in Antonio Negri, *Time for Revolution*, New York: Continuum, 2003, pp. 19–135.
5 'The Revolt at Trani Prison', pp. 253–8 in Negri's *Revolution Retrieved*. Negri describes this experience in a video interview (in Italian) available at http://youtu.be/zTY1Dow6MzU. For further multimedia documentation of Negri's intellectual and political itinerary, see Ed Emery's photo-archive of Negri's personal library at www.flickr.com/photos/105224025@N05/.
6 Many of these charges stemmed from claims made by the convicted kidnapper and murderer Carlo Fioroni to the effect that Negri was involved in Fioroni's own crimes. As a result of his 'evidence', Fioroni's sentence was reduced and the Italian secret service spirited him out of the country. He refused to return for cross-examination during Negri's original trial, but his pre-trial testimony was admitted into evidence nonetheless. His claims were not officially discredited until 1989, when he finally took the stand during the 7 April appeals process. For a more detailed account of Negri's trial, including references, see my introduction, 'Books for Burning', to Negri's *Books for Burning*, pp. ix–xxviii.
7 See Georg Lukács, *A Defence of History and Class Consciousness: Tailism and the Dialectic*, trans. Esther Leslie, New York: Verso, 2000.
8 The phrase 'biographical materialism' was coined by Matteo Mandarini

and Alberto Toscano in their introduction to Antonio Negri, *Political Descartes: Reason, Ideology and the Bourgeois Project*, New York: Verso, 2006, p. 1.

9 Although the character 'David' is a composite, Negri did have a particular reader in mind as he wrote the letters: his friend Yann Moulier Boutang, a French economist who is best known to English-speaking readers for his book *Cognitive Capitalism*, trans. Ed Emery, Cambridge: Polity Press, 2012.

10 Antonio Gramsci, *Letters from Prison*, vols 1–2, ed. Frank Rosengarten, trans. Raymond Rosenthal, New York: Columbia University Press, 1994; George Jackson, *Soledad Brother: The Prison Letters of George Jackson*, New York: Bantam Books, 1970 (with an introduction by Jean Genet).

11 Antonio Negri, *Trilogy of Resistance*, trans. Timothy S. Murphy, Minneapolis: University of Minnesota Press, 2011.

12 Although it has not yet been published, Negri's new play has been staged at the Avignon Festival in France and at the Kotor Art Festival in Montenegro.

13 Einaudi's political engagement came to an end in 1994, when Einaudi Editore was acquired by the Mondadori publishing group, a subsidiary of Silvio Berlusconi's media conglomerate Fininvest.

14 Antonio Negri, *Pipe-Line: Lettere da Rebibbia*, Turin: Giulio Einaudi, 1983.

15 Antonio Negri's *Diary of an Escape*, trans. Ed Emery, Cambridge: Polity, 2010, tells the story of the start of his trial, his election and escape to France in fascinating detail.

16 See Michael Hardt and Antonio Negri, *Multitude: War and Democracy in the Age of Empire*, New York: Penguin Press, 2004, chapter 2.1.

17 See Michael Hardt and Antonio Negri, *Labor of Dionysus: A Critique of the State-Form*, Minneapolis: University of Minnesota Press, 1994, pp. 12–14, 280–1, 309–11.

18 See Hardt and Negri, *Multitude*, chapter 2.3.

19 See Michael Hardt and Antonio Negri, *Empire*, Cambridge: Harvard University Press, 2000, pp. 22–7, 195–8 and chapter 3.6 ('Capitalist Sovereignty, or Administering the Global Society of Control').

Letter One
The Dry Veneto

Rebibbia, 10 October 1981

Cher David,

So you have been in Padua. At last you have seen it – that city, which is a fount of every kind of extremist conspiracy and intrigue. Yet for me it has always seemed worthier of the pen of a Stendhal than of a Dostoevsky. Never mind . . . not only the cities, but above all the ways of the world have changed. So much so that dyspeptic small-time public prosecutors can go round inventing chilling tales to hit the headlines. For some reason it fell to me to be the pivotal point in this game, which was being played (and still is) around falsehood and provocation, because the truth was immediately clear and immediately recognised as unacceptable to the *raison d'état*. The story here is a heavy story and it's already brought me a great many years of prison; besides, at this point I do not want to pull out of the game. So I understand your question, my young friend: tell me your name. A name that has been sullied by the brutality of the political courts and by the violence of the media. Tell me your name, claim what you are. Sure, David, I want to try. Because I like you. But also because this story has not been painless and, in living it – whether with irony or in despair – I've had more than one moment of doubt. Maybe, in explaining things to you, I'll manage to deal with a few uncertainties about my identity. But where shall I begin? Should I call on memory for assistance? I fear memory. Too often it is empty vanity and replaces the real instead of getting immersed in it. It is ideology; it is self-complacency; and, in this prison I inhabit, it is also the torment of a past that is fixed, downcast, turned against life; it is the act of blackmail of solitude against collective desire. There must be something truer, which enabled me both to become a man and to offer you now this bodily thing that I am, declaring myself a collective being, beyond the sour taste of individuality. In the old days I used to attend Jean Bollack's lectures: *animus* – not *anima* – is what Lucretius called that nucleus of very thin material *in quo consilium vitae regimenque locatum est.** Here we are: neither the pure, vital sensibility nor the memory of its illusions – rather it is the *animus* that should speak, against and beyond the triviality of memory. As for our names, we find them assigned to us – they come out slowly from a kind of great indifference in which we recognise ourselves to be immersed. Imagination, then and now, breaks this indifference – and it is a hard nucleus of rationality and passion. It constitutes us as what we are: signs of a relationship between past, future, and the many senses of time; and signs of a collective relationship. I find my name only in relation to a history that has been co-lived with me and in which my being has been formed. A good hermeneutics points to what is most internal with the help of what is most external. So it will be this *cupiditas* that will allow me to tell the story and to set in motion the machine of liberation.

You, David, like many comrades born in this last decade of struggles (and out of its passionate and ruthless critique), are nevertheless deeply puzzled about the ontological compactness to which I refer, and you wonder whether taking it as a starting assumption does not flatten history. That may even be so; for the moment I cannot offer much to counter this puzzlement. I entrust the thesis to history. The canvas is materialist: life is a sacrament, a blend of divinity and reality, and, on this surface, love and violence form social essences and collective identities. A real flow. Pipeline. It is in here that we carve ourselves out. Imagination shows us childhood as a transcendental structure without a subject; the untidiness of memory and the misery of individuality are tempered against this background. We generously seek ourselves within this controverted reality into which we are immersed; it is an astute generosity, à la Lévi-Strauss, that sets us on the hunt, and the ego is the savage. I do not know how to explain this better; it is in the fact of recognising ourselves in a community that we grasp ourselves. It's a tough act. Did you not learn this in your native Brittany?

The people's Veneto, where I grew up, is not a soft land –

---

* Translator's note: 'where life's plan of action and command is located': Lucretius, *De rerum natura*, 3.95.

everything was dry. Dry, the frost that clung to the workers' jackets in the morning, when long queues of bicycles – a huge procession of ants whitened by frost – arrived to assist in the dispersed and primitive accumulation of capital. Dry from the dust that collected on plane trees in the countryside, in the summer heat. That dust was full of pollen in both spring and autumn; it, too, was dry, and always gave me asthma. Dry, the sweet evening air of May – when, after the evening service, we caught fireflies and put them in glasses. Dry, the magnolia leaves – almost wooden by autumn; and when you walked on them they broke with a crack. Recently certain intellectuals have accredited an image of this strong landscape as moist and flaccid. They are bad witnesses. My mother tongue and that of the people were similarly dry and hard. You found Ruzante* in the priest's Sunday sermon, and his sing-song dialect did not diminish the power of the words. My Veneto, the popular and peasant Veneto that I knew in the 1940s and 1950s, had not seen the eighteenth-century bourgeois corruption of morals. It was not Venice, it was the mainland. No religious mysticism. The church was everything in this region, which had no metropolis and had not yet experienced the dispersals of the individual and the exaggerated violence of industrial concentration. The church was a mass organisation. Articulated, loving, omnipresent and powerful. A medieval knight. My relationship with it was physical – a relationship in which the exercise of Christian virtues was dry and natural. I didn't know what torbid meant – neither the melancholy of Rilke's Malte Laurids Brigge nor the emotional upheavals of Musil's young Törless; in the Veneto of my adolescence there was more of Bavaria than of Mitteleuropa. So that's where I grew up – and there, at about the age of eighteen, I learned the magic words that were to enable me to articulate the indistinctness into which I was immersed and to swim freely in that dry sea.

The first magic word that I learned at that time was 'witnessing'. The Catholic movement in the late 1940s and early 1950s was experiencing its first crisis of orientation. Only later did I realise the seriousness of this crisis. My friends and I felt its effects: it was, against the pure and simple political restoration that had happened in Rome, an appeal to the notions of militancy and Christian witnessing in the world. I lived this appeal to witnessing not at the political level but at a human and religious level – this was the concluding phase of

---

* Translator's note: Angelo Beolco, sixteenth-century comedian from Veneto, whose character Ruz(z)ante depicted rustic life through vivid language.

my adolescence. Rather than being grounded in history, my experience was psychologically and ethically defined. I lived an enveloping and indistinct horizon and that was where I built the beginnings of my desire to know – witnessing was, first and foremost, an act of vitality effected from within the conditions that you experienced, a break, a choice between what oppresses you and what liberates you. (Do you recall, cher David, the Saxon witnessing of Hans Jürgen Krahl? When I read it in the middle of the events of 1968 I recognised in that confession the genesis of my own desire for a breaking.) A witnessing – but of what? The community, its needs, its reality, the tension that we recognised in it, between poverty and the desire for happiness. Of course, it was a vicious circle ('there is again a generation that wants to be at the crossroads' – so says Benjamin in the *Metaphysics of Youth* – 'but the crossroads is nowhere to be found').* And yet it was not a vicious circle when the circle was infused with charity – with a stripping bare of oneself in the love of others, which broke indifference and produced the first projects of solidarity. We filled this word with content and with hope, as an alternative to another word, which was also magic but in some ways frightening: 'the priesthood'. It was nevertheless an alternative that we understood well – as a single act of free choice – since it was left to us to take one option or the other, in a world where the abundance of ecclesiastical vocations was accompanied by the urgent need for civil agents of clerical politics. But there was a contradiction – namely this: we were not interested in politics, or at least not in the Christian democrat politics that we saw before us – and we knew no other kind; and yet we wanted to make a stand in the world through radical choices of poverty and of charity. It was clear to us that these choices would not be possible for us as priests, in the world where we lived. In those years, five or six of my friends chose the priesthood, despite everything; but they are all far away now, very far away, as missionaries. We did not understand that the choice of poverty was also an immediately anticapitalist one – only in a distant future could that be argued, not here among us. Here we lived secularism like saints, leaving politics to the priests. What a crazy mix-up. In fact, the decision to opt for poverty and charity broke the indistinction of the world, placed determination as the first element of our ethics – without our knowing it, it was historicising our existence. And perhaps, even though we didn't really understand

---

* Translator's note: the original is to be found in Walter Benjamin's 'Metafisica della gioventù', in *Scritti 1910–1918*, Turin: Einaudi, 1982.

it, we had, in the life of community, intuited communism before we came to understand and critique capitalism. With boundless generosity we lived as communists, and we were at the same time Christians, Catholics and people of the Veneto.

Often today apologists of the bosses' world order accuse me of turning religious sentiment against their works: lack of irony, they tell me. But nothing is more ironic than capital's failure to grasp any of that – religion, youth, and the world. They are bigger than capital. Here's Benjamin: 'The movement of awakening among the new youth shows the direction of that infinitely distant point at which we know religion. And movement in general is for us the deepest guarantee of its proper direction.'* The irony lies entirely here: in the irreducibility of the movement to fixity, of the sacred to capital. However, what ensured that my emotions stayed alive and lasted for the whole of my life was the fact that I was to witness the very rapid maturing of capitalist development in the Veneto, which coincided with the years of my youth. Might one not say, then, that it's been a lucky theoretical situation, the one in which I lived? When, ironically, I was able to amass, in the span of a single lifetime, material for reflection on the birth, the development, and now the crisis of a *morceau* of the *Zivilisation* of capital?

But let's get back to my teenage years and to those magic words: 'the social question'. This was a strange object, because it seemed not to involve us directly. There was no 'social question' in the Veneto, people said, except one that was reflected, experienced at second hand. The social question meant the South – a species of 'third world' that the sudden and rapacious thirst for accumulation (this was the Catholic critique of the Risorgimento) had dragged into our own world, further impoverishing it, plundering it, exploiting it. The social question came to me as a kind of third-worldism. My first real, politically determined intense emotion was for the conditions of the South. I'll tell you in another letter about when I started to go to the South. For now you need only grasp the significance of these polar opposites: the Veneto and the South – on the one hand, a well-constructed community in which I felt myself to be a participant and a witness; on the other, a world of deprivation and poverty to which I was driven by generosity and a desire for love. Also by a

---

* Translator's note: this is the beginning of Benjamin's 1914 essay 'The Religious Position of the New Youth'; see Walter Benjamin, *Early Writings, 1910–1917*, ed. and trans. Howard Eiland, Cambridge, MA: Harvard University Press, 2011, p. 168 (quoted here in Eiland's translation).

desire to know? Not really. This was, in the first instance, a compassion, an inability to bear the weight of a picture of desperation that threw into crisis one's solid illusion of living in a well-ordered world. Compassion is a negative passion – and, like any passion, a spontaneous activity of the soul, but one marked negatively by a suffering that is much stronger than one's ability to react to it. It is a sense of imperfection that becomes a generic sense of responsibility. It also lacked determination, when in fact this is what had to be conquered. To recognise my own name was to be able to give names to things. However, the compassion helped to strengthen the act of witnessing and to disarticulate indistinct participation in the community. The cognitive imaginings that hovered around this emotional upheaval clustered the new image of the South on top of the recent memories of the war: of hunger, death, destruction, bombings, mournings, deaths – ah, what a lovely childhood! So the compassion and its imaginings were taking shape, concretising the image of the poor. The compassion was turning into indignation.

My readings of those years – when, on this crudely formed base, I was beginning to be a Catholic militant – were Mounier, Maritain, Simone Weil, Bernanos ... A thinking of our time, but it was difficult material – rather esoteric for a young Catholic from the provinces. In Italian there was nothing or next to nothing, apart from a few peeks at Dorso and Gramsci. But what good are books before lived experience, or outside of it? My diffidence was a search for determinations. However, Simone Weil struck me: 'Time always takes us where we do not want to go. To love time ...'* A transition was beckoning – charity wanted to reconnect itself to time, breaking anything that stood in its way. Thus a strongly lived passion prevents the indistinctness of the reference to an organic community from being translated into cognitive indifference and from abandoning itself to the customary practice of ethical and political representations. The fact that we were Christians certainly did not mean that we were Christian democrats! The charity and the history had to react immediately on each other. Many of the stimuli of Veneto culture, far from blocking impatience, pushed one into it. With hard work – and much more than one imagined! – but penetrating into the flesh of the matter and building a destiny. Later, when I tried to consider these things in terms of theory and the sociology of community, I reinforced my

---

* Translator's note: As found (in the Italian translation reproduced by Negri) at http://www.bibliomanie.it/alain_paul_valery_simone_weil_traduzioni_adriano_marchetti.htm ('Invito alla lettura di tre pensatori europei del novecento').

conviction that, compared with Tönnies and Max Weber and the rigidity of all dichotomous models, Simmel had best understood the true dynamic of *Gemeinschaft* [communitarian spirit]. The breaking of it, and also the expression of its wealth, which is otherwise greedily guarded, can only take place within an internal act of vital transcending. This, I felt, was needed in my spiritual development. And, while it is true that with this we are on the terrain of a thinking of separation and in the conceptual world of Judaism, it is no less true that my desire for knowledge was recognising this and was pressing its impatience beyond any limit of permissible restlessness, in the dry and Catholic homeland of my Veneto. Dry – and sometimes one noticed this – to the point of risking sterility – and a sterile mother is a *contradictio in adiecto* [contradiction between parts of an argument].

The poor, then. Looking for the poor. From now on, perhaps, cher David, we shall find nothing other than infinite transfigurations of the poor, the proletarian, the immigrant, the emigrant, the peasant of the South, the factory worker, the urban proletarian, the socialised worker [*operaio sociale*], the prisoner, and so on ... *Wanderjahre* in search of this subject – years of vagabondage with this subject.

The first effect of the compassion was a new and ambiguous step in the recognition of my own poverty, and of the poverty of the world in which I lived: a multitude of poor people. Onto each of them, and onto me, there was unloaded, and there came to light, a universe of sufferings and a past history of misery and exploitation. But how could that ambiguous awareness be enough? It seemed to me to be an expression of a world of dead people whose desire for happiness had not been granted. What could it mean, to be the expression of that? Suffering it in religious terms, or seeking an active expression in political terms? The word 'revenge' was not in my vocabulary – and, while being moved by things in a religious sense gave the business of witnessing a long and collective thickness, it failed to show the way to solutions and plucked itself out of historical time. Religious action alone could not support the weight of witnessing! Hence ambiguity, uneasiness. Anyway you have to understand, and also to determine your understanding, bring passion into history. 'Research': now there's another word. But could research ever be practised outside of a concrete and worldly practice? Life as research, life as knowledge: then and now they seem to me to be lifeless and idealistic stereotypes, generic words that have in them elements of softness, perhaps of triviality. But how can you clarify them and express your own self as a historical concreteness, if not through that desire to destroy the ambiguous and the uncertain, which is properly a praxis of transformation? So I began to do politics, without realising it – as a militant in Catholic Action, and not as a member of a political party – and in the end I came to knowledge. And yet it *was* politics. It was a way of approaching reality in order to penetrate it, to grasp it from the point of view of poverty, and to change it. I used to go on early-morning drives around the countryside and the outlying areas of this Veneto, in my dusty FIAT 1100, stopping off to enjoy hot chocolate for breakfast. I began to talk of transformation, of reform, of revolution. There was so much poverty, and so much impatience.

(In retrospect, it occurs to me that my 'political career' – if you want to call it that – has this difference from that of the institutional political classes: it has always been conducted between five and eight in the morning, first with Catholics of the Veneto, then with workers in big factories. Certainly not the kind of hours worked by bureaucrats and trade union officials. I remember good old Piovesan, the trade union official at the Petrolchimico plant: he would always arrive at about ten o'clock – not before *24 Ore* arrived on the Venice news stands: you could see the newspaper sticking out of his pocket, together with *L'Unità* – he was very 'new look', a modern functionary, with his feet on the ground and his head in facts. Who could blame him, poor fellow? Previously he had done thirty years in the factory as a shift worker. Only in '68 were they forced to get up early, and they never forgave us for that. The morning hours, the most productive time of the day. Even before the priests arrived! – Here was a completely different story. The priest could be a property owner and a drunkard, but the community was not corrupted by him. I remember Bortignon, the holy old-style Padovan bishop count. He too was caught up in the entrepreneurial mania of the 1950s, but that never diverted him from his mission.)

But what could it produce, in that strange and ambiguous world and among those unresolved potentials, to speak with so much ardour of transformation and renewal? They asked me, in their usual underhand fashion, if I didn't think that I was doing too much politics. Rightly so. In fact I was arriving at the threshold of the great contradiction; and this could be resolved only at that level. Was it? Certainly not at that point. People were talking about an upcoming Vatican Council, but I didn't really understand . . . So, while I, a little proletarian Wilhelm Meister, did not embark on bourgeois theatrical scenarios, I certainly touched on the grotesque. That of an enthusiastic adherence to a real that did not understand its poverty, of an innocence that did not recognise the degradations of habits and cultures, of an impatience that slipped on the hard times of a powerful tradition. How vague my teenage years were, between an intact idealism and a total compassion, within a tension that left no room for dissonances! But I felt uncomfortable in the presence of the clergy, which was close to the bourgeoisie. Adversary of a feared social revolution, representative of an uncompleted bourgeoisie – a slave of rent, first from land, then from real estate. *Lumen siccum* [dry light]. It was another race. There was a Jesuit who, in order to explain lasciviousness, showed the kids sweets when they hadn't eaten before Communion: the act of swallowing them was followed – vile Pavlovian that he was – by a lecture about desires for women. The desire for wealth was, of course, just as sinful. No question of embroidering it poetically, like Joyce, or mischievously, like Chesterton: this smug frustration of the reference to sexuality anyway remained external, it was something for the rich – Luigi Gonzaga and the stench of his lilies; it was not something for us. Our sex education was something else, rural in its way. Remember always to unite pleasure with love, and vice versa. The first kisses were not sinful. This advice was much like that about combining work with pleasure, and vice versa. And, in consequence, we maintained that – as it says in the Book of Genesis, and contrary to what the priests were now claiming – work could not be seen as humanity's punishment; quite the opposite – Adam worked happily in Eden. What a fascinating anticipation of a hypothesis of liberated labour! And then there were other priests, rich and feared, and creators of municipal entities and marriages – in fact nothing more than excess and corruption. They drained that solidity that the community provided. Ah, my Padova, somebody should write a poem about you. But maybe it would have to be sarcastic, because all this happened when you still had your canals, when rattling trams still ran to the surrounding hills, when the pavements were made of round stones with granite arabesques, when your arcades were still low and arched. But there is, there must be, someone who has survived your destruction: a devil, at least, like the ones drawn by Tono Zancanaro, coming down now from the pinnacles of the basilicas.

So then: with the same sulphurous, insinuating potentiality, little by little, the magic words 'community', 'witnessing' and 'research' became a lever for internal distinction in the world in which we were living. Listen to Simone Weil: 'the concept of leverage applied to inner life (as a function of the notion of energy . . .)'.* The dialectic

---

* Translator's note: unidentified quotation.

of separation that I began to experience was born not from weakness but from energy, not from alienation but from desire. In this form, the vocation of poverty excluded resentment – an emotion characteristic of slaves – something that I have never known. (I leave this vice to the *grunfs* – how many of those I have met in my life! Malevolent geniuses? No; bad dogs, rabid, full of resentfulness, precisely. *Grunf, grunf.* You find them everywhere.) But how was it possible, not in the priesthood, but in rational and secular testimony, to pursue the liberation of this community? Modernisation, crisis and renewal: this was the pitiful proposal propagandised by many Catholics. In my experience, this sequence had no place. The process is internal. In Brittany as in Poland – and in the Veneto region: what determines the crisis in the Catholic social community is a religious motivation, is charity, is the quest for the poor. And then there was another ideological motivation that I experienced in my youth: the driving force of the October Revolution. Obviously there is a lot to say about that, cher David. Now they say that it has run its course. Boh! Why this collapse of pride? *Grunf.* On the other hand, what is certain is that the driving force of Christ is not spent. At least not in my country. And that dry world of negative passions, I see it traversed by feelings of emotional identification with poverty and by the desire for peace, today as yesterday. And I don't know how to offer you, cher David, any other reason by way of explanation – other than the piety of my mother, the physical dryness of Bortignon,* and the Eleusine intensity of my youthful community – to understand how there came to be born in me a need for the world to be transformed – and poverty liberated, and peace consolidated in the happiness of mankind. I hold tight to this heritage as the first inventor of productivity: when you discover that it was not hoarding but investment that made it true to its fortune. And, with the investment, the risk. Of course risk comes in many varieties: there is individual risk, the bourgeois exaltation of the genius, or the hero of the trapeze – the glory of the circus – but no, *ça ne va pas*. Only the choice that comes from within the collective, only this pays. Like when we all used to go on trips out of town on our bicycles – then, having chosen one of the infinitely many little roads in the Po valley landscape, so intensely farmed, so fertile, so shady, you look for a place where you might relax and flirt, a patch of grass or a bar somewhere – places of hospitality that desire sought

---

* Translator's note: Italian prelate who served as bishop of Padua from 1949 to 1982.

out, the desire we had in our bodies. A long and engaging dialogue that involved all of us, sweaty, in this pleasant coolness that was at hand. A surface happiness – but where and what is depth? A collective joy. The choice was waiting to be taken: you could choose the combined possibility (certainly confused, but cheerful) of a rooting among the people, and of knowledge, and of an imagining of how they could be overturned and transformed. The path could not be individual, it had to be collective. The poor is the sign of the collective. This is the subject of transformation. Thus an initial perception of collective being is given: what quantity and quality of effort there was in the journey that lay ahead. But moving forward from a position of richness, as we know, is preferable to moving from poverty. For once it rained on the drowned man, and for me too: the poor person is a rich person. We are happy in this lucky fact of having been born poor.

It's raining again today – on the cement yard of this damned prison. I feel fine, though. How was Padova these past few days? Still so drily sweet? Goodbye for now. A strong hug. Yours, Toni.

Letter Two
The Labour Movement

Rebibbia, 15 October 1981

Cher David,

In 1954 I was twenty. I spent the winter semester in Paris on a scholarship. I was living in a Catholic environment – spending time at the editorial offices of *Esprit* in Rue Jacob and in the tumultuous debate that was developing there – which included the termination of French Indochina, a general enthusiasm for Mendès-France, and Pius XII's elimination of the worker priests. I was living various contradictory experiences. Actually I did not understand all the things I was hearing around me, and at that time it was hard to disentangle reason from emotions. Meanwhile, in Italy, my friends in the central committee of the Gioventù Italiana di Azione Cattolica (GIAC) in Rome were arguing around positions that were similar to the experiences of Catholic protest in France. They were soon removed from their positions. In Paris I worked with Hyppolite, and at the Sorbonne I attended lectures by Alquié, Gurvitch and Bachelard. Fleetingly I was dazzled by Merleau-Ponty. Precious insights and pointless knowledge were piling up in my brain simultaneously – good luck alone saved me from being poisoned. Good luck – and also my working days, which were very long and concentrated, in a way that has never happened with me since – 'in the studious silence of the library of Sainte Geneviève, sheltered from the sin of Paris . . .'* I was beginning, confusedly, to perceive elements of class struggle within the church. I was studying Henri de Lubac and other

---

* Translator's note: James Joyce, *Ulysses*, 2.68.

Letter Two: The Labour Movement

theologians. During the Christmas holiday I travelled to Sicily to meet Danilo Dolci. That was the first time I had been to the South. My impressions were traumatic. The previous spring there had been discussions – equally traumatic – about the swindle law.* It was then that I joined the Socialist Party, which in Padua represented most of the labour movement, both in electoral terms and in terms of its presence in mass organisations.

But let's try to put some order into all this. I was experimenting tirelessly, wandering in various worlds with a youthful sense of intellectual adventure – but starting from a solid anchor point and from a grid of subjective responsibility within which, as if prompted by small stimuli and microscopic accumulations, ideas and decisions were forming. I found it difficult to talk about what was happening to me. But I do remember terrible feelings of pain, as well as moments of high-flown utopianism and sublime imagination. In effect the unitary emotional fabric of my individual culture was being broken – and in such a splitting of one's consciousness it is hard to take a position. It is painful. Love, generosity, and the moment of community clashed with a real negative: I was then a fledgling in the discipline of dialectics and I related the Hegelian *Phenomenology*, which I was learning from Hyppolite, to the whole story of my consciousness. What a confusion. Somehow, however, I sensed that a new and equally damaging form of indistinction could exist: the romantic and Hegelian *geistige Arbeit* [intellectual work], which translates the work of life into the dialectic of consciousness, confusing them and subordinating work to spirit. But mine was a very weak acculturation – culture was not able to pluck me from that grammar of witnessing and from that communion of theory and practice that were the structuring principle of my existence. The only possible solution to this crisis would come through practice.

But this did not happen. My research was twisted around a dialectic that was caught in an all-encompassing vicious circle – my apprenticeship was not creating tools for a lucid discipline. The Catholics – outside of my country, where they put down solid roots, and outside of the Parisian circles, where soft hope was the order of the day – were in a state of agitation that, I had to admit, even when it was theoretically correct, was no more than virtual and when it was effective was a variant of reactionary populism. The likes of Péguy

---

* Translator's note: *la legge-truffa*, a reference to the parliamentary voting law of 1953, deemed by some to have been a swindle.

and Léon Bloiy could too often be glimpsed behind Mounier. In Italy during those years the fascist Sturzo stood in a clear and popular tradition of Murrian descent.* So it was not a time of crisis and disintegration – it was a time of stability, and the word still gives me a bit of a shudder; and there was little to be done except to continue, indeed to understand. The fact that the church – which had been one of the specific elements in the debate that my companions had conducted in the Roman Curia in 1954 and that I heard again in Rue Jacob – did not accept the state of grace associated with the activity of workers, and thus the sanctity of their political actions as a class, offended me deeply, because, for God's sake, it was self-evident that factory workers and workers in general were a collective representation of the poor. And their desires stood for justice and renewal. If grace is the possibility of redemption, the worker in his poverty was a prefiguring of redemption. 'To that extent the worker stands on a higher plane than the capitalist from the outset, since the latter has his roots in the process of alienation and finds absolute satisfaction in it whereas right from the start the worker is a victim who confronts it as a rebel and experiences it as a process of enslavement.' In those days, of course, I did not know Marx's unpublished Chapter 6,† but in the gnostic articulations of research I could have taken up residence in that page.

I was in Sicily that year and, while I had my suspicions about the secular religiosity of Danilo Dolci, I met a number of working-class communist militants who talked to me about land occupations and detailed the fierce and powerful characteristics of agrarian class struggle. Life and death, killings and vendettas – very often intertwined with demands for land and peace – stories of the mafia – and the religious and untamable demands for justice for the poor – this Sicily, so Asiatic, so desperate – Mediterranean and burning – and my attempt to understand love and hate and to set them in the right place – a bit like a blind kitten, impossible. We went down the earth road to the peasants' protest at the dam, and we didn't even take a knife to cut the bread. What could all this mean, these subdued but very violent flashes of peasant revolt and of mafia despotism? When the *carabinieri*

---

* Translator's note: a reference to the radical Catholic Romolo Murri (1870–1944), a priest and politician regarded as an early exponent of Christian democracy.
† Translator's note: this famous chapter from Marx's third draft of Volume 1 of *Capital* was published in English as an appendix (New York, 1977), under the title 'Results of the Immediate Process of Production'. The translation above comes from Karl Marx, *Capital*, Volume 1, London: Penguin, 1976, p. 990.

Letter Two: The Labour Movement

chased me out of Partinico, it completely threw me, in my youthful ingenuousness. Then, crossing the mountains above Palermo, I experienced one of those adolescent moments of clarity in rebellion that last for a lifetime. One has to rebel; it is right to rebel. Poverty is intolerable. So I had to get to know the labour movement – and reinterpret the meaning of justice and transformation, connecting it to a subject that was more real than the one to which, generically and pacifically, I had been relating up to that point.

But it was an impotent desire. I was trying to escape from a situation that was indistinct but firm and solid: the traditional Catholicism of my land, compact and luminous in its isolation – and I was extending to others a hand to help in this somewhat stormy crossing. But I found only crudeness, vulgarity and cynicism. The indistinction of religion had to be broken through class struggle because it was materially traversed and unveiled by it – this is what I told myself. But the real terms of comparison were confused by an overwhelming negativity. When I began to get to know the cadres of the official labour movement, I was disappointed and taken aback. I presented myself, bringing a sweet and combative disposition and an extreme richness of desires. But it was like talking to the wind. A wind that was oppressive and suffocating. Uneducated and arrogant little professors scattered maxims and learned utterances, and every problem was dealt with through quotations or case histories. The few union leaders I met were, if anything, even more crude. Relationships with women were sexually maniacal – was this liberation? Brutality in love, cynicism in hatred. The sense of being part of the working class was marked by a negative – a combination of poverty and resentment. The death throes of a prehistory rather than a foreshadowing of the future history of humanity. In its brutishness, their political behaviour aped that of the bourgeoisie.

In 1953 Joseph Stalin died. The morning the news arrived I was at the university, attending a lecture by Padovani – the Catholic professor of moral philosophy. He spoke highly of Stalin, as a representative of politics *tout court*. The autonomy of the political – the good Lord alone can offer a judgement about its place in the harmony of creation. Furthermore, he added, in a language that sat somewhere between Jean Genet and Baltasar Gracián, the Devil and the Lord work in mysterious ways. This Catholic professor spoke in the same language I was hearing in the Stalinist federation. But there it was even further depleted of meaning because, while the good Catholic taught that the bosses were an irrelevance and that exploitation could be transcended, the Stalinist functionary expressed a bloodless cynicism, like that of a slave. And yet the slave had to be in the right; it was here, in the federation, that you had officials strutting around speaking Italian with a Russian accent ('*Caro compàagno noi sciàamo la richéscia del proletariàato!*' – 'Comrade, we are the richness of the proletariat!'), it was here that you sensed, occasionally, that damnable power, vague but real, of proletarian hope and desire.

Sometimes I talked with my paternal grandfather Enea, who started out as a farm labourer, then worked as a tram driver, and eventually ended up as the doorkeeper at Bologna's Monte di Pietà savings bank. He was a communist. As a child I spent a lot of time with him and he gave me a lot of affection, as a way of compensating for the father I had never known. He used to tell me stories about his arrival in town from rural Romagna in the late 1890s, how they had been driven from the countryside by famine; and then he would go on to tell me about their struggles against the bosses and against the bourgeoisie. In his Emilian accent the word 'bourgeoisie' sounded like the devil incarnate. Then he spoke of his hatred of fascism. And the establishment of the Communist Party. It was an epic tale that he conjured for me each time – but it seemed so far away. A fairy tale. Now he was contemptuous of everyone and everything. Everything was just the same as before. I saw my grandmother: an old lady, all white and gentle in appearance – a seamstress who worked from home, where she would be distracted at any moment by the demands of housework. He, my grandfather, now worked as a doorkeeper. This wasn't work, he said; work is when they put a hundredweight load on your back and off you go! A doorkeeper, but one without a uniform, because he had always refused to wear uniforms. Don't even talk about the blackshirts! Then he told me about my father, also a communist. He suffered from malaria, which he had contracted during the war; and what destroyed his liver was the oil that the fascists had forced him to drink. That, Enea explained, was how my father had died. This positive class hatred left its mark on me, and I tried to understand. But I did not understand. I was looking for happiness, looking for the father whom I didn't have, looking for something to replace the fullness of a community that I had lost – and all I was hearing was about the misery of a relation of power stretched to breaking point. Deceptive and overstated.

What might this ideology be? I came from a maze of passions that were certain, of a love that was proclaimed – and sometimes socially effective. I wanted a horizon where it was not poverty, but the richness of our new motivations that found expression. The indistinct and ultimately dull emotion of the traditional world of the Veneto was coming up against a crude, simple relationship of violence. How many times was I to repeat, later in life, the experience of this absurd reversal! Perhaps it should be read as a pregnant element of the present brutality of domination: and in the very phenomenology of collective praxis, in the desire for revolt, as a pathological condition. Cher David, if I had not only despised its obsolescence but had also at that time understood its practical pregnancy and the dangers, perhaps I would have succeeded better, in more recent years, in controlling the trajectories of extremism. But this is how things were: we grew up in that brutality, and you can't fight the contagion – it was as if we had been pitted by smallpox. Love, violence – and my solitude. On the one hand, indifference of love and of solidarity; on the other, wretched difference and crude emergence of a violent reaction – of resentment.

So I chose solitude – one that embraced me and a small group of close friends. I had joined a party of the working class, as the still Morandian Italian Socialist Party (PSI) proclaimed itself at that time. I was one of the brightest jewels in the crown of the federation – a tangible outcome of the 'dialogue with the Catholics'. But how incredibly alone I was! So I had to study. I had to roll up my sleeves and move onto the only terrain where solitude could be productive: research. A strange paradox, practical choices that were seeking to overcome the abstractness of ourselves as individuals, but that, by the same token, meant that you needed to be alone – abstracted, immersed in study, separated from the totality of practice. Anyway, I worked on historical materialism and materialist dialectics: a first – and last – attempt to match myself to that new society, which might have been thought crude but was desired and real. Cher David, the experience was disastrous. On the advice of small-time professors, I immersed myself in reading Stalin and the book on diamat [dialectical materialism] written by Father Vetter, SJ [Society of Jesus]. It threw me, and I abandoned it. Then various caring friends, solicitous for the welfare of the political neophyte, advised me to get my teeth into Gramsci – and also to do some minor reading of Marx. Only later, tempered by the Italian ideology, would I have been able to approach freshly – and usefully, they assured me – the theology of Marxism–Leninism–Stalinism. The local science and the international science, the ambiguity of the double truth, Soviet science and the Italic, popular–national viewpoint – a fine discovery, and I turned it over in my mind. The fact was that the Catholic world from which I was coming possessed a pastoral theology that was immediately practicable. So was it the case that the old theology was popular, and the new theology was cynical? Why this situation? Why was it that here, in this new society, so many difficulties stood in the way of achieving a balance of theory and practice, and why were the solutions so hard to grasp? I came from a reality of hegemony – the Catholic world of the Veneto. I was accustomed to a condition of correspondence among the various different aspects of the world – the problem was one of 'prudence', in mobilising organically the context of class relations and 'compassion' in making these changes correspond to the needs of the poor. (What the 'ambassadors of the Veneto' – our political patriarchs – were doing was not much different – Ranke and Musil, the political art of the parish priest.) My crisis had grown out of the crisis in the relationship between 'prudence' and 'compassion' – where the first was showing itself increasingly as reactionary regulation and, in consequence, compassion was spiritualised, individualised, and formalised, wrenched away from the materiality of needs. It was no longer the evangelical and theological figure of a collective redemption.

But what exactly were these 'Marxists' offering me? A philosophy of materialism that I found strange, distant, anachronistic – only after many years and many strange crossroads did I finally understood materialism; a dialectic of nature that was very much like that of the neoscholastic texts of Vanni Rovighi; and a debased theory of history, which bore no relation to the heights and luminescence of Hegel – so complex even in its reactionary one-sidedness, as was made clear to me by Hyppolite. In Hegel the dialectic of self-awareness tends towards a theological *escroquerie*, but in passing through unhappy consciousness it overturns the initial attributions of sensible and rational appetites – to the master it grants fear, and in the slave it recognises *cupiditas*. Why step backwards in relation to this role of the subject in history? Yet this theoretical discomfort of mine would have been completely secondary had it not been constantly combined with a practical frustration, which was expressed in the form of party discipline. The act of witnessing was impossible in the official labour movement: the stimulus of collective desire was subordinated not to the creativity that was beginning to be glimpsed in the mass struggles and in the factory struggles, but to a collective alienation in organisation, an alienation similar to that of command and exploitation. Later I learned to interpret this situation and to understand how it was a manifestation of the effects of that cancerous opportunism in the official labour movement that was destroying revolutionary hope. I did not react with attitudes typical of *Edelanarchismus* – that lordly kind of anarchism or intellectualism, so odious to me – instead I suffered the creeping tragedy in silence. Gramscian hegemony as interpreted by Togliatti was a figure of bourgeois cynicism, an idea of the crisis and of disenchantment, as people would say later, a technique of command, not working towards forming the proletarian collective but towards the exercise of power, whatever the circumstances. Reduced to a phantasm, the nostalgic celebration of the people's power manifested in the *soviets* went hand in hand with an emptiness of behaviours and a certain ritualism: this is what communism had become, having been taken over by a bureaucratic mentality, supported by a charismatic legitimation, and made to work in a framework of instrumental rationality. Maybe today I am putting too rational a colouring on all this; maybe at the time it was just an opportunistic mish-mash, half-Giobertian and half-Stalinist. The defeat that had been suffered, between the Resistance and the subsequent restoration, was rife with theoretical ambiguities and – for the working class – with illusion and pain. The fact remains that I learned nothing from Gramsci. In the way he had been handed to me he was the father of the new church. I found his teachings inimical, and occasionally banal or incomprehensible. This was the case until the late 1960s, when I started reading him again and realised the power of what he was saying. I can tell you, David, that I do not forgive the person who originally took that pleasure from me!

As for Marx, I attempted a systematic reading, as I always try to do with authors I'd like to love. Once again, stalemate. On that occasion it was the grand old man himself who denied me access. Alas, I was granted only pieces of the Vulgate. I learned the law of value as objectivistic jargon – this was how I heard it repeated a thousand times by dogmatists in the years that followed, and even nowadays, when it just increases my unhappiness in prison, repeated by so-called 'communists' soiled by heresy and steeped in blood. 'The cold current of Marxism is destructive and can appear as the mirror image of the gear mechanisms of domination.'* So said old Bloch . . . The situation in those days was even worse: the mechanisms of domination were cold-bloodedly manipulating Marxism. To understand that value was not some kind of cement, but a productive human activity, that the whole of human history was based on the exploitation of the freedom to produce and on forcing people into work, and that the exploited subject both fed and overturned the development of capital – for this we would have to wait years. Without that understanding, without grasping the hot and dissolving current of Marxism, how

---

* Translator's note: unidentified quotation, possibly from memory. E. Bloch identified a 'cold' (scientific) and a 'hot' (humanistic) current of Marxism, e.g. in *Ateismo nel cristianesimo*, Milan: Feltrinelli, 1983, pp. 327–8.

could one understand Lenin and *State and Revolution*, the abolition of the state, and the theory of liberation from the slavery of capital? The various versions of the law of the falling rate of profit only made me laugh – even Benedetto Croce could joke about it, and that says it all. Communism is not inevitable, I would tell myself; we have to build it as an act of witnessing a world of suffering that stood behind us and a future of transformation and hope that I could see as our destiny. 'Hope: the last comfort of fools'? I had to confess to myself, though, that my conversion was laborious. So, asking questions to which I received no replies, feeling that the most active stimuli were being frustrated, I went into survival mode and isolated myself more and more.

On the bourgeois side of things new opportunities were opening up for me. This was the season of the first importation of American sociology into Italy. The goods were being offered by professors who combined a firm concept of order with the hope of being able to get a refund for it, after the catastrophe of Croceanism, via the likes of Sorokin, Merton and Parsons . . . (It's amusing to see similar transactions nowadays, but with Luhmann instead of Parsons – no, no, no, the catastrophe today is not in the ideology, it runs in the real: it's not the catastrophe of fascism and idealism, but one within capitalism!) Basically, even then I applied a certain sense of humour when considering the wealth on offer in sociological work. I managed not to end up doing sociology studies at Olivetti, unlike so many of my peers – tortoiseshell glasses, strutting top of the class. Without too much effort, I have to admit. Sociology, with a few notable exceptions, seemed to me a poor example of compensative thinking – when it was not downright mystificatory; and its relation to historical materialism was like that of pornography to love: a heretical and boss class variant of the science of transformation to which one could apply, *mutatis mutandis*, the thought of that obscure seventeenth-century politologist quoted by Koselleck: *'l'héresie n'est plus auiourd'huy en la Religion; elle est en l'Estat'* ['heresy today is no longer in religion; it is in the state'].*
But there was more in this refusal – a something that was rationally hard and ethically uncompromising, a taste of the sacred nature of reason, of its ontological potentiality – an origin that allowed and nourished only certain pathways of the will. 'Since there, where I really want to go, is a place where I already am.' And on the other hand a distaste for fashion and a natural dislike for any culture, which, already

---

* Translator's note: quoted by Koselleck in Chapter 1 ('Modernity and the Planes of Historicity'; and see n. 8 there for the source) of his *Futures Past: On the Semantics of Historical Time*, Cambridge, MA: MIT Press, 1985.

in its genesis, smells of death. Away, away – away with formalisms and hypocrisy, the dress of science – a stalling of reason to conceal its crisis. Can this be called arrogant, this immediate rejection of formalism and of the sterile labours of those who try to climb onto its grill? (Perhaps this terrible period of struggles that we have recently traversed has allowed us to tear away from collective consciousness not only all taste for mannerism, but even the very possibility of that pleasure.)

However, rather than theory my friends and I preferred investigation and fieldwork – we went to see what was happening, to measure the malaise of the first mass emigration and the uprooting of communities. With this, however, the basic question not only remained unanswered, it was not even touched on: how to build a liberation movement of the poor, how to build the working-class movement. Behind me I had that representation of the collective that the church had offered to the imagination of my teenage years: a compact and static world, which tended towards reaction, in order to preserve its own values. On the other hand I had approached the labour movement and, having lifted the veil from the myth, I saw, even in the best of cases, a cynical Jacobinism and a calculating concept of the autonomy of the political. [Palmiro] Togliatti, *The Prince*: small-time professors whispered among themselves, repeating slogans from the dirtiest version of Machiavellianism (or anti-Machiavellianism, which is the same thing). Alongside this was a crudeness, a minoritarian attitude, like that of fractious and resentful slaves. A desert, a world that was *wertfrei*, a *sécheresse*. For me, it stank. If this was the choice, it was better to stay with the priests – there at least, in that world, the prudence would always have been broken by outbursts of compassion – whereas here one drank the milk of the lean cow. But surely there is more than this. Thus, while I was increasingly closing in on myself, defining and measuring the things that I discovered, there emerged, from this objective clash in which I was immersed, a statement as restless in its capacity as it was determined in its intensity. A statement of project: to go ahead with my research, to dig that solid ground (and to hold onto it), that ground from which a lot of love had been expressed and where a lot of violence had been exercised. Beyond the representations there needed to be this vigorous *noumenon*. Where the desire for truth could meet with the *potenza* of the collective. What is communism, other than that?

That's all for now, David. Today is a beautiful day. Here too there is a joy. In our discussions we continue to ask ourselves that selfsame question. I send you a hug.

Letter Three
Souzy

Rebibbia, 23 October 1981

Cher David,

It's a bit odd looking back over history in this schematising fashion. An oversimplification? Maybe. But what does it matter? Midwifery is never easy. So the confusion between love and hate, the immersion into a historical world characterised by the weary regularity of a nature that was overworked – and then the break with all that, but in a way that was harsh and abrupt, so that the hatred did not succeed in becoming productive – all this had reduced me to solitude. My language is also a little comical. But what does that matter? That suffering was real. A solitude fed by the delirium of abstract intellectual work – a pleasure bordering on addiction. Unhappiness was washing over me, like clouds driven by sudden gusts of wind. Being on my own was driving me towards a utopia, but it also brought on me, rather uncomfortably, a nostalgia for the world from which I had excluded myself. The collective comes before my imagination, I told myself repeatedly; it is its precondition, whether positive or negative. For the moment it was only a negative condition, because it was from a lack that I was suffering. I was at a limit. Here's Hegel:

> The nostalgia towards life of those who have developed in themselves nature as an idea . . . Such people cannot live alone, and human beings are always alone, even if they set up their own nature before them, have made themselves a companion of this representation, and take joy from it; but they must also find the represented as a living being.*

---

* Translator's note: This quotation comes from an isolated fragment in a draft prepared by young Hegel for his introduction to a 'German Constitution'

So imagination could either become corrupted into fantasy or reconnect to the real and become vigorous. Growing with me. I knew what I wanted: the collective, recognition as an active participant in a community – and the power to produce change. But I was alone. Luck, however, may be a logical outcome of solitude: perhaps solitary individuals have no vocation to connect themselves to the historical movement, and yet they do so. It is not a gift; it is luck or chance.

Between 1954 and 1955 I found myself in Israel, following a nice girl with whom I'd fallen in love – in Kibbutz Nachsonim, near Petah-Tikva. I worked long hours on the plantations. I slept in a comfortable wooden cabin. The kibbutz was Mapam [United Workers' Party] – left-wing socialists, rigorous kibbutzniks. The languages were English and French – they were immigrants mainly from the shores of the Mediterranean – so they understood each other. That was my base, but on festive days I set off happily travelling round Israel. For a while I worked as a labourer in Eilat, earning money, which you could not do in the kibbutz. Then I left, but without the girl who had drawn me there – we parted company in the foothills of Lake Galilee, because she had fallen for Shlomo . . . Goodbye Israel. I have never been back, and the deep bond that unites me to that land of the fathers has often been subjected to (and has fed) a fierce criticism. (When, dear David, will the ancestral flight come to an end, and when will the Torah no longer be newly foretold? Never – and this is a reason for pride. But sometimes the prophecy is false and treacherous. When pride becomes devastation and hatred, cry your Kaddish then – Jerusalem is Babylon. 'And when thou hast made an end of reading this book, thou shalt tie a stone to it and cast it into the midst of Euphrates: and thou shalt say, Thus shall Babylon sink, and shall not rise again': Jeremiah 51: 63.)

Anyway, back to us. So, Israel was my luck, my chance – and my symbol. When you are looking for a practical foundation of reason, even if it is utopian reason, chance becomes a rich resource. There is no astute foresight in this, nor is there blind happenstance – we move continually within an ensemble of possibilities (which is of course preconstituted), and chance is the condition that slows or accelerates

---

('Die Verfassung Deutschlands'). It can be found in volume 1 (1986) of E. Moldenhauer and K. M. Michel's Frankfurt (Suhrkamp) edition of Hegel's works from the period 1832–45. In Italy the fragment was translated as an autonomous piece under the title 'Libertà e destino'; for a discussion, see Mario Tronti, 'Un frammento hegeliano', *Il Ponte*, November 2009, at http://www.ilponterivista.com/article_view.php?intId=191 (accessed 23 June 2014).

the effects of our liberty. A chance or a miracle of freedom in the midst of the world of phenomena. Like a young man at a dance: after long waiting and much looking, under the sign of desire, he suddenly has the feeling that the 'time has come'. I was ready, from within my solitude, to recompose love and hate into a game of reality.

(Empedocles: magician, man and divine bird. Do the old thinkers provide us with the means to describe the hard and solid elements that remain after the collapse of the bourgeois-philosophical ambition of the past centuries: so many have tried to deal with this mystery, from Hölderlin's anticipation up until Heidegger's reading of it, which was all in terms of death. Love and hate – and their synthesis – and the excavation of the communist way of being: this is what liberates us from the mystery, what dissolves the mystifying attractions of all irrationalist ontologies. The collective can be conjugated with the destruction of the existent, and within this destruction a rebirth of the collective genius of love and of communism is possible.)

There, in Israel, I was living practices of communism that were as radical as they were elementary. This utopia was real; its reality had bite. It was concrete. Souzy, an Egyptian and a former maths teacher, gave me my political grounding. He was a carpenter in the kibbutz, and since he was both a Jew and a communist he had spent many years in the concentration camps of Muhammad Naguib. We maintained an amicable correspondence right up until his death. Souzy talked to me about communism as a necessary development of the human community. He spoke fast and excitedly, like somebody debating fiercely with himself, presumably from his being a former detainee. Then he would stop, he would smile with his extraordinary blue eyes (a comic *tic* would twitch his grizzled brown moustache), his Sephardic belly would wobble – and his exposition would become simple and lucid, his argumentation fraternal and marked by solidarity. His features were as sharp as his hopes: an Arab communism for which Israel had been the crucible. His story was that of all the Jewish communists, namely the desire to destroy, in an extreme act of collective love, all the hereditary handed-down participations in nature and history, to build a world that was free, such as can only be constructed by imagination and separation, by the collective and productive strength of the reason of the masses.

Ernst Bloch again. Differently and yet not differently, Franz Rosenzweig. With this one there is division inside a hope for the future. 'Benediction divides the world into two, to reunite it again in the future. This division runs through the whole life in the form of the sacred and the common, the Sabbath and the working day, the

Torah and the "way of the earth".'* The sacred does not exclude the profane; the opposition is entirely contained within the collective consciousness of the chosen people – it chooses itself in advance and of its own free will; production and creative work are right here, in this division, through this division. Empedocles again? Nowadays one or two of my comrades, a little too hastily inclined to criticism, might say that my views are naive in two respects: that of love and the collective consciousness of a freedom that might have the power to separate itself; and that of the Enlightenment-inspired hope for a practical transformation of nature. This is utopia. So be it! I remain attached to the force of this utopia and I consider it the concluding point of my teenage regeneration. Souzy, thank you, thank you!

At night, from time to time, with our Sten guns, we would go close to the border, partly to take food to the guard, but mostly to check that there was enough food for the pigs, which we hid from the eyes of the Orthodox – making sure that they were also well hidden from Arab snipers. On the hillside we would often stop to watch the sky, chatting and counting the stars. Souzy was a great one for analytical games and philosophical paradoxes. He had studied in England and had attended the lectures of Bertrand Russell. Then, when I inevitably fell into talking about my amorous hardships (which were very unhappy – all because of Shlomo . . .), he would make fun of me. This was our little ritual. Next, having completed these preliminaries, we would start talking about communism. And, as we lay in the grass, the stars were above us and a great intellectual openness between us. Souzy had the same cultural sensibility that, much later, I recognised in other Mediterranean communists, such as Henry Curiel and Samir Amin . . . If it had been possible to translate politically the flexibility and imaginativeness of the ghetto of Cephalonia and of Albert Cohen's heroes, we would have physically configured it in them! In Souzy's view, the central pole in building a revolution is not so much the (albeit essential) relationship between the party and the programme of socialist transition, as the participation of the masses and the immediate efficacy of the transitional programme. From this point of view, the work of the dictatorship of the proletariat was bound to be insufficient: but what was fundamental was the destruction that the proletarian movement carried within the masses – the destruction of the reactionary elements, of ignorance, of poverty – and the

---

* Translator's note: unidentified quotation, possibly from Franz Rosenzweig's (1921) *The Star of Redemption*. (For a modern edition, see Letter 5.)

simultaneous valorisation of elements of community. In the former colonies this programme was bound to be terribly difficult, because the subjective modification had to work within the realities of primitive accumulation; but it was nevertheless possible. This Jewish carpenter was anticipating Mao. In the developed capitalist countries the programme was possible and immediately doable – but was this the project of the western communist parties? Souzy's doubts on this question were coupled with increasingly strong suspicions about the Soviets – even though the USSR had all his sympathies as a militant – albeit very quietly (given the controversy that was raging in the Mapam at that time). (In my memory now, as I write this letter, the words of Souzy mingle in their character with other discourses, which I used to hear some years before, *chez nous*, coming from various former partisans, comrades of one of our relatives, when they held meetings at our house. At a certain point the noise of the discussion would stop, and in a general muttering they would break with the hopes and loyalties they had until then proclaimed vis-à-vis the USSR. Then, after a while, these former combatants would take their leave. Alone, one after the other, like sad shooting stars.) In Souzy the Enlightenment inspiration of the project was accompanied by an attentiveness to the formation of the programme and to the articulations of the transition. He was a true communist, a class democrat in a proletarian sense, opposed to Jacobinism. One of the many deep variants of the proletarian versus the variants of the bourgeois.

But all through that story that I was living and the moral and intellectual growth that came from it, there was also something else. In fact, as if unbeknownst to myself, I was harmoniously conjoining in my mind the peasant origins of my ideology – my Po valley identity – with the hopes of communist transformation. The tearing of the transformation had to be measured in the mass movement, from within it, in its density. It was by a return to the origins that we would invent the future. Because it was on those rhythms of internal rupture and internal recompacting that communism was possible. Does the future have an ancient heart? Certainly not, if this motto hankers after ancient virtues – but certainly yes, if communism seeks to build itself on the compact rhythm of mass consciousness, with its breaks and recompositions. Can there can be a harmony of breakings? A solidity of the discontinuous? I did not know the answer to this, but I felt it as part of the character of the utopia that I was living. I was later to learn that only an overturning constructs the world – but already in Padua I'd caught a whiff of Concetto Marchesi's readings of Lucretius, in the tales told of him by his students – the taste for a creative overturning. Democritus–Epicurus–Marx is a long line of descent but it is direct, renewed by the inversion of the concept of *clinamen* [the swerve] – in the ancients, this was the random production of innovation of the cosmic story, whereas in Marx it was a collective capacity for building, a catastrophic and innovative rationality of history, proletarian dominion and communist community. *Die Formen*. Now Souzy had led me by the hand to that point where, for me (as previously for him), began the possibility of a practical synthesis that placed itself on the human root, both individual and collective, the one in cordial exchange with the other. Nature, just by itself, was insufficient to bring about this synthesis, but collective human action could do it – by building in history a second nature, a new nature. By recreating the world. The kibbutzniks lived on crops and produce that were plucked from the desert and from the rocky hills. They dug and irrigated continuously. This new way of doing agriculture reminded me of the ancient, refined and perfect ways of my homeland in the Po valley. The hand of man had remade nature. (Is it banal, today, to restate this? After Foucault has taught us to make a history of nature, our nature? For me at that time, it was a visceral and hungry discovery.) Why not remake ourselves? It was possible, and it was necessary. Nothing Promethean in all this – for all that Prometheanism contains of the individualistic. The Jewish culture of the colonisation of Israel was rather animated by that other major component – which was Russian, collectivist and Soviet. When I came to read Sereni on the Italian countryside, I found again this emancipated style of the relationship between revolution and nature. For a revolutionary return to the origins – for a radical transformation of our nature: these were the real paradoxes that were expressed in the words of Souzy.

Then, in our discussions, inevitably the question of 1917 came up. When Souzy spoke of revolution, he meant the October Revolution. What was 1917? It was a point of no return – not only in history but also in human nature; the point of a radical transformation in social structure – and only in that transformation was it possible today to speak of humanity. To measure oneself against that reality and to understand that after it nothing was any longer the same in the world and in the individual, that nothing had repeated itself, and that a new human community had become possible, completing the dream and going beyond the malaise of modernity – this was the characteristic line of Souzy's discourse. And he soon brought me into agreement with him. We would leave at first light, coming down the side of the hill that was sheltered from the shooting of the snipers. 'The rosy-fingered Dawn, daughter of the morning.'* So, cher David, in that summer all the scattered elements that I had been collecting were coming together in me. Into my second nature? Certainly not completed, not yet. But certainly into my dream of it – a project.

Back in Italy I threw myself back into my usual solitary way of life. I did a summing-up of my circumstances: a Christian background that gave me a strong orientation towards human beings and their redemption in poverty, and a critique of my background that made me need to overcome the constraints of an organisational terrain that was by now barren, but to preserve and enhance the sense of being that lived *there* and only there – a sense of being that was real and collective, powerful and strong. At my first contact with the official labour movement I saw grudging resentfulness and crudeness as the dominant organisational characteristics – and also an extraordinary poverty of ethics. And yet it was here – it could not have been anywhere else – that the principle that had found its first dramatic incarnation in 1917 would become a reality. Thus, in this maze of uncertainties and doubts, I was wavering; attracted and repelled by these real referents, incapable of making decisions. I had to shun abstractness, I thought – *nun-einmal-so-sein* – to be here and not otherwise. Both in the Catholic world that saw the mystical as the stuff of the devil and in that Stalinist world that exalted politics to the point of becoming coprophiliac, utopia was seen as pure and simple madness. But how to escape the snares of a love that had become such an intense emotion, and the dangers of a hatred that had become crude administration? How to retrieve the potency of poverty and the force of a global transformation? And, I wondered, what if the desire for utopia was more real and historically more active than the ugly realism of the proposals that I was hearing? The first synthesis of the consciousness that seeks to free itself is always utopian.

I found myself moving in small communities of young people who, like me, were experiencing this tension that was simultaneously religious and political. Something was moving around us – we could barely see it but we were sure that it was there, precisely, as a movement and as a real transformation. In fact we were witnessing the onset of the first transformations and contradictions, perceptible and complex, of our world in terms of mature capitalism. But we shall return to a longer discussion of this later, cher David. For the

---

* Translator's note: a conventional epithet and metric formula, often repeated in the *Iliad*.

Letter Three: Souzy

time being we lived this experience of development at a level that was symmetrical but not homologous with it. We carried on in a dream of old-time community that verged on utopianism, while around us new collective subjects were forming and the dialectic of capital was developing its enormous strength. There are people who always live development in this symmetrical position, without interfering with reality: sensitive, intelligent, nonactive. Perhaps the aesthetic theory of modernity, which is also a kind of ethics, is directly prescriptive in this respect: it requires this detachment. As for myself, given my situation, I was (so to speak) ringed in by this contradiction. Caught up not in search of beauty but in search of a true abstract. So: an aesthetic experience, when all's said and done? Maybe – to the extent that it may have been the fulfilment of a metaphysics of youth. But does that remove the truth from it?

I involved myself, it's true, in small *essais* in transformative practice – useful but artisanal. I continued with my sociological fieldwork; I was involved in the student newspaper of the University of Padua; I followed the arguments between those semi-serious organisations known as UNURI (Unione nazionale universitaria rappresentativa italiana), UGI (Unione goliardica italiana) and Intesa; and I had more or less sporadic contacts with the official sections of the labour movement. What boredom, what weariness! We needed to invent the future. I studied; and I travelled a fair bit. In 1956 I was involved in a study commission on the constitution of the workers' councils in Yugoslavia – and from it I concluded that, at least in that phase, these councils were no more than a new form of organising consensus and labour exploitation. 'Thus far constitutions have only perfected the state machine instead of destroying it.' At this point my readings of the history of the labour movement – because that is what I was mostly doing, while for me the classics remained somewhat indigestible (Brecht, 'the intimidatory effect of the classics') – those historical readings, as I say, fitted appropriately into my critical apprenticeship. The October Revolution, fascism and Nazism, the Spanish Civil War, antifascism – in short, a fine encyclopaedia. I began to pick my way through this enormous and formidable ontological spectacle of life and death, of desire and repression. Then the history of the United States, and of Germany. And so on.

Reading, reading – day and night – my distant friend, your inconclusiveness is tiring: even then I experienced this distance between practical consciousness and theoretical knowledge as something of a drama. Books are no use before experience – I was building a latency; but I suffered especially from this latency. Knowledge was not yet making happiness for me. In fact, the heart and mind were driving towards the desire for a politics that was, in immediate terms, construction and liberation. Souzy had taught me this. Utopia is legitimate when it extends towards the concrete, when it is articulated with action – when it is a utopia going towards possibility. The October Revolution and Israel combined pleasingly in my desire. Utopia is a rational construction of the possible – it has nothing to do with the impossible, except for its posing as an impossibility for the enemy, a total alternative against the enemy's plans – utopia is the collective desire to go beyond the limit set up by enemies in order to guarantee their power. Would we ever have succeeded in that, here in Italy? Utopia was the practice of a subject, of a subject who was exploited, of the poor. So it was necessary to work on desire and to attempt small speculations from the starting point of the concept in order to give hope legs on which it could walk. It was necessary to study, to break all the continuities that experience offered, to gain a project that was universal – in order to reintegrate, within being, the surface on which we were moving. The utopia was – and is – a quest for being. It implies the tension of procreating in true love. It is a hypothesis matched to the future, spurred by the critique of the present and by the love of being. Max Scheler and not Karl Mannheim.

Today, when we talk among comrades, utopia has that same good taste. Pathways, once you get beyond the precipices, want to go upwards from the bottom of the valley. Utopia is good because our gaze has already enjoyed – from heights, in the previous journey – the broad landscapes of the border. But in those days, as a kid, I was without experience and alone. I seemed like a crazy person. I have a photograph from that time: hair short and straight, looking like I came from West Point – and my tie crooked. A strange face and laughing eyes, a little wild. Perhaps I understood that the utopia had reached some kind of end point – for me, an outer limit, as I have already said, cher David. There's always an edge to the world as we know it: when we find ourselves standing there, it can be a bit dizzying. I was not armed, but I was ready to fly. It was hard. Often I suffered from asthma at night, and my mother would wipe the sweat from my forehead. It's getting late. I think it's time to say goodnight, David. Till tomorrow.

PS: It's now morning, and I have just reread this letter, which I finished last night. I find it narcissistic, egotistical and manipulative. Yes, there was also something else in Israel – even then. There was the racism of the fair-skinned Jews against those who came from Yemen or Morocco – and the fair-skinned ones disinfected them like you do with pigs, and the fact that the white bird of Isaiah had led them to Tel Aviv did not give them higher wages. Because it remained a wage, and a wretched one at that, even when the paymaster was the kibbutz – a communist boss. All the stigmata of a class society were present in the country and ready to explode outwards. And there was the sense of guilt of the expropriator, who always gives a vulgar colouring to the figure of the coloniser, both in the West and in Palestine. Nor did the epic tale of the motherland regained cancel out the hysterical travail of the diaspora. Today, when the dream of freedom is soiled – that Prussia reborn, which Souzy would have hated – the contradiction seems to annul that hope. But the rebelliousness, the cosmopolitanism and the communism were nevertheless real. And we planted so many, many trees of liberty down there. But then, Souzy, why did we not ask the Arab sniper to come down the mountain and share some of the pork, in a spirit of progressive secularism, solidarity and rebelliousness?

Letter Four
Admiratio

Rebibbia, 3 November 1981

Cher David,

What would you call it today, this topos, the *admiratio* that, in Descartes, lays the basis for the genealogy of the passions? I would call it 'dialectic' – that is, an uncritical adherence to the logic of the existent in the form in which it is given to us, in the splendour of objectivity – a repose of reason in the totality. That the genealogy of the passions always ran the risk of becoming a catalogue of the passions, that much I knew – but that the more mature expressions of the dialectical *Aufhebung* [sublation] effectively represented this, that I did not realise. So it happened – in those decisive years, between 1956 and 1958 – that I fell prey to the confusion of the totality and I deluded myself that the dialectic was capable of containing and developing a utopian matrix. And at the same time I thought it was possible to mediate empirical and pedestrian instances of transformation – as was wished by the so-called 'culture of the left', then dominant. This theoretical situation was imposed on me: the attraction to a middle point, to a fetishism of reality, was in some sense inevitable in that culture, and it was certainly internal to its conditions. Hence the utopian framework on which the research had landed – a beach like that of the mythical Phaeacians in their confused and difficult wandering* – underwent a shift: the *admiratio* became self-complacent, a totality satisfied – and now it called for adequate

---

* Translator's note: allusion to the Phaeacian episode in Book Six of the Homeric *Odyssey*.

nourishment. (To feed on what? We were not capable of making love – brutality, cynicism, a pedestrian *ars amatoria* – the sweetness of the concrete was missing.) Was there deception in all this?

(Intermission: it's a difficult thing, the evaluation of the past – sometimes stupid. Disenchantment is missing. My apologies, David, for the judgements that I hand out and the memories that I distribute: given material. Rough stuff, I'll readily admit; and so is the labour, too. Don't want to justify myself. This return to the past is an insidious thing: I have very little faith in it because in writing big differences are smoothed over, perspectives are wrong, and dimensions are flattened. Everything's running by. Stop the picture!)

And anyway there was something misleading here. Something surreptitiously paid off by the fact that this new presentation of the world was informed by the refinement and sublimation of the elementary theoretical perceptions from which I was moving, and that – consequently – a considerable degree of understanding of cultural relations had been introduced, and that this understanding would serve as a means of reading the generic *Umwelt* [environment]; I was caught within this totality. But in any event there was here a betrayal of the restless and innovative motive forces of the utopian tension. Why did I fall into sin? What was the snake in my Eden? It's good to talk about it, cher David, because we are often tickled by temptation, today no less than yesterday. So what I remember is that my theoretical ambition was perfectly compatible with – indeed was on a par with – the philosophy that was current in the labour movement. And in the meantime I was getting to know this philosophy better and better, in its Italic specificity. So what I shall give you in this letter, David, is, first and foremost, the story of a real deceit, one that was hard to resist: the *admiratio* for the Italic province, the Fellini of revolutionary theory. Then, secondly, we shall try to see how the one-sidedness and the illusory dimension of the humanistic context were broken – and what pathways opened afterwards.

So my approach to the philosophy of the labour movement was the situation in which I moved. Historicism was a comprehensive philosophical perspective, a privileged terrain for alliances, a framework for the forms of tactics and strategy. A philosophy of the Resistance. I accepted it. A setting aside of the utopia, a philosophy of restoration. I did not realise this. I am forever trying to explain to you the reason why I fell for this deception – it does not seem difficult to me. More difficult is to explain how this happened precisely at the point when the ideology of historicism had reached a critical phase: 1956 and the Twentieth Congress of the Communist Party of the Soviet Union introduced frenetic elements of restlessness even before the upheaval of the congress itself. But the inertia was more powerful and had you in its grip: a kind of 'tankism' in philosophy. The dialectic of historicism, whether you took it in its Italic version, smooth and Crocean, or in the more jagged, more nervy German version – that of Ranke, Meinecke, Troeltsch, and the like – was suffering the first decisive attacks. It was not for me. I reacted by being annoyed. I was more of a *realista** than the king. As far as I was concerned, that historicism was a reassurance. From comparisons with the past I drew the illusion of a genealogy of the critical function. In addition, according to a singular heteronomy of ends, the dialectic, in the objective form of its historical unfolding, seemed to satisfy pluralistic and eclectic needs: a totality that was stable and inexhaustible, but also a whole that was multidirectional, a mixture of coherent layers. A multiplicity. And then this totality was something that one could pass through – historicism was also – and especially – a practice of historiography, and the contact with Chabod (whose lectures I had attended at the Istituto Croce during my Naples years) was clarifying for me the infinite and exciting pathways of hermeneutics. Thus the totality of the historical horizon served as a solid foundation (especially since in those days the analytical objections were presented in the pretentious utterances of the likes of Talcott Parsons and Pietro Rossi). Nor did the decidedly reactionary elements of the historicist tradition offend me – although I punctiliously fought them. The fact is that historicism presented itself as a projection of traditional humanism – in its democratic and optimistic version. The whole framework elicited admiration, and upon it, upon the complexity of the functions it held (an objective totality and a sort of subjective unanimism), it was even possible for my desire for utopia to be laid, a figure that was cut out and manageable. This is probably the reason why I persevered. A Cartesian, reasoning enchantment. But there was more. There was the question of the dialectic. Curiously, rather than presenting itself as a struggle of historical subjects, in that context it appeared more as the logical shell of a world of communicating vessels – it was a sort of historical Neoplatonism, a Neoplatonism without mystical excesses and without irreducible physical or theological elements. The gnostic protest, the restlessness of the young Fichte or Schelling against the sweet taste of this reductionism, against the manoeuvre

---

* Translator's note: this is a play on the double meaning of the Italian word ('realist'/'royalist').

of undervaluing the irrational or the utopia, did not touch me. Yet, paradoxically, how much more realistic was their *Je méprise Locke*! [I despise Locke]. The systematic elasticity of objective idealism and historicism allowed them to be used in ways that were ambiguous, versatile and astute: by all those who had made it their trade, both in the Catholic movement – where the great tradition of the history of the two cities, of heaven and hell, was manoeuvred within the hybrid framework of the hegemony of the church, from Cardinal Newman to the Dominican Sertillanges – and in the area of the labour movement – especially there, where the historical necessity of a succession of modes of production meant that revolution (and the human articulations of exploitation) became an ontological platitude when it was not merely an agitational argument. The splendours of the Stalinist theory of the stages of development. (They were all inebriated with them.) It was in this context that Gramscianism operated: its lessons were further vulgarised by charlatanism – self-justifying historical interpretations, pseudocontinuities, Masonic stories. For what it was worth, a philosophy of history: pacified, organic, evolutionist, reformist – a quietistic usage of the category of 'hegemony'. A truly vulgar *maquillage* [makeup] for that fine Leninist face of Gramsci.

(And then I found out – I justify myself with the horrified good faith of a German after Auschwitz – I found out that in those years there were the exile departments in FIAT, and so many communists in jail, and yellow unions in the factories and in society at large, and shit pensions, and people going to work with the boss's union card – how fine to talk about historicism! Is it possible, after Auschwitz, to be objective?)

The sea was full of oil – and the sand of tar. But we still believed in humanism. We dug below the tar. And this (confused) digging, we took it for a promise of liberation. Was it? In some ways it worked as if it was. It is for this reason, cher David, that I would still insist on the humanistic ambiguity of historicism, because the force of deception and its effectiveness depended on ambiguity. Humanistic historicism in a historiographic sense – as another of the teachers of those years, Eugenio Garin, explained very attractively; humanistic historicism in a political sense – because what there was of a politically progressive element expressed itself in those terms. So I have some supporting evidence to justify the tangle in which I found myself and to recognise that I was not wholly responsible for it. Pitiful justifications: from the point of view of the class struggle, this philosophy produced in effect only a single slogan, vague and repeated: let us pick up the banners that the bourgeoisie has dropped – let us go deeper and re-create the accumulation of capital inside socialism. In myself, at that time, the dislike for such stereotypes had not yet become a rejection. I endured that philosophy of castration. The fact that, at that moment, compassion for the world, hatred and love for the way things were, and a commitment to communist knowledge ended up resting impotently in a state of *admiratio* can only be explained as fascination and surrender.

However, they are correct – the suspicion and reproach that I see on your face. I can only reiterate: remember that historicism at that time presented itself as an effective cultural mediation, it was the philosophy of the people who had played their part in the Resistance, against fascism. It was a civil and political fact. This was the fundamental fact about the imbroglio, and I was a newcomer to politics. (The imbroglio was in fact far more tragic than that – and now we're all paying a high price for it. A political class was overturned by it – precisely the political class of the Resistance. Historicism in fact soon became the philosophy of administrators and its ideological flexibility was a justification for their surrender, a corruption disguised as wisdom, a cover for cynicism, a restoration. And, in this dynamic, humanistic tensions were put second to the urgencies of *Realpolitik* – and became faded, reduced to a witnessing of the past and to impotent nostalgia. Today we recognise them immediately, more for their weariness than for their hypocrisy, more for their rhetoric than for their falsehood – these mediocre representatives of the mediocre mediation that followed on the Resistance, these vulgar symbols of a huge – and ultimately fraudulent – historical failure.)

But the mystifying calm did not last long. Consider a few factors: the ambiguity of this patriotic humanism contained in itself elements of rupture. After the Twentieth Congress the political landscape began to change very rapidly. Personally I followed these changes in the collective cultural sensitivity with a great deal of work and worry. So let us now start again from the last point, because it is easier, cher David – and certainly not to erect my personal experience into moral allegory. Having finished my thesis on contemporary German historicism and its re-elaboration, I began working on Hegel. I translated some of his youthful writings into Italian – I spent a number of years working on this, as well as on the culture of the period and on the Hegelian project. Did this bring me to the end of the first (corrupt and opportunistic) fascination with historicism? Did it open a really new perspective? I don't think so. I ran into more trouble. It was no longer provincialism, however. The debate was spreading like wildfire. New bacteria were beginning to ferment. Hegel was like a funnel: he brought together in himself, more or less tumultuously – or so it seemed to me – everything that the history of thought had produced after him. Hegel was as big as a pyramid of Egypt, everyone had put a brick in, slaves and masters alike, no chance of being able to shift him. Now everybody was climbing him. The young Hegel was giving rise to neohumanist readings, which put the young Marx together with Hegel – the themes of alienation, community, and the liberation/realisation of *Menschenwesen*. Was it possible that, with the young Hegel, an alternative to historicist humanism was opening? No. It was just a dynamic variant within that horizon. But the game was complex and potentially innovative, not reductionist and historicist. I adopted a tactic: not to jump beyond the horizon of humanism, but simply to grasp the dialectic in terms that were more properly conflictual and subjectively relevant, even if not exhaustive of the thematic of subjectivity. The general picture remained as it was, solid; but the *admiratio* was subjected to a more refined fusion, and thus its elements began to split apart – the philosophical work was shaking off the ecstasy. The first ferments of the post-Twentieth Congress situation were experienced by myself through the optic of this problematic. And there is no doubt that it was a life event. In the same way in which the magnet attracts iron filings and makes patterns with them, aggressive and diffuse tendencies and tensions clustered magnetically around this new excavation of Hegelianism. In particular around a Hegel who was nostalgic for the *polis*, who denounced bourgeois alienation, and who saw in labour the laborious key to a recomposition of humanity. In those luxuriant and violent analyses of the passions that were born in Jena and culminated in *The Phenomenology of the Spirit*. Recalling the masterly acuteness of Hyppolite, I recomposed many suggestive aspects of postwar French philosophy, with which I was familiar. The systematic figure of the mature Hegel had been torn apart – and this meant that the connections – obscure and ambiguous, but certainly pacificatory – that had formed in academic historicism and in the labour movement's philosophy of alliances had been broken too: the breaking of the system made it possible to identify its components, led back to practice, revealed the material dynamics. Once again I ask myself whether all this was decisive and broke the fascination of the totality that was *admiranda* [to be admired]. And again I answer in the negative. Nevertheless it is true that, in the new authors that I was beginning to read – be they Sartre and Merleau-Ponty or Enzo Paci and Preti in Italy – I saw the analytic of that *admiranda* totality developing into a constitutive function rather than as a harmonious definition.

As we know, in Spinoza – when he takes up the Cartesian genealogy of morality – *admiratio* is not presented as the founder, the first among the passions, but as the fourth in the catalogue, paired with *contemptus* [contempt] and (this is the important thing) preceded by *cupiditas, amor et odium* [desire, love and hate]. So, from the point of view of the passions (and this was the dimension on which my mind was defining itself at that time: besides, is it not a reactionary fable that simple *contemplatio* could constitute philosophy, as an alternative to the study of passion? that philosophy could exist without a practical foundation?), the totality is not the foundation but only a medium – ideology filtered by desire. Probably my thoughts, which were in tune with a very European line of thinking, did undergo an initial Spinozan conversion. In fact I began to ask myself: is it possible to have a dialectic that does not move to, or that does not lead back to, a total foundation? With this, the bacillus of the negative finally began to infect my culture – which still remained, however, frankly dialectical. The conquest of the materialistic sense of the determination was a long way away – but I suppose I was making progress. Humanism was no longer, beyond any doubt, historicism, and the justificationist function of that great machine was misfiring. (Another self-criticism: would this *mélange* of utopia and the negative have ever been capable of breaking the iron mask of dialectic? In short, we – or I – were only deluding ourselves.)

Cher David, they will certainly have filled your head with the generation of postwar French philosophy, which grew up on the 'three Hs': Hegel, Husserl and Heidegger. But the real journey takes place, logically and historically, on an opposite path: from the assumption of the Heideggerian existent to a methodical renewal of the constitutive function of Husserl, to the determined reappropriation of the dialectical schema proper to progressive humanism. Personally, I was tying myself to that determination with ever greater conviction. And I had made my own the presuppositions of this disposition of the spirit: to paraphrase Hegel's exclamation about Spinoza, I could say here that, unless you knew and loved Hegel, you were not a philosopher. The curious thing was that this reaffirmation of philosophy was aimed at its destruction: the primacy of the dialectic was not directed at reconstruction, but at the dissolution of the abstract and the absolute. And, whether or not it was aware of it, at the consequent foundation of a concrete practice, a material rooting of thought. It is now clear that here, on this form of Hegelianism, was where the young Marx came in, and that here, on this radical humanism, the hope of formulating politically the theory of transformation was renewed – inside and after the crisis of the Soviet vulgate in the years immediately following the

Twentieth Congress. At that time it was not obvious to me – but this does not mean that the research did not push very hard. The climate of the period was leading to radical humanism. Hegel was the master, reinterpreted and renovated, and standing centre-stage. As I have said and continue to repeat, cher David, the dialectic had become new. Because the exercise was to take Hegel to pieces and then put him together again – dismantle his systematics with a view to finding the anthropological basis of each concept, reassemble the concepts in hypothetical and imaginative functions, which would make possible new and more adventurous practices. It was really an orgy of subjectivity, what we were witnessing. Given this state of things, it is easy to understand the irritation and reaction of the structuralists – the claim for a 'transcendental field without a subject', which the Hegelian Hyppolite himself was to propose for analysis a few years later – and the frenetic anxiety of 'deconstruction' that followed this proposal.

In Italy these currents were felt much less. The resistances were infinite. It was only later that these themes made their entry – I remember, for example, Franco Fortini's *Argomenti* – but here they were more centred on the re-creation of the (still Hegelian) subversivism of the communist left of the 1920s than on the French experience. On a strictly philosophical terrain, the academic and the official world tended rather to relegitimate, through exchange, both the historicist culture and the socialist reformism. And, if you leave aside that extraordinary freelance, Enzo Paci, little was discussed, destroyed, or invented in cultural circles. But there was a lot of discussion among the younger generations, who were cut out from the channels of official culture after the Twentieth Congress and were now definitively hostile to all variants of the Croce–Gramsci hybrid and nauseated by Soviet scholasticism.

What I'm trying to say, as I look at myself and the world in which I was living, is basically that this neohumanism, which was so widespread in literary circles, was a focal point of renovation and the true cultural birthright of a whole generation. Post-existentialist ideology provided a positive, albeit vague foundation for a theoretical and political initiative, reproposing the centrality of man, of dialectical anthropology, of a sense of the destruction of systems, and of the practical renovation of project and horizon. Much irony was expended on this transition in subsequent years. The subjectivism it contained was so strong that – as was rightly noted at the time – the humanisation of the world often became a personification of nothingness. Empty figures, theatrical ghosts. This strange Hegelianism, which knew only Hegel's *Darstellung* and not the *Logos*, they said, was an itch, not philosophy. Yet it seems to me that this progressive religion of the human being was a frontier – or, if you prefer, a trench – essential if you wanted to defend the communist hope as you faced the U turn of Soviet ideology and the elements of radical discontinuity with the labour movement's traditions that the Twentieth Congress presented. The year 1968 cannot be understood without this theoretical passage: in its genesis, the three Hs counted for much more than the three Ms. A generic proposition, an indistinctness of the project – and yet this aggressive humanism made possible the secular proposal of an absolute Pascalian wager. *L'existentialisme est un humanisme*. The liberation of Algeria was a universal sign. (In those days philosophers did not baulk at carrying weapons to the rebels; they considered freedom to be a right for all and torture to be disgrace for all. Is it possible that the days in which the simplicity of rebellion and the firmness of solidarity had value are past and gone? Must ethical revolt now be timidly handed over to Amnesty International?)

There was a strange frenzy around, and it was gradually spreading. The insistence on the problem and the urgency of a renewal were therefore not only my own – indeed there was a worldwide reevaluation of the pre-reflexive elements of the revolt in philosophy and politics. I remember that in those years I was attending the classes of Eugenio Garin. I recall the famous statement by Kojève, in his *Introduzione alla fenomenologia*, which runs more or less like this: 'if the real totality implies man, and man is dialectical, then man is totality.' The Italian historicists took this on their own, well aware of the foundational and ontological centrality that human operation thereby assumed. And, through an identical epic transformation, the 'the rational is real' became a mode of the anthropological node: a *verum ipsum factum* [truth itself is made]. The sense of crisis, the abandonment of the old horizon became, for all of us, a bedrock for new initiatives. Pure subjectivist hysteria? *Individuelle Kompensationskunst* [individual art of compensation]? Maybe. But, for me and for many of us, it was a further support for, and a profound corroboration of, our commitment to revolutionary discourse; a twisting path, perhaps even folkloric and provincial, but it brought us closer to materialist analysis. More of this, cher David, in another letter.

(But why have you forced me into this very tough game? I can sense your being ironical as you read these letters. That's not fair. Did I laugh when you were getting all agitated because you wanted the seashores of Brittany to be free of oil and tar? Everything is contradictory in the fables of lived experience: ingenuousness and reflection change roles. Utopianism and realism are two faces of one practice – and only this justifies us. It is only by throwing ourselves in the sea of philosophy that we learn to swim in it.)

In any case, in what I've written thus far there are empty spaces, which you of course, educated as you are in the rigorous outcomes of structuralism and in the *potenza* of Deleuzian difference, will not let pass. But, setting aside irony and with a little goodwill, I persist in asking: How was it possible to turn all those ghosts of totality and all that sublime ethical void of the subject into the key to a transition to a revolutionary undertaking? They were gadgets, not concepts. The answer can only recall the misery of those times – across all its coordinates: we were attempting to bring together a religious rooting and a desire for revolutionary transformation, a metaphysical sense of being, and a desire for a communist reconstruction of nature! Put the sea in a bucket! Yes, this was a life experience. Often in the history of culture we have, as stereotypes or as problems, incredible intercrossings of paradigms, ideologies and meanings. But all this only shows that the history of culture in no sense constitutes a logic; in it are combined, under different names, problems that have their origin in practice. And at that time the practical problem was the caesura effected in the history of the revolutionary movement. Certainly, most of its militants chose – in the face of disillusion – ways of retreat, opting instead for choices between an acritical continuity, a new resistance movement, or technological reformism. But that was not the case with the younger generation – indeed it reinforced its break with the past, and thus its autonomous quest for a practical restitching of the break in revolutionary continuity. *Cupiditates* [desires] were being expressed – but revolutionary needs, in order to express themselves, needed to find mediation and theoretical expression. Thus Hegel functioned as a catalysing pole. Eros was the son of Penia:* theoretical gropings, confusion, bogus alternatives – our poverty was great, but so too was the great love and freedom that all those fantastic abstract Hegelian totalities could feed. Pages such as those of the *Phenomenology of the Spirit* on 'the slave and the master' were used in order to imagine the first processes of collective liberation from alienation – and it was as if a philosophical epic was being configured in those adventurous experiments. A philosophical epic that, initially, I felt to be all my own – but then gradually I realised

---

* Translator's note: Penia, the famous mythical figure in Plato's *Symposium*, was a personification of 'poverty' or 'need'.

that it was widespread – perhaps marginal in the sense that it was still extraneous and did not affect the terrible tedium of the dominant culture, yet it could be seen circulating in the discourse between young researchers and academics of the most famous circuits of interacademic communication, between Pisa and Padua, between Rome, Milan and Naples. (Turin was out of this circuit – shortly we shall see why. But this did not concern me particularly at the time. The fact that the city of industry and the labour movement, and its problems, still did not enter into my frame of thinking can only be understood if you bear in mind the long journey of my emigration from the peasant majority to the centrality of industry: when one looks at those years, it is like saying that the working class was on a long journey towards becoming a social majority.)

In short, what sustained me was a fine humanism, much admired; it enabled me to make a first synthesis of my journey, which in part mystified the utopian passion but at the same time presented relations that were critical and articulated on many elements of transformation. With this conquest – of a humanism that was radical, liberal and critical – I had begun to live the metaphor – it was just a metaphor, but that was no small thing – of a process of liberation that, beyond all the difficulties, I sensed as having real legs. I had a vague awareness of this. To be able to stand up, after having played at allowing yourself to be knocked over and kept head down, is a long and complex operation. Do you remember, David, when we did that exercise in Brittany, riding the big rollers from the Atlantic? When shall we return to play on the waves of the sea, and on the waves of philosophy and politics? Ciao. A hug . . .

PS: I'm adding a note that I wrote – as a memo to myself – after I sent you my last letter. 'This writing about myself, about the prehistory – it's hard – but more particularly it scares me. What explodes and comes to the surface is a pre-reflexive reality. Pre-memory. Finding myself outside of the control of reason almost paralyses me. Petty bourgeois decorum? When we had arguments in the family, my mother always used to say: "Children, there's no need to shout." And then: "One can be poor and still be clean." I, on the other hand, I quarrel with myself, and I put my poverty out in public. That seems to me somehow ugly, unseemly. The flow needs to be dominated by reason. On the other hand: involuntary memory: Deleuze on Proust . . . reason and the body. There is energy in what I am expressing. But is my writing up to it? Energy – flow – a gas pipeline – an oil pipeline – a pipeline – it is moving forward, but it's filthy. A tunnel of mud. Is poverty dirty? Is my writing filthy? Everything is so shorthand in my description. I'll try to be more lucid from now on. Lucid – but does not reason itself have thickness and body? Is poverty unsayable? No – the pipeline is fed by the earth, it has to run, it brings energy. One time I saw small flames flickering and flaring from control points on the gas pipeline: releases of pressure. These reflections of mine must also serve a purpose – a small fire – to relaunch from afar.'

Letter Five
Jürgen

Rebibbia, 14 November 1981

Cher David,

At this point the prehistory comes to an end. I could recount to you, in the manner of the Freemasons, how it happened that I entered into the universe of wisdom! But I'm sure that your concern for that kind of wisdom is as scant as mine is ironic, so there is no point in constructing here aphorisms à la Lessing. However, I do have the ingredients of my didactic 'trip' to hand, and I can spell them out. My peregrinations during those years, in the Neckar valley and the Black Forest, were a journey through the seventeenth century and the romantics – Tübingen, Freiburg, followed by Heidelberg, Hanover, Munich and Frankfurt. 1957–1958–1959. A rediscovery of the homelands of German philosophy, after the Parisian elegance of the preceding years. In retrospect, I realise that I was, however, missing a 'stove' around which my animal spirits could warm themselves and make room for the phantasms of theoretical imagination. Indeed the physical sensations were minimal: a Rosicrucian degree of chastity – what remains most solidly from that period is the cold and the fact that you needed woollen gloves to read in the library . . . But, as I say, at this point prehistory comes to an end. A big blast of brass and massed voices, like at the end of the *Magic Flute* – that amazing 'beat' spectacle.

Around this time I got my hands on copies of *Geschichte und Klassenbewusstsein* and the *Dialektik der Aufklärung*. And there began a headlong descent into the forerunners of those works, a reordering of the ad hoc library that I had been building in the preceding years. On the one hand, the Hegelian thread – here Marcuse's book on Hegel's ontology was a happy discovery; on the other, readings from Heidegger, and the laborious but extremely productive reconstruction of the philosophy of crisis in the first three decades of the twentieth century – and an understanding of critical, material and present being (which is a form of liberation from the last Platonic mystifications of philosophical thought). I was discovering the centrality of the problem of the meaning of being. '"It's clear that you have long been familiar with what you mean when you use the term *existent*; we too hope that we shall understand it one day, but for now we have fallen into perplexity." ... It is therefore necessary to re-examine *the problem of the meaning of being*.'* This passage, entirely Heideggerian, was central to that German philosophical world. To identify this whole line of thought, it's worth quoting Rosenzweig (and it is clear that irrationalism has absolutely no place here): 'Schopenhauer was the first among the great thinkers to be concerned, not with the essence, but with the value of the world.'† So this was the order and the direction of my philosophical readings. Husserl and Wittgenstein, under the spotlight; a set of lights and shadows. And then, consequently and in parallel, a reordering of the basics of sociology and of critical reflection on history (as the history of capitalism): from von List to the academic socialists, from Max Weber to Simmel to the Frankfurt School. The fine progressive humanism in which I found myself involved did not give much account of itself in this new temple. As I advanced, the progressive tendency, typical of the culture of the Italian left, turned out to be literary and rhetorical when it intersected with a systematic approach to the world – as capitalist relations, as the being of alienation. Instead the approach of critique – which would soon become, by inner coherence, a communist critique – finally made it possible to grasp the relationship with the adversary.

How difficult it is to learn the critical function of knowledge! In other words to practise knowledge like a scalpel that cuts into being, and distinguishes and fixes things, and gives them different names, often inimical. Like calling on the sun to stop. As an ability to take sides, to remove oneself from the ecstasy of the self as a subject, from the indifference of nonproblematised foundations, from the

---

* Translator's note: the first sentence comes from Plato's *Sophist*, 244a; it is quoted by Heidegger right at the beginning of his *Sein und Zeit* – which is the source of this entire quotation.

† Translator's note: Franz Rosenzweig, *The Star of Redemption*, trans. Barbara E. Galli, Madison: University of Wisconsin Press, 2005, p. 14.

complacency of assumed certainties. When truth becomes a victory over an adversary, only then does it have the meaning of a truth. Only separation and antagonism bring out truth. It is for this reason, David, that I say: prehistory had come to an end. From Jericho there extends the Promised Land. This world into which I was now inserting myself with a new intelligence was no longer a world made of shadows – I was beginning to recognise certain shapes, material logics, irreversible contradictions and oppositions. The years of vagabondage were coming to an end.

The critique of the philosophical universe in which I had previously lived became radical: I saw the general humanism on which I had built my youthful philosophical illusion enter into crisis along two lines – Husserlian asceticism and Wittgensteinian mysticism – the one opposed to the other, but the two concomitant in their outcomes. This age into which the force of capitalist development had placed us was an age of crisis. An open dialectic, of which we were the subjects, presented itself now. Any abstract compensation for the totality that was coming undone was impossible. Building and dismantling the dialectical schema was no longer a literary exercise but was becoming a hands-on mode of liberating the world. I had finally arrived at the base – and neither above nor next to the Christ triumphant – in that huge Last Judgement. The arrogance of ideology no longer had any place. Both asceticism and mysticism were now following lines subordinated to the scission of being – to its loss of human signification. Husserl and Wittgenstein were a delusion: teleology and mystical *Jetzt* became equivalent. A world that was not making sense. No polytheism – capable, by polite ideological convention, of comforting and removing desperation – could compensate for the loss of human signification; no, I rejected any *Plädoyer für aufgeklärte Polymythie* [plea for an enlightened polymythy] that sought to recreate illusion, and I saw no illuminating force in it. The real, the real, this is the cry of the truth seekers who, after a long homeward journey, stand on the shores of their native land.

The loss of the human meaning of the world is the system of exploitation. Hence it is on this that intelligence needs to be sharpened – on the splitting of the world, on the separateness that generates crisis. The solution can only be practical. But the practice is just as split as the theoretical conception of being: in the world of practice, asceticism is matched by the emptiness of critical rationalism, of reformism; and mysticism is matched by the foolish vitality of decisionism, of conceptions of the autonomy of the political. In neither case does humanism hold. The refounding of revolutionary

Letter Five: Jürgen

thought can only emerge from between this Scylla and Charybdis – in other words from beyond humanism. As an act of recognition of real determinations and of a practice of mass transformation – and as a submission of ourselves to this practice and to its laws. The communist critique, coupled with the hope of a humanism that sees itself not as foundation but as horizon, poses a subject that is capable of passing through all negativity and can discriminate and overturn all transcendence of being – and this is a practical operation, a theoretical practice exercised by a collective subject. I want to be a political activist, and my theory can only be communist practice. In those same years Louis Althusser, for his part, was forcing French philosophical thought to a similar horizon, albeit within a different cocktail of theoretical elements: I discussed this with him many years later. He told me that he had a similar sense of urgency. The theoretical conjuncture and the political conjuncture were destroying any possibility of moving within a phenomenology of simple consciousness and imposed a *coupure* that involved work of critique within real being, which meant in turn that theoretical work became productive work. *Pour Marx*.

With that I now reclaim for my generation here in Italy the merit and the good fortune of having been, with an inevitable originality of approach, the first European generation – in our arrival at maturity and in our manner of building. And, compared with the operating conditions of our peers elsewhere in Europe, we had the advantage of being immersed in an effectual practice. While we did not actually draw anything from the Italian Communist Party (PCI) and from its Italian ideological archaeology, it is to this party that we owed the possibility of the immediate relationship between theory and practice that characterised the – ineradicable – historical presence of our generation. It was for this reason that the Italian 1968 would be so different – because we, the European generation, had enjoyed that formidable Introit into the life of the masses that had been the PCI.

But now let us return to ourselves, cher David. And I mean to that total shift of discourse made possible at the time by contact with German philosophy. Those repeated journeys of mine over the Brenner started from a Paduan philosophical institute – the Institute of the Philosophy of Law – into which I had fortunately and fortuitously enrolled a few years earlier. I wasn't earning a penny but, ahead of the times, I had long since acquired a sleeping bag and a restlessness that I made use of, and I was living a healthy, mobile and multifaceted life of Zen simplicity. The institute had an extraordinarily rich library – Ravà, Capograssi, Bobbio, Opocher and Caiani had all contributed to it over the years, and they had built a place of study that was a rarity in Italy. Here, in the most total solitude, I could prepare my journeys. And each time I moved, my thought was that I would make a small contribution to the destruction of the academic vices that still penetrated that little backwater. The cynicism, the cliques, the blind conservatism, the social climbing, the general ignorance of a profession that had been exclusive until that point – the academy of the barons – a parasitic mode of existence: I saw with increasing anger how all this was attaching itself to and feeding on the sense of the sanctity of the institutions and of the law, holy in their formalism, beyond the doors of the seminary of philosophy – which is precisely where law institutes began. What a great reactionary *mélange*, what an incredible waxworks that Faculty of Jurisprudence was! There you learned how to identify and classify every species and subspecies of the fauna of 'the right' – the pure reactionary and the good-natured conservative, the fascist and the Catholic centrist, the royalist and the sex maniac, the fascist terrorist and the special branch police officer, the former partisan and the repentant communist, the reformist snob (but not too much) and the opportunist, the Nazi and the mystic, the Spaniard and the South African . . . All this in an atmosphere of great decorum. So that was the environment in which I, the cold entomologist, was spending my days. With a heavy irony: today I would be accused of having been an infiltrator. It's true – my clandestinity was total. I worked with discipline and earned academic qualifications with ease. But my really solitary adventure was happening on the other side of the Brenner Pass. I made my escape. Every couple of months I left, and every couple of months I returned.

Towards the end of this period of scholarly nomadism, in 1959, I happened to meet a wonderful person in Tübingen. This was Jürgen, formerly professor of theology and now a sociologist. They were blooming then, in the existential void of the Cold War, of the *Schuldfrage* [problem of guilt], of the internal migration, of the restoration – these exceptional Germans, new people who seemed to come from some ancient time. Big, solidly built, brown hair, blue eyes. Many years later Peter Brückner struck me as being made of that same stuff. I met Jürgen at an Ernst Bloch seminar. He had the air of a southerner, a Mediterranean Norman. We talked for a long time as we strolled beneath the willows of the Neckar. He was active in the antinuclear movement. For him Hiroshima was, rightly, a metaphysical sign. With him I was able to take a cool look at the various things that had happened to me. The scattered bits of my experience began to fit together. Jürgen explained to me

Letter Five: Jürgen

the continuity between the communist utopia and the analysis of the everyday – developing the ethical discourse and its evangelical significance directly into a practical definition of anticapitalist insurgency. He believed strongly that war, destruction and fascism were inherent in the mode of production founded on capital and that, in consequence, this was not just a neutral economic essence; because of the effects it produced, it was also an ethical essence. German self-criticism regarding Nazism, the subtle analyses of Neumann, Kirchheimer and Gurland, recovered the historical density of class hatred. So why should one not personify the evil? Why not bring back critical reason to ethical reason? In short, capitalism is evil. On the other hand, why can the communist utopia not be real – a concrete project, subject to and practised in the story of everyday life? Why do we not recognise in this huge potential of alternative constitution the best quality of our humanity? For Jürgen, who came from East Germany, communist practice had no exemplary representations, in either the East or the West. Germany, the one single Germany, which included all the Germans, would sooner or later find itself again in the common struggle against oppression. Jokingly he added that Marx, in foreseeing the revolution in Germany, would never have guessed what history had in store for him – 'the revolution in the two Germanys'. We both read the *Deutsche Zeitschrift für Philosophie*, the East Berlin philosophical journal, and we joked about its obscene bureaucratic rigour; and from West Germany we read the *Kölner Zeitschrift für Soziologie*, observing its vacuousness and its commodified problematics. But the real dialogue had shifted entirely to the concrete utopia, or rather to the translation of the concrete utopia into a practice of militant life. Jürgen died a couple of years later, as a result of a fall in the mountains. Where would you be today, my old friend – in Stammheim Prison or in the Teutonic forest battles over Startbahn-West? I am grateful for your appearance in the world, chosen spirit! But Jürgen went further, much further, in his positive critique of Marxism. Critique, in his view, could become revolutionary practice only depending on how much it could be extended, with full application, over the fabric of alienated being. Critique could and should pass through all the veins of totality – of the negative totality of power and of the positive totality of the social. Jürgen explained the Twentieth Congress through a materialistic analytic of the productive society of socialism. The capitalist transition in which we found ourselves, in both the East and the West, was marked by a productive reconstruction of the whole of being, of the extension of exploitation to the sectors of reproduction – and thus by the appearance of new structural dimensions of conflict in this transition. (The books of Kosik and Kołakowski were circulating widely at that time.) It was on the basis of this transformation that Stalinism collapsed. Berlin 1953, Budapest 1956. In the western world the crisis was pressing, and it was all the more mature as the relations of production were more advanced, and more evident in its subjective aspects. Not only the critique of political economy, but also a critique of the sociology of society as a whole was thus necessary to permit us to grasp the human totality of the antagonistic subject. Horkheimer had been saying this since 1933: 'the misery of the present is intrinsic to the social structure. Therefore the theory of society constitutes the actual content of today's materialism.'* Not only: *so fort* [onwards]! Marx had to be conjugated with Heidegger. At this level of intensity and quality, thought reaches the real – and, insofar as it does, it makes possible the exercise of revolutionary transformation. And it guarantees ethical action.

(Here I had difficulty following the development of the argument. In this plunge into being, I found it hard to understand how a desperate realism could become such an acute cognitive force. And the reversal and destruction of any possible mythical or metaphysical horizon. That damnable second-hand Platonism that, having read the *Symposium*, we carried around with us from a young age – that bright-eyed philosophising – let us sweep it away: the way of thinking of the masters, the way of thinking of the temple. I want to join my seed with that of the earth – even if this were the realm of aridity. But it is not.)

The methodological discipline of Jürgen's discourse was linear – the centre of the analysis consisted of a critique of all objectivist and mechanicist deformations of the revolutionary method. But, unlike in Korsch, Lukács and the polemic of 1920s' western Marxism, here the critique was directed towards a dynamic unification of the self-understanding of science and the orientation of praxis: the criterion of truth was not transcendent, external, party-based; it could no longer be that. Subjectivity was an element inseparable from science. That statement was true for theoretical practice at both the individual and the collective level: Adorno – 'in such a construction, the working class returns to itself.' Now the elementary words of the communist struggle all reappeared in front of me, but freed from shreds of abstraction or sentimentality. Now they no longer represented only

---

* Translator's note: unidentified quotation from Max Horkheimer (1895–1973), the famous Frankfurt School sociologist.

Letter Five: Jürgen

concepts, but desires or things. They did not contain just a vague protest, but the basic – material – reason for the transformation. The critical potency became materialistic potency: we talked about things, about person a and person b, about classes, poverty, hunger, exploitation and war. And then: no more war, no more poverty, no more death. No more masters – all of us together, we can be masters of ourselves. This world is developing towards an exasperation about command and death. Necessarily. And, equally necessarily, that logic has to be broken. Violence is internal to society, and thus to science. The mechanism can be blocked, and therefore the possibility of critique asserted, only through collective initiative. This collective task is determinate: *Bruch mit der herrschenden technologischen Rationalität* ['a break with the dominant technological rationality']. The dominant technology is powerful and destructive – impossible to think of it as neutral, it is the bosses' means of conducting their never-ending war on the working day. Rationality is the word they use for this kind of mechanism. In this sense, the break occurs and grows as an element that is ethical, autonomous and free. It applies, inasmuch as it is an autonomous breaking, also in the field of development, because development, far from being constrained within the pure expansion of its technical base (and therefore far from being defined in terms of neutrality and indifference), can be qualified by and refounded on proletarian needs. The servant does not need dialectics in order to rid himself of the master. The dialectic of servitude can and must transform itself into a separate logic of proletarian revolution. So enough of the dialectical, of that figure of thought that always reproduces negativity and transcendence and their impotent pacification. It reproduces religion – and all religions, even those resolved into sectarian thought, affirm dialectics, and in that way they sanctify exploitation and negate the ethical. Except for Judaism, the Aryan Jürgen added. On the other hand, when we have constructed within ourselves the political as ethics, we can reproduce the desire for liberation in the mass subjects and develop against capital their separate reality and their solidarity. Historical materialism is a methodology of liberation.

Jürgen joked: *zum Bauernkrieg*! Let's go to the Peasants' War! No, it was not this, really not. But we had to deal with that sense of radical separation in order to render visible the object of our hatred and the subject of our love. The ontological implantation of negative thinking, which articulated the rigour of the techniques of formal and systematic inquiry of the new (but already experienced) Frankfurt School of sociology; the political passion of humanism and antifascism; and, finally, a radical critique of capitalist alienation – all these allowed us to situate ourselves appropriately in relation to our present tasks. They were tasks of militancy, and at the same time tasks related to the effective determination of theoretical analysis. The criticisms renewed later, after 1968 (and still today) – against the one-sidedness and abstract radicalism of the Frankfurt School and of the militant sociology that was beginning to become a weapon of the youth movement in those years (Habermas: the Frankfurt School did not give normative substance to the critique of instrumental reason! Bon, cher David, so it was he who gave it? A fine hypocrite!) – those critiques, then, do not take into account that those were hard times when it was difficult to build an alternative horizon – in a European society in which the restoration was in full swing.

So, David, it was at this point that prehistory came to an end for me. Obviously I continued to work around philosophical arguments in the following years, but without believing in them much – in the sense that I'd already built myself a solid niche. And from this I settled down to a work of empirical analysis, to a commitment to political activism. *Skepsis als Endlichkeit*: translation of critical behaviour into finiteness. Later on, the revival of philosophical discourse, for me, represented a return to life's restlessness – and, why not admit it, to certain political defeats suffered on the ground made up of the philosophical positions that I was now taking. But we shall speak more of this later. What I feel right now is the satisfaction of those years. Not a presumptuous attitude, not some supposedly admirable possession of truth, but a relatively secure arrival at a critical method. And at its ontological basis of separation (which my memories of Souzy confirmed, and where I took comfort in the tradition of thinking of the division – the basis of testimony and conquest: the great eternal Israel!). It was not a critical method that developed in leisurely fashion, down known routes and pathways, nor was it neutral knowledge – but rather a capacity for concrete analyses and for mobilising them into antagonism. It was a thinking of tendency – where the link between subjectivity and objectivity was recycled within the risky dynamics of relations of power. The rule of the class struggle, the method of overturning and of the antagonistic explanation of all events, and an ability to analyse in parallel two logics, that of capital and that of class – these were the tools that I had won for myself.

I was happy with all this. I was looking ahead, with a certain timidity; at the same time I was looking back in amazement and could not understand how I had managed to extricate myself from so many false roads and such powerful temptations, to reach the serenity of performing a job that needed to be done. Without having paid too high a price in terms of life difficulties – even with a certain fidelity to myself and my world. I was coming closer to Marxism – I did not feel that I was betraying other beliefs. I had been a communist from way back. Could Marxism be capable of organising communist hope in an appropriate manner? The renewal of the Frankfurt School, which seemed to me so strong and positive, was successfully grafted onto a radical ethical dimension; and this led to a rediscovery of the Jewish origins of the separation, the true meaning of prophetism, on this road – twisting and scary, but emancipatory – that humanity travelled. Meanwhile I read and reread the authors of that silver German age – everything I could get my hands on, starting with the Hegelians and going back through the century. The historical disaster of that culture did not spoil its very pure capacity of being the conscience of the world. And meanwhile, like a sailor returning from a long and happy journey and seeing the coastline of his native land – and, nostalgically, his mind goes back to the ports he has visited, the cities he has seen, and the adventures he has experienced – I was happy to be returning but worried about the changes I would find, possibly hostile, and certainly about new jobs waiting to be done; this was how I was – nervous about my return. Was my period of travels and the emotions of theory over? Was I finally a full-fledged communist political militant? Yes, certainly. Now the important thing was being able to be poor – poor as an heir to the great disaster of European culture and of its crisis, poor in order to be able to talk to workers about communist hope. However, these edifying thoughts did not trouble me much, because there was always at hand some ironic line of my old friend Bertolt Brecht – my daily reading at that time – to correct them with a dose of realism and to steer me clear of the pathetic and passivity. Goodbye to my childhood friends, goodbye Souzy, master of my apprenticeship, goodbye Jürgen, my brother in research.

Goodnight, David. Do you remember our shared reading of Gershom Scholem, how excited we were about the antinomic ferments of the Kabbala, and how we concluded that Judaism is neither dialectics nor religion? Rather it is a religious exception, because it is an exclusion of dialectics. The element of separation, as universal potentiality, reaches us and traverses contemporaneity through Judaism. Marx's 'Jewish question' cannot be read simply as the attribution of alienation to a historical subject – but also, and above all, as a way of understanding how, within capitalist development, this separation can transfigure itself and become a foundational element of theoretical intelligence and of practical transformation. The Nazis had seen in the Jew the communist and the revolutionary worker; today Israeli fascists see and hate and kill the Jew in the form of the Palestinian and his wife and children; we could see in the Jewish separation the sacred history of the proletariat. Here, on these trips into German things, the antagonist logic of the Kabbala had revealed itself to me. But Zohar's dream of liberation was also urgent and pressing, and it was possible. I send a hug. I'll write soon . . .

Letter Six
Turin

Rebibbia, 26 November 1981

Cher David,

In those years of my political absence incredible things had been happening in the Veneto. A kind of 'once upon a time' story, now long past and gone. The story of the boom. In 1959 I returned from my long theoretical journey and came back to socialist militancy and practical political intervention. The differences and the newness of things were a real challenge. The continuous flow of change had created a qualitative leap. As you went round the outlying parts of the main cities, following the main arteries of communication, you entered onto the old B-roads, and there you hit on an endless landscape of cranes, factories, chimneys, billboards. Big lorries all over the place. Was this the Veneto or the Ruhr? As if a big beehive had been broken open and was now exposed to the light of day. I began to know the outlying branch offices of the Communist Party and local *camere del lavoro*. I was amazed. Contrary to what I had seen some years before and what people had repeatedly told me, those sections of the labour movement were not peasant-minded in their outlook. In fact everywhere I found a working-class composition that was alert and mobile. As if class reality was also a construction site, a work in progress. In particular I found no pathologies of nostalgia, regret for the past and rejection of the coming changes. Indeed these new workers hated the peasant life, which they saw as clammy and dirty, something to be ashamed of, good only for weekend visits (and then only as long as you didn't have to work there). Instead there was an enthusiastic adjustment to the new demands of struggle, a determination not to end up paying costs that would outweigh the benefits of development. They also had a confidence that they would succeed in this. The major waves of emigration from the Veneto region had already ended by the second half of the 1950s – now what we had was a huge internal circulation of labour power. Like insects in springtime searching for pollen. So, for the second time in my (admittedly brief) experience, I allowed myself to be drawn into the movement of this new Veneto totality, observing its qualities and its labours. It was a nascent state. It had a powerful materiality. Life was changing impetuously. The contradictions were piling up, and if, for the time being, they tended to represent themselves in traditional terms (in the Catholic majority and in the left minority), this was only skin-deep: the representation of the new was embracing everything and was transcribing itself into new symbols of antagonism. The parish priest spoke against 'development' from the pulpit and denounced the girls in overalls who used to come out of the factory and sit in his churchyard: it was shameful, he said, girls should not wear trousers. But a few months later you found the same priest in his shirtsleeves trying to understand what was happening as the first little groups and clusters of trade unionisation crept into the square of his churchyard. And you could hardly complain about consumerism here: at that time the proletarian families of the Veneto were reaching income levels not much above the poverty line. Refrigerators and televisions were beginning to pop up between the peeling paint on the walls, the washed-out colours and the yellow damp spots in the low-ceilinged working-class apartments. One by one, those peasant caverns would fall – ye gods, that was progress! Without a sense of glorious ongoing traditions, a fresh wind of class struggle was beginning to blow.

Obviously, cher David, I too was becoming changed by my immersion in this reality. But in a quiet way, because it was not my thinking that was changing, but only its relationship with experience. Representations determined by pre-reflexive conditions. In the Veneto the equilibrium on which the nascent state rested was large scale and paradoxical. Critique was obliged to develop itself in terms of translations of values, and these presented themselves more as development than as a break. So that, already then, one could say *Wertkonservativ gegen Strukturkonservativ* [value-conservative against structure-conservative]. This slogan of the more recent green revolution – values against structures . . . Could the discontinuity be balanced out? Here it was, but this did not mean that it was any less radical. And this equilibrium derived from the fact that the transformation of the structure of capitalist production and powers was matched by the immediate formation of antagonistic subjects and contractual moments – the decline of the old community did not bring with it, for the moment, an explosion of its contours. My Veneto was living up to its past. I was working there politically, albeit still in limited circles, learning the craft of the trade unionist and agitator – with tranquillity and commitment.

(Isn't it strange how an enlightenment attitude manages to stay on course even in the face of such major changes in the fabric of society? Much later, faced with the phenomena of postmodernism and with the computerised transformation of the social, I was in some ways to experience similar paths of critique – namely the possibility that the rational tendency of the changes presented itself in a manner compatible with the organic nature of the cultural fabric. When subjects render the transformation effective and retain the contradictions within the project – then, in an organic society they feel that their power is growing within the transformation, even if the latter is managed by the enemy.

Up until the moment of the necessary breakpoint. In these processes utopia fulfils people's needs without separating itself from their materiality. And that is how things were, back then, in the Veneto. Just as they are now, in so-called postmodernity.)

But at that time everything was singularly Veneto – even though this feeling was to last only for a short while. During that period I often had to travel to Turin, for reasons of study. It was a plunge into an unknown world, wild and terrible. Fellow students and political activist friends guided me through the thickets of this monstrous and chaotic reality. I began to learn about the metropolis. Here the labour market is a fact, not a theoretical representation: a market of human flesh. Here the infinite variety of paths that traverse the Veneto in a spectacle of indescribable entrepreneurial and proletarian vitality, here they are all narrowed down into one single crazy roadway. Only poverty, the most absurd poverty, unfolds in a variety of dirty rivulets – dispersive structures, a licentious disseminating – everything else flows towards the mighty monster. The market as a rational solution? Never was rationality more vulgar. I was living in Porta Nuova and I had friends at Porta Palazzo. A nightmare of a journey. And yet it was the same capitalist project that I had seen growing and spreading in the Veneto. But, whereas in the Veneto it was a soft Dantesque Purgatory – here it was the circles of Hell. In Turin I began to meet people in the labour movement, in the trade unions, in the Communist Party. At the heart of the storm, towered over by an overweening and ungraspable machine.

(I now understood the enormity of this abstraction – 'the mass relationship' – as a fundamental element of theory. This enormous concept, rendering itself little by little manoeuvrable, was to remove from us all pessimism of the intellect. Great concepts, conceived of as great tools of collective thinking. But then, in that situation, the mass relationship was unshakable: a *bateau ivre* [a drunken boat].)

Among these activists you found a desire to break things down and to build anew – but, as they confessed frankly, they had nothing that they could build on, because 1953 represented a defeat from which they had not recovered. The freshness of my hopes and the Germanic clarity of my analysis made me acceptable – albeit perhaps a little pathetic – in that hell. One evening I had an official of the *camera del lavoro* cry on my shoulder: my theoretical musings had moved him. He thought and thought, in a circular fashion, with dogged alcoholic determination. The logical schema was looking for a verification that it could not find. He broached various opportunistic hypotheses, persuading himself that they could be used tactically – but then he withdrew, scary and muttering. He swore. It seemed like he was trying to climb a mountain of sand. The heaviness of the body aggravated the problems. He recounted episodes, details, and became excited in in his description of the struggles. But he found nostalgia disgusting, 'I would be a Bordigist if I enjoyed memories!' He sobbed big sobs – the Barbera had something to do with this – but not with tears, only with his belly. I was overcome by the hardness of the class relation, by the ferocity of social constitution. I tried desperately to understand.

(In certain situations trying to understand is a priceless virtue. Detaching onself by a tiny amount, to be always – only with your brain – a millimetre outside of the extreme urgency of the things into which you are immersed. This is something to hold on to. You're lucky when you have this ability – otherwise known as education. A kind of ironical qualification of reason – not romantic, not destructive, not mawkish, but critical.)

Turin confirmed, through dramatic images, the German parameters of my theoretical consideration of mature capitalism. Its capacity for extreme articulation, which had already happened in the Veneto, was here developing in a kind of wild puzzle: it was a fullness that was continuously expanding and, as it did so, it left residual holes and pores; in these a new, formless matter precipitated, to re-establish the compactness of the fabric. A seventeenth-century physics. Then this huge figure began to move of its own accord, writhing, stretching, sometimes apparently close to breaking. I confirmed myself in the observation that only this – the rupture, the explosion of this huge mechanical body – is an expression of life. All the utopian determinations of knowledge crash on this breaking point. But they are no longer utopia – rather, they contain the hugeness of the comprehension of a universal phenomenon. The abstract here is the only concrete. But this is not enough: we have to be within this reality. Once again, generosity has a cognitive potentiality. The whole has a sublime force: at the moment when it smashes, it will produce that life and that freedom that, at present, it holds imprisoned. We have to be inside it. The experience of the Veneto, where the articulations of the overall framework of capitalist command were obvious to behold, helped me develop possible analytical readings on the compactness of this monster and on the mobile pathways of command.

The trade union people were not much use for what I was seeking. Even when you could persuade them of the immediacy of action – action that was heroic, hard-fought and blind – they started spouting ideology. You had the usual mutterings – about the Twentieth Congress, about Khrushchev's ineptness, about Togliatti's clever trench warfare, about the ambiguity of Nenni – and then came a further distraction: someone suddenly remembers that he attended the Communist Party's school and pours over you kilos of useless dialectical materialism shit. Steam-age Marxism in a city where rampant Taylorism was the rule. The few factory cadres whom I knew at that time struck me as being mentally unbalanced – completely. What sustained their communist struggle – a fierce, unrelenting, everyday struggle – on issues they did not understand and in a tangle of dynamics they were unable to bring to an antagonistic synthesis, was simply faith. They had no way of connecting with the tens of thousands of workers who were pouring into the factories for the first time. They despised them, but at the same time they were forced to take and use this huge new accumulation of labour power as an Archimedean lever for any eventual overthrow of the system.

As a good historical materialist, I understood just one thing in this bedlam: that theory had to be brought back into this huge melting pot of class recomposition. Solidly inside it, because everything had changed. The southern Italian prostitutes made you understand Turin more than any union official or professor of Marxism. But how were we to move forward? The working class is a body, a productive body: what was the key to its logic and its physics? Out of everything I had learned, the only thing that I was left with, vigorously and realistically, was this unique methodological tool: bringing theory back into practice. That was no small thing. But the German theory was objective to the utmost degree – and left room only for the exasperated subjectivity of the global alternative and for the working-class use of the overthrow. The dialectic of separation was at all times close to extremism. The conditions I was experiencing were not of a nature to permit it. Instead you had to build the theoretical framework from the bottom, recomposing the subjective instances, in the objective dimension of production, of technology, and of restructuring. Theory had to be rebuilt starting from the factory floor up. So now was the time to make contact with the workers.

Easier said than done! Here, in the factory, the difficulties already visible at the level of the trade unions were multiplied: the structures of the (real) working-class movement, of self-determination, of the 'making' of the class were nonexistent in the factory. And where they did exist, albeit weakly, they did not provide an adequate basis for an inquiry into the new figure of the working class. The obstacle, once again, was mainly the old working-class militants, who were characterised by their heroic warrior ethic, expressed in Piedmontese dialect, and also by their dusty awareness of their status as skilled workers and by their incomprehension of the present in the face of the emergence of the mass worker. The leap forward in the mechanisation and massification of production had thrown them to one side; it had dissolved the possibility of grasping the bigger picture and the articulations of exploitation. The *officine-confino* ['exile departments'] were a real ghetto – a cage violently imposed by the bosses, in which an endangered species now managed to survive. So I was forced into a long roundabout route to arrive at my destination. A long journey that had me bouncing around between the Veneto and Turin, between a vision of the articulations and an analysis of the whole – but the whole is *das Mehr als Vergleich des Vergleichs*, in other words it's that part of comparison that is more than comparison – only a practical act would have the possibility of resolving a mass relationship – therefore we had to set up methodological approaches that could match this new system of production and these new potentials of struggle.

Arriving at a suitable methodology. Again, easier said than done! There was not much evidence of an emerging culture of modernisation – what was emerging at that time was precisely that discipline, halfway between economics and industrial sociology, that mixture of management science and administration, which was highly regarded as the magic key to the programming of development. Giolitti, Leonardi, Momigliano . . . was this science, or art, or magicianship of development? It was a hybrid proposition and not at all attractive – to me it seemed less than rigorous and very makeshift.

As a theory, it claimed to be socialist (indeed many communists were beginning to use its concepts); but it failed to address the problem of exploitation. Was it a new formulation of reformism? And what if it was? Cher David, I have never had a gut opposition to reformism – I am happy to admit that: I say and I repeat, reformism is sacrosanct and can be an effective programme when understood as a schema for advancing relations between class subjects. Unfortunately, and certainly not through any fault of my own, every time in my political history when I have crossed paths with reformism, it has shown itself only as a policy of repression. So I learned that, when reformism talks of conflict, it is only because it wants to control and reduce it; and, when it speaks of progress, it sees it as a market to be extended. To be a true reformist, one has in fact to be a true revolutionary: reformism is a sociopolitical structure that can only exist as a strong dynamic of class relations in equilibrium – and only as validation of a strong subjective drive. For the rest, reformism was and remained sheer mystification – one of the very many versions of the indecent theory of development *sans phrase* [without rhetoric] and of its uniform mediation. Formalism of capital. Any approach to the new reality therefore had to avoid the strictures of formalism. Formalism of a fierce industrial reformism. Formalism of an unwarriorlike union reformism. Yes, because at that time, in that desperate situation of the working class, there were people in the union who were trying to make a shift – albeit a very cynical, very pretentious and utterly opportunistic one – towards a perspective of institutionalisation. But more on this anon. Here I just want to make the point that these were the obstacles and limitations that were blocking me as I sought to re-engage with the labour movement.

Gradually, however, I began to be no longer a free and isolated wanderer. In the Veneto, in particular between Padua and Venice, a network began to form towards the end of the 1950s around that core of problems; at first it was workers and intellectuals and party activists, but then, gradually, you began to find solid points of reference for debate in local cultural clubs and journals, as well as around grassroots trade unions. Bringing theory into practice and reviving theory on the basis of practice. It was at that time, around 1959, that I embarked on a new reading of *Capital*. I read and I took notes. I continuously related the scientific gains and the logic of *Capital* to the everyday experience of class relations. Sometimes I gave talks about various chapters of the first volume of *Capital* for a group of workers from the big factories in Porto Marghera. It was incredible: the theory of value could be applied to describe the everyday realities of exploitation. The workers were sometimes amazed that what I was reading out was actually written down there. What – it describes exactly what happened to me in the factory today? We began to understand that the dialectic of capital was open in a downward direction, towards the subjects of exploitation, and could be turned upward only as a work of destruction of exploitation. Not the anatomy of capital but the political logic of a relation of power, a revolutionary weapon. Marx. Today, cher David, it is hard for me to talk of Marx in the terms of yesterday – we have moved so far and often 'beyond Marx'. But I have to try to tell you what Marx represented for me at that time. It was the certainty of a method that gave a foundation for rational behaviours of rebellion: I seemed to have grasped that the possibility of predicting the progress of the command of capital was, in itself, a possibility of blocking its movements, of disarticulating it, of destroying it. Intellectualism? Utopia? No. Knowledge is power. Every worker, within the civil war that is the working day, saw and acted according to this necessary logic – of antagonism. The political problem, the problem of power, thus emerged in a pure form: as a solution to the antagonism – and thus as a tendency in society that brought against power (the power of the bosses and their institutions) the entire accumulation of the needs and hopes of the proletariat. In my case, the communist revolution was never conceived outside of the prospect of liberation: now Marxism revealed itself as a theory of liberation. The communist movement as subject.

Really something damnably innovative had happened in my life, in my experience, and in my brain: I was in a world that had the complex density of an origin – the world of the working class, the proletarian totality that capitalist development had created. God willing, the last product of dialectics. Creating a subject is the end of dialectics, as every parent knows when their children reach the age of majority, freedom, and the practical possibility of realising their imagination. (Anna, my daughter, is seventeen now. Did you know that, David? It's so strange – but at the same time a very pleasing sensation – to encounter her now as a woman – a living desire, tensions, maturation, this completed adolescence, this maturity. The dialecticians are dogs – it seems to me that they deny me the possibility of loving this great person whom I now have in front of me – no more a daughter, a kitten, an object, a projection, a protection – but a daughter, a lovable woman and a developed rationality. A miracle of transformation that produces desire.) Anyway, as I was saying, in that environment theory no longer had difficulty in matching itself immediately to the practice of the subject. As for myself, the nostalgia for an old-style compact world transferred into the awaited practice of transformation – and into working for that. A reactionary leftover of my upbringing? Oh, come on, let's not joke. Rebellion does not despise the strong thighs from which the subject is spawned. Now the theoretical practice could run on sure tracks. Of course, at this level, a lot of indistinctness still characterised the immediacy of the picture. Turin was the monster and an unknown terrain. The work I had done, my *Wanderjahre* spent in research, which seemed to have produced the concreteness of a given approach to theory, now came up against the difficulties and mysteries of a path that was inductive and rooted in the concrete. Was there discomfort? Lamentations and loss of faith? Certainly. But it was not worth the trouble – soon the facts would have told this with a biting capacity for conviction; and, until then, so much the worse for the facts. Theoretical practice had to develop itself, to articulate itself, to make itself accurate – but the tracks on which it could run were in place. That absurd and powerful world of mature capitalism, of the industrial metropolis, of the continuous subsumption of every aspect of life, Turin – was excessively all-embracing. But theory traversed it like an oxyacetylene flame welding steel. Because inside that all-embracing reality – neither above nor below it, but right inside it – ran the permanence and the forward-moving transmutation of antagonism. It was as if I had defined that second nature of which I had heard so much, and as if I knew the physiology of its development. It was as if I had understood the witchcraft of this second nature and now I had the power to exercise a thaumaturgy of liberation from it.

Some evenings, sitting in the hills above Turin and drinking good Barbera, we would look down the valley: the sweetness of the evening, thinning and diffusing the smoke from the big factories, encouraged flights of fancy. We used to fantasise about that class unity that the reformists and bureaucrats had perhaps only allowed us to sniff – but what different things they were for us, the infinite and possible paths for the restructuring of consciousness, and how human and close this explosion was! We had no idea of how the struggle would be concretely conducted, we were only aware of its necessity. But, at this testing point, the power of imagination was articulated and supported by such a lively vein of theory that nothing seemed impossible. 'The *cupiditas* [desire] that comes from reason does not know excess.' Turin, *cupiditas*. And that is how the fabulous years of the 1960s found us. Cher David, I send you a hug. Goodbye.

Letter Seven
July 1960

Rebibbia, 8 December 1981

Cher David,

July 1960 was a decisive experience, and one that was so pregnant with consequences for many – indeed very many – of my political generation! I really don't know how best to explain to you what happened. Cause: an attempt to shift the axis of government to the right; a fascist provocation in Genoa, a city with a strong working-class tradition; a violent police response in Emilia; the deaths of workers and communists in the streets; a wind of revolt that for the first time affected the new layers of the proletariat – of that social subject that had been forming in the processes of restructuring during the preceding years. Effect: demonstrations in the streets; mass action all over Italy; the Tambroni government falls; and that brings to an end the big period of calm that had followed the defeat of the working class in the early 1950s. These are the bare facts. But they are also history – the emergence of a great mass movement. The truth was on the surface in this case. It seems miraculous that a reality made up of facets of an infinite variety, with such complexity of behaviours, and even with contradictions and divergent trajectories, can finally produce a unitary representation; but this was indeed what happened. It was the first time that I saw the break develop itself in terms that were so global, so outside of even the semblance of any ideological sign – and I saw it constitute itself into a fistful of hate and class revolt that were both rational and matched to the scale of the political task at hand. It was during that phase that there began to be talk among us of 'mass vanguards' – a concept that, as you know, cher David, would have a long history as a direct forerunner of the

Letter Seven: July 1960

political hypothesis of the 'class subject'. The mass vanguard as the personification of the most advanced political interest of the working-class movement. A class subject as a conscious and fully developed figure of proletarian strata brought to maturity by the struggle.

But let us return to those days, to that history. A large number of elements were in play. As I said, simplifying a little: the will of the masses was substantially homogeneous; the differences were to be found mainly in the political leadership. In the previous winter, big demonstrations and workers' struggles had fired people's spirits and had shown that the reactionary stability of the political centre could not hold. Realising that this was the case, both the socialists and the communists began arguing for strike action. But, when it came to defining the modalities of that action, we sensed a split between the socialists, who took more extremist positions, and the communists, who took the more cautious positions. Togliatti advised everyone to stay calm and quiet – so we were told by the honourable secretary of the communist federation of Padua when he returned from attending funerals in Reggio Emilia. Who would have expected a different recommendation! Tactical caution becomes vulgar and banal when it is repeated too often. The institutional effect of the July movement was enormous: not only did it sweep out Tambroni, it also shifted the axis of any possible legitimacy definitively towards the centre-left and in favour of reform, both on the workers' side and on the capitalist side. It was not until the start of the years of tough reaction – the second half of the 1970s, the years of 'national solidarity' – that we would move backwards in comparison to what we had in 1960. So 1960 marked a lengthy historical breakpoint. And it was here that the differences of opinion about how to carry the struggle forward affected the objectives of the confrontation. Nenni was ready for government there and then. Togliatti wanted a leftward shift of the political axis, but he feared that such a shift would favour the socialists and might end up creating a new structure that excluded the communists. So he prevaricated and manoeuvred the timings of the operation. These disagreements developed before the effects of the formidable unity that had matured in the struggles and at the mass level became apparent.

But, at the level of the province and from within the struggle, the ins and outs of formal politics were entirely secondary, in the sense that we, the generation that had entered into the labour movement in those years, understood that what was coming out of the struggle was above all the emergence of the subject and the new composition of the mass vanguard. If we ever were anarcho-syndicalists, it was then. What a leap forward in our awareness! And yet (you see, cher David, the maturity and the independence that the spontaneity of the movement was already expressing?) there was not one among us – the many comrades who started living together the great adventure of those years – there was not one to press in extremist terms for an immediate deepening of the struggle. The fall of Tambroni was considered objective enough in itself. A beginning. In one of the meetings an old partisan showed the butt of a submachine gun from under his coat – a moment of astonishment, and then a brief political discussion concluded the show. (Guns are a normal thing in the history of the working-class movement. Guns, and their appearance, often represent a beginning. A new beginning? Here the old partisan came across to us as a symbol of the old – the revenging father, the avenger. Comical, in fact. That was also a period of rhetoric, with talk of a 'new Resistance'. But the partisan's gun seemed to us antiquated from the standpoint of both theory and practice. Because, while it is true that in the working-class movement there are always guns, it is also true that they don't pass down by way of inheritance. Never. Whoever wants them has to go and get them. That's the way it is. At that time it was the Algerians who were teaching us – no longer, pathetically the old partisans. At most you might tolerate listening to the stories of the GAP [Gruppi di Azione Patriottica] resistance . . .)

So that was a beginning. At the time I was involved in a public meeting – a big one, for those days – in a town square somewhere near Padua. As usual, the priest was ringing the church bells to disrupt the meeting – big bells, famous throughout the area for their workmanship and power to drown out our makeshift sound systems. And then the news came: Tambroni had fallen. I announced this news from the back of the truck, and a roar of joy went up, so great that for a moment it seemed that the bells were actually ringing to celebrate our joy, our victory. The priest immediately stopped his bell-ringing. And there you had thousands and thousands of people laughing, shouting, and making fun of the class enemy – our own local one, and the one in Rome. It was a great party.

Precisely here – with the certainty of instinct – the extremism of objectives was set aside. There was something more important and fearsome that those days had revealed and made explicit to all of us: the possibility and the urgency of the reconstruction of the revolutionary mass movement. Around this problem, in a very short time, there emerged a whole set of breaks and innovations. This is a date of birth: July 1960. But of what? There were many proposals. The immediate assessment that a single generation had achieved great

Letter Seven: July 1960

collective means that were appropriate for the class, together with the recognition of the winning nature of mass violence, translated into a choice of battlefields and a decision for action in the shorter term. Whereas the official labour movement took July 1960 as indicating the possibility of a long march through institutions and the trade unions took 1960 as a confirmation of the possibility of a dynamic and reformist insertion into the system, we, on the other hand – that is, many, very many comrades, both singly and in groups, even without yet knowing each other, without knowing one from the other – were looking for ways of rebuilding the movement. The revolution in production that was taking place had built a new class composition – it was realistic to think of turning composition into consciousness and subjective will. But how? Who knows, what does it matter? There are laws that govern the collective practice of which we are part: in approaching them we have to start from ourselves. As I go through life, I have found myself many times in historical relationships that have opened new pathways in real and necessary terms. In this particular case it was evident that the recognition of this major and renewed social unity of the proletariat had to be followed by choices of action that simultaneously affirmed and negated, and in any case prioritised the subjective centrality and the development of that unity. Was this a displacement? Was it an innovative pulsation of the great animal body of the proletariat? Whatever the case, a renewed theoretical practice had led me to discover and embrace a new class reality. I was aware of how solid it was, but I was caught up in the complexity of the relationships and therefore liable to end up dissipating my energies. But now July confirmed this reality and broke apart and articulated its complexity, negating its indifference. It was the kind of breakpoint that identifies the subject.

Then the tension melted way: the young people in stripey T-shirts swapped the political headlines for the beach. It seemed that the rule of the media had been reaffirmed. For a short while everything went quiet. But many people were left with the bitter taste of an opportunity lost. Furthermore, the songs of revolt, the photos of the crouching sniper killing the communist worker, the big demonstrations, the physical clashes, the massive strikes – all this fixed itself in the collective imagination of a generation. Once you've lifted the veil from Isis, the vision remains unforgettably in your mind's eye. And if, as a good materialist, you consider the vision only as an indication to be verified – then you give it a go.

Raniero Panzieri was the first total materialist whom I met in my life. He liked to try and try again. As a good materialist, he knew that artisanal work is often a rich prefiguration of industrial work. There was something Baconian about him, a materialism that was fresh and light-hearted as well as aggressive and well ordered, an irony about the lack of rigour that was the best legacy of Gramscianism – along with an irony about the lack of concrete experience, which was a first-rate weapon against the timorous, pallid Togliattian elites. Raniero taught the generation of July 1960 how to identify – and therefore how you could develop a critique of – the many idols that prevented the official labour movement from becoming a real movement of the working class. There was something about him that I found exciting: his uncertainty – which meant a humility in the face of reality that, if supported by rigour, is the only human grid of a correct revolutionary methodology. Optimism of the will and pessimism of the intellect: he was a good example of this maxim. A radicalism of reason and a respect for life, for diversity, for plurality.

With 1960 the strangest bands of Marxist heretics started arriving in Italy. It seemed to me that the only ones among them who had the dignity of an intellectual radicalism of great historical proportions were the people from Socialisme ou Barbarie. Raniero found them congenial. We avidly read their first articulated critiques of social capital, and we picked up the first allusions to the 'refusal of work'. After July 1960 I spent a few months on a trip to the USSR for heroic apparatchiks who had been battle-hardened in that struggle. I had never understood whether that *ou* between *socialisme* and *barbarie* meant to indicate choice or equivalence between the two terms. My *retour de l'USSR* resulted in my opting for the explanatory meaning, which creates an equivalence: *Socialisme est barbarie*. This arose out of my instinctive – and on that occasion traumatic – rejection of the vulgarity of socialised capital. Only Raniero explained to me, with the prudence and attention of a great teacher, what it meant to go beyond this ill-considered point of view. To go beyond betrayed hopes and demystified illusion. He put it in positive terms:

> The process of renewal in which the labour movement is engaged manifests itself on the one hand as a restitution of Marxist method to its original terms and as a reaffirmation of some basic principles of socialism, and on the other as a growing awareness of a new development of reality, as a dissolution of the dogmatic crystallisation of strategy, and therefore as a qualitative enrichment of that method and of its results. For this reason the affirmation of the current process as a breakpoint is the only way to affirm the historical continuity of the movement.

Letter Seven: July 1960

Raniero taught me to reject the philosophy of resentment always and everywhere. What was in play here was not a question of betrayal: real socialism was planned capitalism, a law and a grid of the same process of development of exploitation. Looking back today, I have to recognise that Raniero played a crucial role in my intellectual and ethical development: he forced what I was, the yearnings for truth that I had inside me, to become political, to develop as a practice of collective action, to recognise themselves as action always geared to the genealogy of revolution.

Thus there were two workers' movements: the official one and the real one. The first developed its ideology and practice merely as an alternative management of capitalist society: planning instead of exploitation; capitalist reformism; and/or socialism instead of capital. The second struggled against exploitation. All of us found it easy to argue for the distinction: we had before us July 1960 and the obvious split between the institutional project of the official labour movement and, on the other hand, the tenseness of the attempt at working-class self-determination. It was here that Raniero inserted his own proposal for a method: to rebuild working-class knowledge of the production of exploitation and of its destruction – starting from the shop floor. Grasping the irreducibility of the working-class presence in the capitalist organisation of production; denouncing the technocratic mania of any project of planned production for socialist monkeys; following autonomous dynamics in the real movement of working-class production and destroying capital's appropriation of them. This was good fuel for my brain. The preconditions, the driving motor, already existed; but here the political analysis was expanded by means of an effective method; the dynamism of the project was supported in real terms by evident historical contingencies – the continuity of a weapon, a unity of collective theory and desires. A continuous thread extended from the factory to society; it was represented by capitalist command, but it could be traced – and used in alternative ways – from the working-class point of view. Raniero taught the proper use of the dichotomous model, rescuing it from baleful catastrophist and insurrectionist interpretations. There were two roads that could be followed: one was that of a continuous technological restructuring of the organisation for exploitation, between factory and society – and that was the viewpoint of capital; the other, reversing the optic, followed the continuous recomposition of the proletariat, through struggles, between factory and society. Both lines of research, however, focused on and took strength from emphasising the basic experience of capitalist development: from the cell of exploitation represented by the factory. A scientific method that moved from simple to complex was thus proposed and developed with rigour. *Das Kapital* ceased to be a sacred text and became an operational schema.

This brings us to the beginnings of *Quaderni Rossi*. This journal was not some kind of rare flower blooming in a desert. In that period *Quaderni Rossi* provided a focal point for discussion of the scientific and political problems of the new generation of revolutionaries.

> The reconstruction of a strategy of the labour movement, which we *see* so clearly reproposing itself urgently today, is not a spontaneous process. The fact that we *see* it determines our tasks of today, tasks that are really new. The characteristics of the material figure of the collective worker are not simply hidden in the womb of capital (for all its becoming itself collective and self-aware in its own way). They are anticipated in struggles, and it is there that their unifying and revolutionary potential grows. It is not from capitalist planning that the (new) possibilities of revolution are born, but from the working-class anticipation/overturning of the fundamental elements of 'capitalist planning'.*

On the one hand, then, *Quaderni Rossi* represented both the figure and the radicalisation of a first Marxist usage of sociological tools – and this path was also being followed by a fair proportion of the younger trade-union left, or at least of that section which, prompted by the presentiment of a new phase of struggle, was addressing problems of institutional modernisation. The break would come later, although some of its terms were already implicit in the reductive judgements expressed regarding July 1960. But in immediate terms the context provided by *Quaderni Rossi* was unifying and set the pace of things. At the same time, *Quaderni Rossi* was a central hub in the refounding of a revolutionary way of doing politics.

I would say that, for everyone, including myself, the combination between the sense of this huge revival of the mass movement and the definition of a new analytical method of research and organisation served a little as a means of freeing us from a romantic and rebellious anticapitalism. (But of confirming both anticapitalism and rebellion. Rationality was the new wine – more rationality equals more freedom – the relationship was direct and linear – rationality was the form of a life that was liberating itself. The theorists of formal and functional rationality were dogs. Raniero, they say that you and I and many other comrades were evil teachers. Myself, perhaps yes,

---

* Translator's note: unidentified quotation.

but you – you are a genuine DOC [*d'origine controllata*] Socrates, not watered down with Platonism: Antonio Labriola has spoken with philological penetration of that love that sensuously defines Socratic reasoning, and you, with passion, have shown it in action.) So the task was to find the explosive connection between factory and society, but to refind it as a unity that could be articulated through scientific pathways – long but reliable in evidencing the antinomies of capitalist development. So, cher David, this was an incredible growth in maturity for all of us. The scattered threads of people's various discourses came together: the interest in the new technologies and in restructuring, the critique of reformism and of the political system – but above all a vocation, armed with scientific instruments that seemed to us matched to the task, for a militancy capable of rebuilding, on the basis of the new and given class composition, a revolutionary perspective. But what exactly was the communist revolution? In those days there was no doubt about the answer: the seizure of power by the working class. And what to do with power after that? Socialise the means of production and establish a state of equals. And with what tools? Through a soviet-style organising of the proletariat, through the action of the party vanguard, within a project of abolition of the state. And so on.

Among the texts that did not feature in our exclusive focus on, and usage of, Marxian thought was Lenin's *State and Revolution*. But our attention started to turn more and more precisely and continuously to the analysis of these questions. The critique of Stalinism was conducted in positive terms – themes of self-management and critique of bureaucracy, and the analysis of the instruments and institutions of working-class democracy, became central. There were, it is true, huge gaps at the level of a proper analysis of the institutions. In fact in our experience we ran up against reformism and its disarming effects each time we took for granted what was simply science in the eyes of the bourgeoisie (our academic teachers, or grand culture, and the like): sociology, economics, the analysis of concrete reality, planification, socialism. The scientific tools were in the hands of the bosses. Overturn them and reinvent them: our lack at the level of institutional analysis could be made up for by working the other way round – by research from the bottom up. How was it possible, working against reformism, to carry into concrete reality, and in ways that were not romantic and ideological, the necessity of transformation, and of destruction, of the present state of things? How might it be possible to set in motion knowledge processes that embodied class love and class hate, and science and practice? We were rather passionate in our commitment to finding positive answers to these questions. Obviously I cannot forget the simple-mindedness and the sheer quantity of nonsense that were often perpetrated on our side. But Raniero was there to impose a strict rigour. We went to our meetings like timid students. The essential thing was to move along a road that made no concessions either to the official culture or to the cynicism of exploitation (even when the latter came from the socialist side) and that was renewed in the culture of communist revolutionaries. Panzieri addressed critically the unresolved drama and the failure of his generation and restated them as a problem for the next generation – showing the limits of the old and the hopes for the new. The *impasse* of having to choose between reformism and catastrophism could be overcome. Raniero posed the problem of the past with one foot in the future.

Without the lucky conjunction between the political emotionality of July 1960 and the new method of analysis and intervention, now on its way to becoming hegemonic, the history of the Italian workers' movement in the years that followed would certainly have been different. And our impulse to move in that direction did not derive solely from that historical moment of happiness that we had lived. For the first time we were reconstructing, as a grounding, as a horizon of possibilities, the totality of that great revolutionary adventure that, from China to Cuba, was traversing the third world. And alongside it, with much greater attention – inspired partly by a re-examination of Algeria, that incredibly rich crossroads between the third world and the first – we were following the workers' struggles that were beginning to re-emerge in Europe: the Belgian miners, the strikes in Lorraine, the endemic strikes and wildcat actions in Britain. Meanwhile in Turin there was a continuous and growing development of struggles. Elements of politics – demands for power – were visible everywhere, but they were blocked by the official party lines. There is, in the construction of each generation of revolutionary militants, a point of internal equilibrium – a kind of toolbag that everyone will carry around, whatever their future experiences. In my opinion this point of equilibrium, this determined potentiality, was formed precisely then – in the events that took place around July 1960. This was true for my generation – even though I was somewhat older. It also applied to me, to my life and my destiny.

(But was it only to me? No, really not. In prison I watched, from close up, a man dying – a comrade from those years, Gianfranco from Genova, a brother from way back – no matter the political distance. We carried on our backs that same bag of tools and that great love for humanity and for liberation. With a smile that you would expect, Gianfranco, I'm smoking a Gauloise in your memory.)

It was sometimes difficult to get on with Raniero. (Good old Gianfranco knew something about this.) As a fine intellectual, Raniero fascinated me; as a politician of long experience, he intimidated me. His intellectual restlessness sometimes affected his judgements of that pure reality, of that concrete reality that he was always spelling out for me in theoretical terms. And this puzzled me, because I was neither an intellectual of that standing nor a political professional, but just a young provincial philosopher who was looking to this new practice to provide an outlet and the happiness of a pristine desire. Maybe my faith in the real, in the things that had to be done, was a little stupid, but I felt that there was a broad and genuine practice to support my stance. And also theoretical. Thus I found myself in sympathy with the militant community that was beginning to form up. Raniero was not. He confessed: 'I see all the roads blocked, the "return to the private" gives me the shivers, and the possibility of ending up in some small sect terrifies me.' He hid from himself the fact that the historical context of militancy had changed completely. We were in a sea, a beautiful sea, and we were learning to swim, to resolve metaphysics and politics in a single act of mass love. But what was the point of talking about that?

Nowadays it is important that we remember Raniero, that little great demiurge of my generation, that classical teacher of communist militancy. And while I'm on the subject, it was precisely in those years that the terminological and political distinction between 'socialism' and 'communism' became, for us, primary and continuous: a new and essential conceptual restoration of Marxism. Socialism was for the reorganisation of work, communism was for the liberation of and from work. This distinction, too, was due to Raniero, but his biographers fail to mention it. I remind people of it, as he would have wished, with a touch of irony: it is true, his intelligence was greater than his will. Cher David, this is a problem – and one that affects many people. It would have been so good if you could have met him. But the fact of liking him created big problems – because the inflexibility of his analytical reason and of his ethics, the force of his intellectual style – all this fed on itself. It was a war machine, powerful and manoeuvrable, with perfectly rational mechanisms and gears – and a kind of circularity – and a jealous defence of this independence of judgement of his, which sometimes deprived itself of the hermeneutic pleasure, the pleasure of making reason the handmaid of the movement. And also of the joy of listening. (A great musician deaf? This is not a paradox – or, if it is, it has been concretely solved. Rational and ethical inflexibility can mysteriously – but no less effectually – join together with body and love. How I wish that this might also be possible in writing!)

Goodbye for now, David. I send you a kiss, with the sadness of these memories and of these foggy days – and with affection, as ever . . .

Letter Eight
Piazza Statuto

Rebibbia, 20 December 1981

Cher David,

So then, how did our imagination of the transformation become physical fact? How was it possible to construct a process that would enable us to prefigure, in the singular and in the particular, the great extent and generality of people's interest in liberation? The theoretical discovery consisted, I believe, in counting not on the continuity but on the discontinuity of the processes. In other words, we had to exclude from the outset any idea that the continuity was linear – we had to exclude any Prometheanism of research, any sense that the result is proportional with its cause and the will commensurate with reason. How did we come to this awareness? And how, furthermore, did a belief in the non-inevitability of communism become a motor that drove increasingly our commitment to research and struggle? In my view, the critical point of the experience was the working-class revolt in Turin in 1962, the clashes in and around Piazza Statuto.

Up until then, the work carried out in *Quaderni Rossi* had been characterised by great critical and analytical rigour. The analysis of the factory and the analysis of the restructuring of capitalist society – in short, the two faces of neocapitalism, as it was called in those days with a horrible pleonasm (when has capitalism been anything but change, even if not necessarily productive change?) – we began to follow these two aspects through the entire arc of their logic of development. There is no doubt, however, that some activists close to Raniero Panzieri had given this research a very positivistic imprint. As often happens in cases of contamination between positivist methodologies and revolutionary instances, the former – at least initially – tend to get the upper hand. I remember having been personally touched by the compelling logic of the reversal that emerged from the empirical analysis of the increase in the organic composition of capital – studied not at the ethereal and meaningless level of general laws, but in the stamping press department of FIAT-Mirafiori and at Olivetti in Ivrea. At this point, however, Raniero's genius and restlessness reacted: communism is not inevitable. What came to the fore here was the dogged lucidity and impatience of the research done by Romano Alquati, that extraordinary Louis-Ferdinand Céline of the revolutionary sociology of the factory. Romano objected that, if the research is done with workers and is done as a moment of agitation, the focus shifts immediately to the residues of capitalist logic – in other words, not to the abstract logic of capital but to the capitalist activity of rationalisation: this is the moment of confrontation, and it is ongoing and decisive. 'The crucial element in the growth of the organic composition of capital is the discontinuity of its relationship – the relationships of exploitation and struggle that constitute it.'* Synchronic discontinuity of the class relation that constitutes capital, diachronic discontinuity of the class relations that capital tries to rationalise over time. So this is the horizon that we all have to address, these discontinuities of relationships, foregrounding their complete irreversibility. When I reread those debates today, cher David, I'm amazed at our intelligence during those years: on the one hand, a scientific reading of the administration of capital that largely anticipated functionalism and Luhmann; on the other hand, an analysis of the physiological fabric of the struggle that carries you directly to the physics of Serres and Prigogine. So there we had it, that otherwise inconceivable physics of transformation, spreading out before us. But the problem could not be posed solely in terms of intensity, in the daily microphysics of the relations of production – it also had to be present in the great expansion of the social. The precise analysis of the discontinuous links had to be located in terms of historical extension. On the one hand, the factory; on the other, society and history. Only in this way, if we succeeded in grasping the global pulsation of the working-class body, could the wretchedness of factoryism – which was understood by us in a Leninist sense – have been overcome. The foreseen event was, however, in psychological terms, disproportionately small compared to its ontological emergence; the living form is always redundant in relation to the form imagined in thought.

---

* Translator's note: unidentified quotation.

Letter Eight: Piazza Statuto

Piazza Statuto was a shock for everyone, but especially for us, even though we had been expecting a violent reaction to the trade unions' betrayal of the struggle. The basic facts are well known. After several days of strikes in Mirafiori, at SPA-Stura and other factories (all-out strikes, for the first time in years and years of trade union peace and after a long and careful preparation by the vanguards inside the factory), one of the trade unions, the UIL [Unione Italiana del Lavoro], went for a separate agreement with the company. The workers walked out of the factory and tried to attack the office of the scab union. They also protested violently against the FIOM and the leaderships of the other unions, which were trying to calm everyone down and stop the strike from turning violent. In the end, acting on their own, the workers took over the streets – on their own, but maintaining and renewing for a couple of days the composition of the pickets, operating their own system of shift work on the pickets, matched to the shift times in factories – clashing violently with the police and the various peacemongers. After the events in Genoa, at Piazza Statuto the 'Padova' battalion lost a fair amount of its reputation as an unbeatable police force. The cobblestones, the rocks, the chains from the parking lots, reminded the proletarian police that the proletarian rebels are the womb from which they had become detached – sometimes proletarian struggle is a subjective choice, a vocation, but for proletarians it is always their destiny. Gramsci, the brother of so many proletarians, reminds us of this insistently – can we perhaps, with Pasolini, scatter his ashes, chatting amicably about policemen – sometimes murderers, always scorned by the great proletarian belly?

The *Quaderni Rossi* were caught up in all this, willy-nilly. In their intervention they proposed that the struggles should be escalated, so as to prevent any betrayal. 'The only possible answer now is out-of-hand rejection of this agreement, a heightening of the struggle at all levels, its organisation in an anticapitalist sense, grassroots control of the struggle with the collective worker, without the false problems of top-level unity and of workers assistance to public capitalism.'* The factory cadres – extremely few – who had some contact with *Quaderni Rossi* found themselves at the head of this street uprising. What then happened within *Quaderni Rossi* was a bit comical. A great timidity, a deep uncertainty, contradictions and polemics led to a paralysis. A few wild outbursts. Accusations of anarcho-syndicalism,

---

* Translator's note: unidentified quotation.

of extremism and infantilism . . . Boh. A ping-pong of hysterics. The big trade unionists who had initially regarded the *Quaderni Rossi* sympathetically now withdrew in terror, but not before launching anathemas against them. The young workers who had participated in this experience as a precursor of political intervention and in the hope of creating organisation also withdrew – cursing, but not understanding, naively feeling betrayed. Meanwhile the press launched a witch hunt, hunting down the provocateurs – 'fascists', of course, as it was customary to call activists in those days, and continued to be so for a long time to come. 'Who is paying them?' Stop. But what had happened in reality? A FIAT workers' struggle had exploded after about a decade and had moved from the factory floor to the streets. Unexpected. An attack on trade union normality and on the institutional power of the negotiating process, a refusal to be represented by the official labour movement. Unexpected and impermissible. A mass rejection of the dominant ideology of progressive reformism in the relations of production. In short, nothing more or less than the emergence of a discontinuity in the physics of imagination. The reality of daily struggle, the rejection of command geared to exploitation had expressed themselves collectively and globally – the atoms, in their fall, had invented a *clinamen* [swerve]. Venus had risen from the waters. That sea of workers that poured into the organisational system of the factory every morning, every afternoon, every night, in the inexorability of the shift system, violently directed through a thousand channels like an irrigation system of surplus value, had now found its own logic of identity, which was violent and massified.

But there was more: the vanguard of workers who were leading the struggle and the rejection of the separate agreement reunified all sectors of the proletariat within the metropolis. Within the anti-union revolt there was a direct political representation of the entire people of the metropolis. Everyone was there, in Piazza Statuto – they arrived there as if at a ceremony of purification from the filth of the working-class meat market, and they stayed there as if at a big country festival, without a precise organisation but with a physical identity. A while ago, in one of the special prisons, I was talking with Sante Notarnicola about that festival, in which we had both taken part. He spoke particularly about the ritual significance of that struggle – about the fullness of the renewal that the spectacle of liberatory violence created in the consciousnesses of individual proletarians. If I had been a writer on political matters in the bosses' employment, I would have brought them here, to observe these extraordinary displacements of mass consciousness, teaching them cynically that, when you are forced to endure them, you have to react radically, eliminating any possibility of their reproduction and imposing exemplary punishments for those who took part. There is no Machiavellian weaponry or Pinkertonian provocation that might not be used in such situations. Schmittian *Entscheidung* [decision] – boss-class hatred, pure and simple. 'At this point, in this kingdom, there is no tangible authority except power and the might of the sword.'* But would a ferocious repression be sufficient? According to the physics of the imagination, no. The structural playing out of the displacement consists in the fact that what was hitherto positive now becomes negative and what was negative becomes positive. The metropolitan market of human flesh – special meat, exclusively for work: even the Piedmontese prostitutes scorn the peasant southerner – is thrown into turmoil. The positivity of the market for capital, in other words the traction it exerts on the well-ordered world of those who are paid wages, is dissolved, demystified, unmasked. On the other hand, working-class negativity – that mysterious productive force that, albeit left to one side, lives and alone determines value – well, this has made its appearance on the stage, once and for all, against the market. Once and for all – at least for those who attended the unveiling ceremony. 'The poor, the illiterate, the mechanics have turned the world upside down.'† These were old proletarians from the South who had chosen emigration in preference to the defeat that followed on the land occupation movement; they were young Piedmontese who had grown up with the dream of a partisan rebellion that was ongoing; they were Rocco and his brothers, drifting through the metropolis; they were communists humiliated in 1953 by the violence of Valletta and of the yellow unions; finally, they were us – the generation awakened to politics with the thaw of the labour movement, delicate flowers with strong seeds. Piazza Statuto became an extraordinary symbol.

Then there was a pause – it was summer. People returned to the factories in small groups, as in the preceding years. But we already knew that there had been a huge increase in the amount of waste output. A little newssheet was doing the rounds – *Il Gatto selvaggio* (*The Wild Cat*) – which detailed sabotage in the factories. The bosses and the judiciary accused it of condoning crime. Was that true? Perhaps they had more fear of this than we had foresight. The

---

* Translator's note: unidentified quotation.
† Translator's note: unidentified quotation.

rain of atoms continued. Beyond the first *clinamen*, towards a second. Solitude had turned into violence; now it had to turn into hope.

We followed the articulations of the violence manifested by the workers' activity with all the attention that the mode of production deserves. And we discovered that core of thought and revolutionary perspective that only the fact of the working class finding its own path – already strong in its metropolitan dimension – could permit the concrete utopia of communism to affirm: the 'refusal of work'. Starting there, at the heart of the factory, on the shop floor, from the analysis of the job functions of the individual worker, we analysed the worker's relation to the machine and its product – a relation that was ambiguous. But if the analysis went a bit deeper and sought to qualify this ambiguity, we found a long series of alternatives: there were elements of indiscipline pure and simple – against and the opposite of the attitudes of the skilled workers (the machine cannot do what I know how to do); but between these extremes, permanently neglected by the frustrated utopia of trade union negotiations, one found the negation of capitalist command – not so much over society, not so much over the totality of production (because indeed these conditions were generally overlooked and regarded as non-negotiable and preexisting), but more over the organisation of work, over the specificity of the elements that made it up: from the fact of coming to the factory at a certain time and of having to reproduce the absurdity of the hours of the working day for the whole duration of one's life to the fact of having become – in the workplace – an idiotic appendage to a piece of machinery. A short while after that, other slaves of that same exploitation were to write:

> Workers don't go into factories to do research but because they are forced to. Work is not a way of living but the obligation to sell oneself for a living. And it is by struggling against work, against this forced selling of ourselves, that they clash with all the rules of society. And it is by struggling to work less, and no longer to be poisoned at work, that they are also struggling against toxicity at work. Because it is toxic to have to get up every morning to go to work, it is harmful to have to do shift work, and it is harmful to go home with a wage so low that it forces you to return day after day to the factory.*

Wage labour is against humanity. I don't think I need to return to Volume 1 of *Capital* or to the *Grundrisse* to explain what alienated

---

* Translator's note: Assemblea autonoma di P. Marghera, 1974; see http://www.chicago86.org/archivio-storico/254-assemblea-autonoma-di-p-marghera-1974.html (accessed 29 June 2014).

labour is – nor do I need to stress what the Taylorisation of the workplace has done to deepen this desperate situation. The *quid novi* [something new] in our analysis was not the mournful restatement of this proletarian misery. Something else was in play: first, to grasp the unificatory elements in the refusal that this condition brought about; and, second, to grasp the communist quality of that refusal. In other words every worker's behaviour in the face of the machine was, naturally, one of refusal. Only artificially could the worker be forced to the norm. But this violent enforcement produced an immediate effect: the worker generalised the refusal in violent forms – on those same dimensions of massification that the norm of command produced. This happened through an extraordinary symbiosis of positive and negative behaviours, both subjective and objective. The smallest, most unnoticeable defect – a nut that was not properly tightened, or paint that was a bit streaky – meant a waste product emerging at the end of the production line. The collapse of the working hours system and the rampant absenteeism destroyed the composition of the workteams. The mobility used by the bosses – whether calculatedly or by trial and error – in order to break up the lines that were producing too much waste and the changes in workteams made necessary by the high degree of absenteeism became a great resource for the circulation of information. And there was the other aspect, equally important – namely what was revealed when, faced with disorder and chaos on the assembly lines, foremen, engineers and so on arrived trying to restore order and regularity – or to study innovations that might simplify the production line and functionally modify the labour process. Now, any change was usually the exact opposite of what had been done in the act of sabotage – whether the operation had been deliberate or not. Innovation by way of sabotage. So who was doing the inventing – the saboteur or the engineer? The worker asked himself – if the machine is a product of necessity, on what is its necessity based, if not on my struggle? That struggles are a way to produce innovation is a commonplace, among reactionaries as much as among social reformists. 'The machine runs to places where there is struggle.'* But to say that the refusal of work was the necessary and exclusive factor of innovation, of the progress of productivity – this was a truth of communism. And they say that communism is utopian!

---

* Translator's note: this seems to be a free quotation from the famous 'unpublished Chapter 6' of Marx's *Capital* (on which see note in Letter Two, p. 26).

The refusal of work, cher David, became and remains a creative point of communist thinking for this reason: because it is an immediate synthesis of struggle and innovation, of life and productivity. It is the potency of the negative. Obviously, of that which the bosses call negative – inasmuch as it is a denial of their rationality. But their rationality is the expropriation of the innovative capacity, of the productive force, of the working class; it is command over the working day. Whereas the rationality of the working class is to increase the productivity of labour. For the benefit of all. Within a social organisation that permits its development and thus offers wealth and happiness to all. The measure of the struggle is thus born from the refusal of work, and then it extends positively in the social programming of equality and of the development of productive forces. From the factory to the social, from Mirafiori to Piazza Statuto. And vice versa – to rebuild within the factory nuclei, together with the sabotage, the collective potency of the expansion and unification of social struggles.

How much time has passed since then! Today the struggle, constructing itself in the social, encircles and penetrates the plant. The sequences of struggles have become further massified and socialised, as has the subject who sustains them. Only trade union corporatism remained firmly attached to the factory – and not in all cases . . . not even those dinosaurs could manage that! But then, finding this point of strength (call it sabotage if you like) and grabbing it in that huge social chaos of the workshops and assembly lines at FIAT – this was a great laying of a foundation. When I heard bourgeois sociologists talk about the factory, it was something that I really did not recognise: their abstract theorems, their Olivettian mystifications, their rationalistic illusions made me chuckle. I chuckled because, above all, they were only capable of perverse effects. The factory was struggle, it was a huge and confused army, which produced to order and to deadlines that were entirely massified – Kutuzov rather than Napoleon. And this army could become a people of free partisan bands. I spent whole years seeing the analyses of my comrades find continuous verifications – whereas those of the bourgeoisie fantasised means of control that had absolutely no effect on the growth of the collective paths of the refusal of work. Invisible to power, and clandestine in relation to command. But, in a huge process of recomposition of the proletariat, we were marching forward. The metropolis was all around: we went to the gates, crossing this territory whose ugliness and ecological disaster revealed it to be hostile. But behind every new barbarous emergence you saw running a thread of recomposition, of reunification between people who were forced into waged work,

Letter Eight: Piazza Statuto

rebellious against power and full of desire for liberation. 'The voice of the Kingdom of Christ will come first and foremost from those who are part of the multitude, those same people who are so contemptible in the eyes of the spirits possessed by the Antichrist, and of the clergy.'* The journey was long, we thought. In thinking that, we ourselves made the mistake of considering the future as a continuum. No, the journey was not long: it was discontinuous. The space in which we were moving was a frontier, a Wild West – on multiple tracks, in many directions, *tout azimut*. It was a modern Odysseus: as the geographer Eratosthenes put it, fixing a route is impossible because only the person who stitches the skin of the wind knows that. As Piazza Statuto had shown us, we had lived the sudden pulsations of the working-class body, the irreversibility of the paths it had taken, the expansion of its desire for revolution. And also the defeats.

Defeats – but never defeat. The red thread of the science of revolution, the hope of liberation – for sure these were good compasses in this traversing of space. Piazza Statuto shows the workerist how irreversible and all-encircling passion is – from the factory floor to society, from utopia to science. So the solitude of man, articulating itself on the sabotage of the producer, finds the invention of communism. I had the paradigm, this new paradigm that plucked me out of the normal science of the official labour movement – this, cher David, is how I experienced things, and I was excited by the fact of using this paradigm both as a scientific lever and as a practical tool. It was a fever, a passion. It was the same as when, cher David, many years later (but having become young again), we followed the struggles of Lorraine in 1977–8: once again it was people from the Veneto and immigrants from the South who, alongside us, in Longwy, were planning disasters for the bosses. *Ciao, compagno mio bello* . . .

PS Cher David, in my recent letters I have talked about Raniero. About a pedagogical relationship. About his love and the seductiveness of the man. But still in abstract terms. I cannot do better than that. It happens that I maintain, or undergo, relationships at the pedagogical level – I avoid talking specifically of either of them, the disciple or the teacher. Evading the tangle of emotions, sensations, upheavals and enthusiasms. I establish and satisfy relationships that are full of sensuality in purely conventional terms. How unjust all this is! How much sensuality political pedagogy contains! Here, in

---

* Translator's note: unidentified quotation.

my narrative, there are no passions, betrayals and abandonments – and this is wrong, because the abstraction of concepts does not remove from politics the concreteness of *cupiditas* [desire]. And, for a voyeur, you and I, as well as Raniero and I, might seem to have been locked into a homosexual relationship that we hypocritically do not recognise. Maybe it's true. But it's not completely true. Because vulgar voyeurs spy in private and in all their grumbling inconsistency; but between us we – and I enjoyably on other occasions – had that *aufklärische Erziehung*, that relationship of communist education, which unfolds sensuality in a relationship that is universal, schizophrenic, collective and joyous. It is the private element that renders the experience prurient – but concepts can be full of a free sensuality. I try again and again to write about this complexity of political relations. I can't do it. But I believe that enlightened education also has to pose unresolved problems. This certainly means that some of my arguments are rather dull. But . . . Take writing: it is a limit – perhaps it is a world that precisely this conquered, mature concept of eros shows to be preterite, old, outdated. Eros calls on life to build forms of expression that are denser and more complex. As regards my poverty of expression: could it not perhaps indicate a deficit (historically clear-cut) of narrative in the form of writing? Of the impossibility, not of expressing eros through writing, but of saying it collectively, publicly, wholeheartedly, as something that concerns all of us? Interchangeable and full and concrete in its collective relation? The end of the Gutenberg galaxy? Books teach us only after the experience has become a given. Books become less and less useful, less and less . . . Allusions, traces. But then why do I write?

Letter Nine

Autonomy

Rebibbia, 26 December 1981

Cher David,

I want to tell you about the year Togliatti died. I'm talking about 1964, but in a sense I could be talking about any of the years between 1962 and 1967, because they were lived as a continuity in the deepening of the new theoretical practice. But the death of Togliatti is too important an event to pass over. Togliatti left an ambiguous legacy as regards method – and he also left a great party that was on the defensive in the face of capitalist reformism and developments on the international front. Togliatti represented a kind of universal 'third way' – you never knew if this was a way of getting around problems or a problem that remained unsolved. From this point of view Togliatti's funeral provided a snapshot of a generation of schizoid and frustrated intellectuals. Renato Guttuso [the painter] unconsciously succeeded in showing it, portraying his ideology, not the truth of art. But the funeral was also, and above all, the expression of an untamable proletariat – and it showed the extent to which communism, that century-long hope, was alive in people's consciences! Millions of proletarians saluted with clenched fists, and the mourning was inseparable from pride. At that time it was impossible not to feel both the present and the longer-term action of this symbol. In our memories he did not yet represent betrayal. So the emotion of the moment translated into restlessness, and this sad and dignified proletarian festival became an incitement to renew the strength and historic density of this mass. The tasks of the new generation were thus clear: they had to create a break in the theoretical practice of the proletariat, so as to renew its revolutionary potential. A new tactics for an old strategy: and new political personnel

– but we could not forget, and we did not want to forget, that we were *there* – in those masses and within that tradition.

I went to Togliatti's funeral with militant workers from the Vetrocoke plant at Porto Marghera – older workers with whom, the previous year, we had set up one of the most hard-fought and costly wildcat strikes ever seen in Italian industry: the molten glass spilled out over the gears, and it took them weeks to chip it all away. The plant manager came to see what was happening. They grabbed him and passed him, hand over hand, right up to the mouth of the furnace: his managerial arrogance gave way and he shat himself, and only then was the furnace door shut – the manager stank too much – among the laughter of men who were half-naked and drunk with the heat, those divine beings who fed this volcano with the finest crystals. (The manager was later made Knight of Labour.) Alongside us were some communist workers from the Petrolchimico plant – the initial core of the future Potere Operaio of Porto Marghera – who in the previous year had organised the first lightning mass strike at what was then a very young factory. When the machinery of a continuous flow production process stopped, the comrades understood their own strength. (David, do you have any idea what it means to block the continuous production cycle of a petrochemical plant? It's like a huge body that is dying. The mechanical fixity of relations that were previously flowing, the fatal predetermination, hundreds of millions of dollars of fixed capital per employee – all of that goes into short circuit. The heart comes last – first come the arteries, veins, liver, and kidneys . . . Now we have this man-made anatomy in our grip, and we can either feed or block its physiology – but in any event we can exercise power over them! This recognition is an extraordinary acquisition of class consciousness. Our ignorance alone allows us to be commanded and exploited – the boss is the embodiment of our lack of dignity. The alternative – just the knowledge that an alternative is possible – is a priceless gift.) So they, the comrades at Petrolchimico, sensed the possibility of a new beginning. Indeed: maybe we had already started. There was much that was sacred and powerful on that day in Rome. That is how they experienced the situation, both the older workers from Vetrocoke and the young ones from Petrolchimico.

It was on our return from Togliatti's funeral that we began to distribute joint political leaflets in all the factories in Marghera, moving beyond the fragmentation of the small factory intervention groups. These were political leaflets that played on two sides of the capitalist development plan – the reformist face and the working-class face, that of command and that of wages – pitting the one against the other, pressing wage demands as a way of destabilising the political equilibrium of command. The discourse was explicit. In our view the younger Togliatti would have been happy with our strategic cunning; you could have laid money on it. And the Togliattian approach found a continuity in the practice of the 'workerists'. There was no aspect of the wage or of the organisation of labour that we were not able, with duplicity and working-class astuteness, to resolve within our paradoxical reading of the topos of 'limits to development' – the limits of 'their' development, that of the bosses. 'Workers' autonomy against the plan', that was the slogan. In 1964 the boom was also running out of steam in psychological terms; in material terms, we were seeing the beginnings of that historical downturn of the level of investment that has not picked up since. Not that we had foreseen it with clarity, of course. But we had understood clearly that, in the hysterical specificity of Italian-style development, there would inevitably be a contradictory relationship between economic crisis and political crisis – that the whole structure could only stand up if there was economic development, and that there was no force capable of managing the economic crisis. So that was the understanding on which we had to move – that potential asymmetry was a weak point where we could strike. And within this ongoing action we could build organisation. On the one hand, the use of a kind of wage Keynesianism, a reformism of the real wage, passing through the immediacy of working-class needs and interpreted as a tool of destabilisation; on the other, a realist view of the Italian state's inability to mediate the economic crisis and the major changes in class relationships that prefigured that crisis. Throughout those years we firmly believed that, once a solid level of crises had been established and those moments of organisation had been built, the official labour movement would align itself with the revolutionary process. It would have had no choice. What a terrible mistake! What naivety and short-sightedness on our part – not to have understood that the K factor was not a possible strength but a congenital weakness of the labour movement!

Yet not even today can I manage a smile when I think back to that period – sharp as doves, that was our watchword. Never in the history of the labour movement had the truth been exposed more forcefully, more rigorously, and so forthrightly: a message to the bosses – we want money, and we shall lead you to ruin. And as for the unions, the new functionaries of social capital, we were the precursors of the working-class slogan that was later to emerge with Solidarność: we will win because the lie cannot last. Short is the path of words in working-class struggle, and profound are their effects. In this game, once again, there were just two players – servants and bosses, proletarians and capitalists – eliminating the third term – mediation and the political. We talked straight – *da cristiani*, as we say in the Veneto – as we were reviving the Hobbesian geometry of the 'market society'. We often quarrelled among ourselves, as happens in all vanguard episodes of the labour movement and of the renewal of its nascent state. But we had learned from the refusal of ideology and from the working-class discipline of speaking clearly, so our quarrels never resulted in irreparable breaks or breakdowns in our common cause. In any event, the logic of our association for communist agitation was reaffirmed. When one aggregation was blocked, another would begin. Later, in more recent times, this metamorphosis and this process of growth by division, this 'go forth and multiply' that lay at the origins of our practice – because I think that ours was a practice strongly and radically characterised by theory – were so overvalued as to be seen as deliberate decisions taken in order to perpetrate crimes: dividing in order to set up plots, secret intrigues, infiltrations, and so on . . . How disgusting these suspicions were! *Grunf* stuff. We were never infected by the behaviours of defeat and resentment, the dead nucleus of the Trotskyist atom. What later happened – and what continued to happen, all the time – was the opposite of what our enemies insinuated: we divided in order to swarm everywhere, so as to apply our theoretical practice to the complexity of the situations in which we were involved. Sharp as doves. What was developing from that time onwards was a kind of Franciscanism – a living of the class struggle in its immediate conditions, in the richness of its poverty, bringing it to politics. In relation to the class struggle, what politics meant was what poetics is for poetry: a reflection on concrete action and on its effectual results.

Cher David, if, now, I think about myself in that period, I find a big change in that old character whom I have described hitherto. I always carried my political vocation with me: but the fact is that I had always lived a certain dualism of theoretical and practical experience, so that I always had to reread the latter between the intellectualistic twin poles of sociology and utopia. Now this dualism was over. Precisely as I was concluding a theoretical trajectory that led me implicitly to adhere to the productive conclusions of European philosophy – enough of descriptions, we want only deconstructions; enough *Aufhebung*, we just want destructuration, *assez d'idéologie*, we want the concrete – these conclusions seemed to me to be supported by a collective subject. A collective subject that was not only what political analysis proposed as an empirical reference point, but also the mobile internal product of all thinking about destructuration of the enemy horizon, the continuous reappearance of a multiple activity of resistance and destruction wherever command signalled its logical emergence. That collective subject was not a principle but rather the force capable of breaking all command, all mastery and logos of capital. A collective subject as a horizon that was epistemological before being historical. Was this a remake of the proletariat inherited from classical German philosophy? Not at all, because this subject that was being built was subordinated to the same law of destructuration that we were applying to the enemy. The strategies that pervaded the real also pervaded the subject. So: wiles and stratagems. Thus it was a historic gamble – only the result could justify it; communism is not inevitable. What we were bringing to the construction of the working-class political was not a metaphysics but a technique, full of irony and hope. That horizon of destructuration could only be closed, of course, in relation to a signifying subject – but this subject, which we could qualify as collective and communist, was not a given. It built itself during the course of destructuration. It could not be given either as relic of the past or as a prefiguration of the future – but only as a continuous work of – simultaneously – destruction of the enemy and construction of itself. As a tension that passed through this destructured time. All final cause had to be dissolved; its discrediting was for us total. Here is Bacon: 'The research into Final Causes, like a virgin dedicated to God, is barren and produces nothing.'* Later, reading and rereading Derrida and Bataille and early Foucault, I found myself thinking of them as big brothers who, in the abstruse regions of thought – like lucid meteorological sensors – were grasping pieces of the reality that we were living. And so it happened, cher David, that, in the name of a destructuring practice, we were able in the major journals of those years, from *Quaderni rossi* to *Classe operaia* and *Contropiano*, to analyse the crisis of instrumental reason, and we were able in our books, from Tronti's *Operai e capitale* to my essays in *Forma stato*, to bring into a critical synthesis the motifs of a working-class structuralism, and on the other hand an absolute rationalism of the collective subject. Wise as doves in practice, angels of destruction and hope in theory. We had little time in those days to theorise about ourselves – so why not do it now, when we have infinite years

---

* Translator's note: Francis Bacon, 'On the Dignity and Advancement of Learning', 3.5.

of imprisonment hanging over us? There was nothing juvenile in our experience, nothing experimental – even if everything was young and experimental. Rather we were an outcome of the working-class revolution in industry, a point of self-consciousness of the class of the future. We were – and we are even more so today – the only generation of revolutionary intellectuals produced by the working class in the period after the second great imperialist war. (Of course, there will be some who will have a good laugh at this: intellectuals produced by the working class! I don't want to push this risky claim to the point of having to defend it. But then to have believed in this is no less risky than never to have asked oneself about the relationship between intellectuals and the working class – and it is certainly less comical than to have disowned it.) And let this stand as a mark of our dignity. However, the period of commemorations had not yet begun, and Giordano Bruno had not yet been led anew to the stake.

So let us return, cher David, to our own history in those days. How many stories I could tell you! But I prefer to tell you about my Virgil. He guided me through the difficulties of my journey into the entrails of the great machine – it was no accident that he was a control engineer in a chemical plant – and he steered me through it in a way worthy of Virgil himself, the poet of the *Aeneid* and the teacher of Dante. All around that machine – namely the Petrolchimico plant in Porto Marghera – that great nodal point, sometimes starry and throbbing, sometimes monstrous and poisonous – there spread the territory of the working class – the neighbourhoods, the towns, the bars, the parish rooms, the party offices. And here the picture changed by comparison with the factory, because in the factory we were deconstructing the organisation of labour within the continuity of a bosses' command that we could not think of breaking except in some imagined future. In the territory surrounding the factory, on the other hand, the bosses were violently destructing the organised proletarian community; but here the community was resisting and organising, and only in some imagined future could the bosses think of winning. Unlike in Turin – the great metropolis – in Marghera and throughout the whole industrial region where we were beginning to operate, from Schio to Pordenone to Trieste, from Thiene to Padua, from Conegliano to Monfalcone, the relationship between factory and working-class society, between capitalist structure and antagonistic subject, resisted the internal tendency towards an extreme mechanical dissolution. My Virgil led me to an understanding of the territorial networks that constituted the composition of the workforce in the factory. So that, gradually, the relationship between

Letter Nine: Autonomy

the factory and society went beyond the fuzziness of mere theoretical definitions, and also beyond the great historical longing for an assault on the heavens, as had happened in Turin: it became viable in precise terms of struggle. 'Sabotage the plan on all fronts.' On the buses, which were the embodiment of territorial mobility, the mass subject could be followed and recomposed, reversing the trajectories and the directions of the spatial processes of exploitation. Our first intervention was in the area of the Brenta, where thirty thousand proletarians were packed into factories – making shoes, breathing in the benzene until they become addicted to it (and then, after this vile apprenticeship, going on to promotion and a right to the poisoned air of the Petrolchimico plant: higher wages for the same amount of poison – a step up!). Then we began to operate more around Venice. And then in the zone of the Piave, which was effectively a watershed between Marghera and the swampland of industries that extended from Treviso to Friuli. And then we headed south from Padua, to the Montedison plant in Ferrara, in Emilia, where the exploitation was co-managed by the official labour movement.

At each of these nodes of agitation and organisation we met and clashed with the suffocating structure of the trade union and party bureaucracies. Struggles, small and large, followed one after the other during those years. Every strike was a clash with both the bosses and the trade unions. Mr Bloom: 'I can't stand pigs at table.'* Virgil, who had had some experience of demons, camouflaged himself well – in the characteristic style of a chemical industry worker: he had something of the sulphurous cunning of those beings. (But my Virgil was not like the Virgil of the famous engravings by Doré – a thin, dry figure, elusive in the shadows of engravings, not easy to distinguish from the devils. This worker-Virgil was a bit prematurely bald, and he was tubby, affectionate, argumentative, lively, and sometimes sarcastic – a plump demon. One would have said he was Irish, were it not that he was from Chirignago . . . no, there was no mistaking him for Mephistopheles.) This is the birthplace of much of our linguistic arsenal: it was born out of a semantic overturning and an empirical specification of the misleading abstract names that the union was giving things. Leftist jargon? Maybe. But it was working-class usage of trade union language – and its overturning. Chomskian genealogies

---

* Translator's note: this appears to be a misquotation from Dylan Thomas, *Under Milk Wood: A Play for Voices*, London: J. M. Dent & Sons, 1995, p. 47: 'MRS PUGH: Persons with manners do not read at table [. . .] Some persons were brought up in pigsties.'

and grammars of demystification. Autonomy: was that not what the unions were calling for? There was so much – too much – talk of trade union autonomy. Did they want it or did they not? But it is clear that there is true autonomy and false autonomy, as my Virgil explained, having armed himself with an incisive Enlightenment logic. *Der Doppelcharakter der Gewerkschaften, Fetischismus der Gewerkschaft* [The dual nature of trade unions, fetishism of the trade union]. Only real autonomy is to our advantage. The autonomy that the union talks about, does it put anything in our pockets? No, it does not. So what kind of autonomy is it? Those union people are just hacks. 'The triangle of the economic plan: employers, government, union.' 'One single struggle – against the reformists in the party and against the bosses in the factory.' So let's roll up our sleeves and set about making a real autonomy ourselves. When you find that the totality in which we are inserted has no foundations, what meaning can words have any more? Anything that does not further our class interest is just ideology. Let us bring words back to their meanings, Virgil added. Let us place them in a given cognitive field – the process of bringing new life into the world is a practical operation. Virgil was pushing us to a concrete dramatisation of the word, of the materialistic destruction of all its ambiguity – in other words, he was inciting us to dissolve all idealistic univocality. This genealogy was thus a radical operation: it could not limit itself to effecting a kind of striptease on the trade union's rhetoric; it had to reformulate the subject theoretically and reshape it physically, outside of any dialectic.

Virgil expressed his project neither in Augustan Latin nor in Florentine Italian, but in the dialect of the Veneto. Maybe the extraordinary importance of the experience we were going through also derived from that fact. Dialect is a useful reminder of the characteristics of industrial development in the Veneto in that period: the Veneto is not a metropolis, so – unlike what has happened in the big cities, with the churning effects of immigration – it maintains an identifiable proletarian substrate that is still structured, stable, and directly translatable into a new subjectivity. Furthermore, by that time the Veneto had become one of the major industrial areas of Europe, and the confrontation was taking place at the highest levels of the composition of capital. An averageness thus applies to all aspects of the experiment – a good situation, a favourable opportunity. So at this point Virgil becomes an alchemist and pushes ahead to the *experientia crucis* [decisive experiment], to that experimental transition that creates a reaction in all the items selected and assembled. Years and years of daily political work, thousands upon thousands of leaflets, the extensive range of organisational experiences – everything was boiled down and reconcentrated. *Paracelsus redivivus*.

Genealogy has to produce difference. I was overwhelmed by the density of the reference material of this new philosophy of ours, cher David – and never did I honour humanity more than when I found myself among these strong men, who were focusing on the will of one great violence, the accumulation of poverty, suffering and falsehoods they had endured. Virgil insisted on the need to intensify, to push, to provoke the clash. There was no need – the outcome was already building itself. We had a huge mass movement that was about to speak. 'Mass intervention.' 'Against the swindle contacts.' 'Now let's move against the contracts.' 'Piecework = Exploitation.' 'Enough.' 'No to the Framework Agreement.' 'Let's go beyond the contract.' 'Let's strike first.' 'Hit the bosses before they hit us.' Those were some of the slogans that the leftist newspapers of the period were scattering around, in hundreds of thousands of copies. But it was important not to end up in isolation, to identify other experiences of movement that had been started and were moving in this direction, and to reunite the scattered elements of theoretical practice. So we were moving continuously from meeting to meeting, and from strike to strike. And difficulties did not scare us.

What did scare us was the sectarianism: residues of a clapped-out Italiot ideology that, at that time, was beginning to wallow in Marxism–Leninism. *Grunf, grunf.* What a pain that was! And then the fashionable third-worldism of the time – Virgil was the only one who pretended to be interested in it, forgetting that he could perform his role as guide in Hell and in Purgatory; but in Paradise – in ideological and artificial Paradises – really not! He sent me off to meetings of the most varied and useless committees. 'Victory to the Vietcong.' What a bore. *Grunf, grunf.*

We used to meet, and often on Friday evenings, when the afternoon shift came out of the factory, we would go to a big bar where we would discuss revolutionary theory . . . And the wine flowed by the gallon. Because communism could not be abject misery – and only if we regained for ourselves the productive potential of the working class, only then could we think of those peoples with black or yellow faces and empty stomachs. What united us in brotherhood was strength, not pity. The Vietcong soldiers are winning – yes, because they are putting up a strong fight. Internationalism is not a holy relic, it is a task. Third-worldist language was part of that totality of distorted meanings that we had to dissolve. A hypocrisy that had to be fought if we were to get back to real values. Struggles only win if they constitute the materiality of the subject. What could come from abstract solidarity, if not the confirmation and the exaltation of the windbag virtues that swindlers have always proclaimed? So let us take aim, comrades – with all the force of which we are capable, with all the necessary caution, and with all the hope we can muster – on our target – and on the cycle of struggles that will have to open. Our analysis requires it. A match, now, just one match for this dry prairie. Either the communist revolution moves where the working class is strongest, or it does not happen. The night of the Veneto, sweet as the passion of its people, is so soft as to give a semblance of reality even to the dreams of these Pantagruelian drunkards. But was all this really an illusion? I send you a big hug, dear friend . . .

Letter Ten
New Year's Eve 1968

Rebibbia, 7 January 1982

Cher David,

Christmas and the New Year are past and gone. This is the third time I spend the festivities in prison. Sheltered from the madness of the world? If only . . . However, this time was better than the others. Better than the end of 1979, when I was in the special prison at Palmi, among enemies. Better than the end of 1980, when the revolt in Trani was sprung on me and I spent New Year with broken ribs and a broken head – I was one of the lucky ones in that slaughterhouse! Now, New Year 1982, among friends and in fraternal solidarity. I shall write to you later about these prison events, in another letter. Now the New Year puts me back into circuits of imagination. New Year 1968: the wires of this story hum and tinkle sharply, like telephone wires in the wind in the old days. We had been through an exciting time. In August we had a baby – and Virgilio had a son, too – both were born in that August of 1967, when the comrades had led the first great autonomous mass struggle at the Petrolchimico plant. Leadership of the struggle, forms, objectives, method of negotiation – they ran all this by themselves, with finesse, these barbarian autonomists. Before becoming a subject of analysis, the nascent collective state is a new subject, a birth in fact, a displacement, a strategy. Attempting to understand in a dynamic sense, in a Marxian comprehension of practice. Yet that New Year was the most restless one I've ever lived. From all over Europe came signals of struggle. In Berlin the policeman Kurras had killed Benno Ohnesorg – an unarmed student with no sense of his impending death. In Nanterre there was a growing contagion of German anarchist banners. A savage anomaly, with young people and of young people, was traversing the world. My wife Paola and I had been on holiday to Madrid. There we met people coming over from Cuba – frenetically active, alert, intense. (How much fragility there was in those professional revolutionaries – their third-worldism was as intellectualistic as their understanding of the class struggle in Europe was devoid of material supports – but these limits were understandable at the time: the first was driven by passion, the second was idealistic. Nobility and dedication rather than ignorance. I sensed, however, the lurking danger that the lack of realism might turn into cynicism.) So at that time there was joy in our hearts. But what restlessness of reason, too! The birth of our child – in that Porto Marghera August – absorbed all my thoughts. One's expectation of the event does not lessen the surprise. A small Hercules who already in the cradle was struggling against the serpent.

At Marghera the struggle had begun, as we used to say in those days, in articulated form, led by the vinyl chloride production departments – autonomous decisions of workers over three shifts and in four workteams. When one department stopped, another would take over, then another, then another, and so on – this was planning completely from below. A war machine of working-class freedom – *Mille Plateaux* – mobile, flowing, lively, constructive, strong, rational, intuitive, agile, intelligent, expansive. The workers from the warehouses and maintenance, the only ones who could move around the big area of a petrochemical plant – nomadic trajectories on bicycles – they were the ones who communicated the struggle. Then other departments began. That was May and June. In July the unions stepped in and tried to stop the struggle – then came negotiations, postponement until September, and the summer holidays. But in a continuous-cycle factory it's only the trade union officials who take holidays. On 17 August all the departments in struggle unified their action and blocked the factory. We called for strike action, we formed picket lines, we organised assemblies. Rubbing their eyes at this rude awakening, a few trade union officials arrived in dribs and drabs to view the new working-class legitimacy. Gradually the employer gave in – on wages and on many issues regarding the organisation of work. It was a victory. The prestige of the committee was sky-high. Now it was September, and we could relax a bit – watching our unruly children as they rocked between cradle and bath and mother's breast.

Then the demands began to pile up: struggle pays. More and more meetings were being organised. From other factories in the Combine messages arrived, telling of similar experiences: Azotati,

Letter Ten: New Year's Eve 1968

Leghe Leggere, Acsa, Sava Nuova. A territorial network of proletarian initiative was being established. In the surrounding villages, in the parishes, in the bars, the stories of struggle immediately became epic; and they were contagious. What for many of us had involved the construction of collective consciousness over a period of many years, here, in the working-class collectivity, was now exploding with immediacy. Just as a stone thrown into water makes concentric ripples, so we were seeing a growing relationship between the workers' committee and the informal organisation of struggle, both in the factories and in the surrounding areas. We were spreading out in Veneto style – good solid chats, *paciole*, good drinking sessions. How I love you, my old Bavaria! The fried fish of Chioggia and the chicken of Treviso are tastier than anywhere. But what restlessness! The struggle was moving ahead, it was growing with the force of a rising tide – but then . . . then what?

There was another circumstance surprised us: the willingness of the younger generations of intellectuals and students to engage with the factory and with working-class power. You saw a whole lot of young people at the factory gates. With them began again the Virgilian pedagogy of the masses. The reactions of the official labour movement were increasingly harsh and insolent – they were forever asking us: 'Who is paying you?' Now and then it all ended in fights. They didn't try it with me: they invited me for discussions – to the *camera del lavoro*, then to the federation. Once again I found crudeness, and a certain streak of Levantine cunning: I was enjoying myself. In the squares of Venice, between Dorsoduro, Canareggio and the Giudecca people were now talking about the struggles – it was exciting, this new grafting of the new onto the old, and it even began to have a slight influence on the intellectual strata of the big institutions. We were feeling rather pleased with ourselves. But then what?

Each of our meetings gave a further stimulus to struggle, but they gave no answer to the problems of perspective. That winter brought an incredible tension to the struggle. I was tired. Virgil was destroyed. In fact, for the period we were living and the medium term of our politics, Virgil and I and many comrades had not thought about anything but this mass practice, which today the Polish writer Kuron calls 'a self-limiting revolution'. The dimensions within which the struggle presented itself escaped us. Meanwhile other comrades were beginning to emerge as mass leaders. One of them was punished by being transferred elsewhere in the company. Hard to respond to that; a lot of impotent rage. A growing state of restlessness, and then the problem of what to do next, and the expansion of the movement. An urgent need to generalise the struggles. Local contacts were resumed with officials at the *camera del lavoro* and with the official labour movement, both locally and nationally, to discuss this issue. It immediately became clear that all of us had an interest in the generalisation of struggles, particularly those in the chemical sector: we, in extending the movement, they, in keeping it controlled in an area large enough to bring them gratification – namely by encircling the vanguards of Porto Marghera. The first clashes in the committees: we give them those struggles on a plate, those dogs. They generalised the struggles in order to take them out of the hands of working-class autonomy. There was good reason to be worried about this. In fact, only a crazy hope could have predicted what would happen. On the horizon was not just a high tide; it was a flood, a storm. Nobody could hope to control the rising tide – only Caliban, who was an element of that nature, would have enjoyed the joy of this storm. But how to develop this fury and this urgency into consciousness? We were shaken by restlessness – far from being clear, the picture was blustery. And meanwhile the stormy seas were rising.

In the universities of Venice and Padua we saw a growing number of autonomous activist committees. The old culture, protected by its lifeless niceties, could not hold. Its operators would often claim that the inputs of protest and the demands for renewal were simply behaviours of irrationality. The output was repressive – culturally, politically and legally. The honour lost at that time has never since been redeemed. They did not realise that a new intellectual workforce was demanding from the education system methods and routes of collective and conscious reconstruction of knowledge – strategies that could be socially productive and valorising from within the social self-determination of the subjects. Culture is not a mirror of reality – a past that repeats itself – but a thousand mirrors, and a thousand angles of refraction that the subjects constitute into a technique for reconstructing the world. To the demand for a creative and collective mediation of knowledge, the profs responded by behaving like men of power. Much good may it do them: let the dead bury the dead. The cultural revolution thus makes itself – and rightly so – independent of the institutional channels, indeed takes them as its enemy – and turns to working-class autonomy in order to achieve its consolidation. We imposed a hard style of work onto the committees of students and intellectuals: in the morning, at the factory gates; then to the university, to the meetings, to the printing of leaflets, to the workshops for militants. A hard style of work, but not self-obsessed: the experiences of liberation were mixed with those of the class struggle – the working-class anthems were Beatles songs. Then there were the senile ones, the bores, the fanatics, the hysterical ones, the romantics – every movement brings a weight of passive elements in its trail. I have always called them (and shall continue to do so) the *grunfs*. But the richness of things was enormous. And the unrest did not abate; rather it multiplied. I feared like the plague the heroic indistinction I sensed around me – I wanted determination. That concrete determination that I found in the course of working-class struggle eluded me in the complexity of the movement. Sometimes I sensed the growth of elements of contradiction within that indistinct relationship and, above all, alongside the increasing difficulties, the manifestation of elements of cynicism and manipulation in our style of work – old habits and the no less dangerous behaviours of professional revolutionaries who were false and treacherous. Once again, the *grunfs*. Hey, no! Ours was not a movement of alliances between different class strata, it was not a chromosome of the party, or even an external vanguard – ours was a forward recomposition of the proletariat.

I'm reading Moses Finley, the scholar of classical Greece: when the Greek territory was entirely occupied and Hercules came down from wild Thrace to the compact expanse of the marble-like Aegean, human beings leapt beyond the limits of the human as it had been understood up to that point, and this leap forward was a modification of their own nature, a discovery and a maximal extension of the truth that is in the people themselves. The occupied nature was a microcosm and the interiority of the subject was a macrocosm. On the border arose a new subject without borders. Ulysses. The materiality of the process had to be defended in its unity, which had been won, and in its new subjectivity. All our work was about to take the test of fire. But how do you go beyond the test? The dimensions of the political weighed on us. We were alone – in the Veneto, and in a few other parts of Italy – and then what? How were we to connect these scattered elements, these fragments of hegemony?

Cher David, I'm telling you about a precious experiment. To us it felt like a test tube experiment, and our fears that the glass might shatter were justified, albeit perhaps a little hysterical. But you, who with precocious maturity acquired some experience of full-on struggles in those years, you may be wondering: isn't what you are saying now contradictory with what you said earlier? How is it that you all felt that you were on your own, you who had just had a Europe-wide experience and a fascinating apprenticeship in impacting the concrete? Did you not feel the growing chorus of European struggles?

How could you be – in that given conjuncture – so short-sighted? Now I can answer you: we were not, in fact – but our behaviour was discreet and guarded, as the first and pure experiences of a constitutive practice of an initial genealogy of revolution always are. The potentiality saved us, that *potenza* that is not afraid of installing itself at the limits of being. As the comrades of Solidarność say today, 'what we are doing is at the same time both impossible and necessary'. So you will have to allow me the unease, this existential feeling of the unknown, this inner pendulum between hope and unknowing.

And now the picture opens out again. Young Hercules has strangled the serpent in the cradle. It was an impressive scenario: the struggle was spreading everywhere. Sunday afternoon: all the matches, minute by minute – day after day. Fortunately we had managed to avoid connecting the birth and the generalisation of our discourse and of our political activity to anything negative – by refusing the ambiguous and compromising offers of the trade union officials. Today, looking at us in prison, an organic evolutionist – one who sees himself as being a little pessimistic, a little wise, but in any event victorious – could still reproach us for this. But how could such doubts touch our innocence? Believe me, cher David, I am not taking innocence as a hostage, or as a cover. Really not. That innocence was the catastrophic sign of the innovation we had produced. And it was necessary in order for the dislocation to happen and to follow a subjective thread, because of the paralysing dilemma that was posed by our circumstances: either accentuation of our isolation or regression into the murky generality of political party representation. It was necessary, in other words, in order for this dilemma (a perennial problem of the communist left) to be cut away on the indigenous track we were following. In short, the movement was present everywhere – and we had avoided the 'all round alibi' typical of bourgeois political behaviour. You old, perverse, heteronomous Rousseau, how far you are from our political passion – which despises the cold abstractness of the general will, its latent Stalinism, its mystifying dialectic. No, we had not chosen the totalising and empty alibi and the void of representation as against the *potenza* of the singular rooting.

So – there we were on that New Year's Eve of 1968, in the middle of these choices and of the logical and theoretical projections that extended from them. In play was the entire nexus of problems related to a healthy practice of the political *Beruf* [vocation]. So let's talk about it again, cher David, to remove any cause of restlessness. From restlessness comes uncertainty, and at that time a large quantity of uncertainty was threatening to paralyse me. As regards the little that

Letter Ten: New Year's Eve 1968

involved me directly and depended on me for what was collectively decided about it, I had the sense that the future was presenting itself as a fierce tearing away – yes, implanted in loyalty to our action and to the subversive innocence of the project, but in such a way as to upset any continuity in our lives. Just as the lover hesitates in the face of the violence of penetration, which nonetheless completes and heightens his desire, so I followed individually and uncertainly the phantasms of imagination as they entered into the future. There are of course those who will argue, with old rhetoric and weary cynicism, that these problems are appropriate for the collective agitator. I really do not think so: in the communist community it is the principle of responsibility that lies at the basis of social living and project – and not some transcendent legitimacy. How, then, can you make responsibility live through uncertainty? How can you mobilise a wholesome will across a risky range of collective alternatives?

Effectively, then, the choice was determined and supported by the power of the collective in movement, which reduced the complexity of the situation and provided an ethical guarantee of the choice. (Today the philosophers of *Verantwortung* [responsibility] have, from within the German context, created an ideal model of this situation. Community versus consensus versus responsibility. But theirs is a formalism pure and simple. A philosophy of those who control the mass media, which downgrades community into consensus. Formal or institutional sequences; transcendentalism instead of transcendence; and what changes? These are itineraries that are privative of responsibility. It's just a little game of impoverishment and of mystification of reality.) The solution of responsibility, in its subjective aspects, comes from other and more encompassing conditions. It arises from the recognition that we are collective beings before being alone, that we cannot conceive of ourselves in solitude – just as we cannot be born in solitude. What founds critical intelligence and the will to project is an act of love, and it empowers them and makes them answerable. Only in this way can uncertainty and its sister, unease, be resolved. But there arose a second problem, and it was not raised by the non-institutionality and fragility of the logical schema that the collective action, albeit powerful, was exhibiting. It was good to recognise oneself in it; it was good, this snatching of oneself upwards out of solitude, and the denunciation and overcoming of its empty abstractness – but who guarantees for whom, in the collective? This Prometheanism that was being developed by the collective subject, might it not reveal itself as pure narcissism – and debase itself into a dialectic of a thousand mirrors, deluding itself that it was the real movement? It was in fact on this passage that the tearing was strongest. But here we also have history recomposing itself, and it is a love that is no longer a pre-reflexive act – but an adjectivisation, a predication, a story of many subjects. It is a present ever renewed, a density never resolved, a potentiality of being. Determination: this word is magical – there is no being, there is only the being *there*, in the here and now; there is only this complexion of the collective; there is our new composition. The fluidity of the emergence, the non-institutionality of the process, are inevitably scary: the determinations have to consolidate themselves into composition.

So here was what could resolve my uncertainty and guarantee that the mirror with a thousand angles would not create a collective illusion: the refractions, if controlled, could indeed be reduced to strategies – paths, subjective trajectories, known and understood. Commitment is born as a moral act, and then translates into a cognitive task and into an action of transformation, into an ethical–political project. So let's take another long look at everything, that's what I was telling myself on that New Year's Eve. And I had to start from the small–big problems that I had before me. The labour movement: was it ethically right and rationally correct to push for it to be broken? An 'other' movement had emerged: it had no need of icons to bow to or of the beacons of socialism, with its magnificent and progressive futures languishing somewhere on the horizon. These had given us nothing. We had had to take everything for ourselves, even a glorious part of that tradition: a paradoxical form of continuity and of memory. The *potenza* of breaking, of separation, had grown and had organised itself into a development of unprecedented struggles. Kill the father? The clash became inevitable, because the principle of certainty that presented itself in the practice of the new working-class movement drew its strength from the responsibility of the subjects, from their actions, by the very form in which they constituted themselves into the collective. Kill the father to love the brother. Choose your poor brother instead of your rich father. Turn the parable of the prodigal son on its head, while maintaining its evangelical overtones. The mechanisms of formation and circulation of struggle were signs of the truth of the movement that they constituted. There was no difference between the movement and its objectives, because the objectives of the workers – wages and the attack on how the working day was organised – were establishing themselves in the movement and developing compactly and simultaneously into a discourse, theory and practice of liberation. Once again, from the factory to the social. From the working class to the class of social producers.

Letter Ten: New Year's Eve 1968

From the struggle for emancipation to the struggle for liberation. Why, given these determinations and these certainties, avoid the risk of going ahead? And then, was it really a risk? Can you call it risk, the bursting into new life of a potent being? Only the melancholy of the individual can declare it. But when he intuits the collective, he himself, the hunchback of Recanati, my great poet, puts grudgingness aside and raises the desperate broom flower again – a sign of unity against inimical nature:

> . . . and since he thinks,
> What is the simple truth,
> Mankind has been united, organized
> Against her from the first,
> He sees all men as allies of each other,
> And he accepts them all
> With true affection, giving
> The prompt assistance he expects from them
> In all the varying danger and the troubles
> Their common war gives rise to.*

Here we ourselves move entirely from the collective. Life, the given life of a particular subject whom only the collective sustains and for whose needs only it provides – not the indeterminacy of any old romantic *Leben*. Life stretched across a bitter border, which has to be traversed and conquered – a distinct materiality of interests – not the indefiniteness of any old nature: this was, both in form and in content, what we were pursuing. Why, then, not lead the project to a determination? To be frank, there was not much talk of philosophy in collectives and committees at that time. There was much talk of politics, about how to destructure it in order to free oneself from it, about how to substitute a positive mode of expression for the relentless pattern of negativity that it was producing. Authoritarianism, total institutions, Molochs of the political and of the system: the critique, although it was tempted by the global opposition and by the misdeeds of a mirroring dialectic, was traversed by the deepening of the individual fields and by determined and centrifugal destructurings – the expansion of the critical dimensions did not confuse the picture but produced an irreversibility of trajectories. Marcuse supporting Basaglia. We talked above all about concrete tactics – a method

---

* Translator's note: Leopardi, 'La ginestra, o il fiore del deserto' ('The Broom, or the Flower of the Desert'), in *Canti*, Manchester: Carcanet, 1994, ll. 114–123; trans. J. G. Nichols.

and its articulations, to make the collective grow – a reconstructive surgery to recompose the subjects in the project. Perhaps, given the ontological scale of the innovation, a real and actual biological engineering.

I am rereading what I've written, cher David. How hard it is to explain all this! How to tell someone who was born with 1968 how 1968 was constructed, at the time and subsequently? The literature of the bourgeoisie presents it to us as an irrational event, a great emotion of the (slightly stupid) psychology of the masses – Le Bon and his foolish stories reborn.* Otherwise a product of modernisation – what trouble, that modernisation! Otherwise, again – and here we have the progressives to suggest it – a worldwide circulation of struggles: a circulation without an engine! While 1968 – like everything constructed by human beings who are liberating themselves – was the powerful limit of a hard and continuous production of elements of potentiality, of small conquests, of minute radical transformations. The accumulation of innumerable chunks of movement – from all over the world. Each little piece is an engine, a dynamic and a transcription – genetic acids. Until the soul of the world, recompacting the infinite variety of the drives of liberation that compose it, displaces itself. Listen to Spinoza: 'For since being able to exist is power, it follows that the more reality belongs to the nature of a thing, the more powers it has, of itself, to exist.'† In this dislocation the new humans burst forth – and everything that is not filtered by them becomes, from that moment, reactionary and enemy. And so, cher David, you who are already born to culture and politics as a new man: I am explaining to you the mechanism of your conception. Now you can see it, and you can understand the countless acts of love and of project that have given you this irreducibly new identity. As for us, we feel the uncertainties of those times as variants of a criterion of truth that we were constructing: if the truth is built, it is very human to tremble between the before and the after. (Blip blop, blap, why so much comical pedagogical pathos and this slightly prophetic spirit? An ironic tootle of the flute to discharge the tension, a student wisecrack – a chance comment by one of your children, devastating in its ingenuousness . . .

---

* Translator's note: a reference to Gustave Le Bon (1841–1931), French anthropologist, popular among other things for his 1895 study *The Crowd: A Study of the Popular Mind*.

† Translator's note: Spinoza, *Ethics*, Part I, Proposition 11, scholium; as translated by Edwin Curley in his *A Spinoza Reader*, Princeton: Princeton University Press, 1994. The term translated here 'power' is *potenza*.

Letter Ten: New Year's Eve 1968

Just what would be needed, as it has always been in the real world of this story. But to what effect? Paradoxically, that of raising the aim. Always. Like a bunch of tragic actors – who in the grotesque and sarcasm of a dinner after the show create a new play. Is the play of the world also capable of this low and generous knowledge? Yes – and it flows into prophesy.) Ciao, my dear brother . . .

Letter Eleven
Golem 1968–70

Rebibbia, 16 January 1982

A few days ago, cher David, my mother died. Old Aldina, a sweet Lombard Niobe who had known every kind of pain. We wrote to each other every week, for three years – mother and I – and she urged me – always, but especially while I was in prison – to faith and to testimony. Old Aldina departed with a smile, they tell me, without pain, and went back to that nature that she always loved, into the eternal and ever-renewed cycle of creation. May she rest in peace. The law did not grant me the ancient right to see her before she was buried. I write to you today with tenderness and with pain – and this presence of my mother pushes me to seek for, to grasp, that deep core where life and death are woven together seamlessly and love and violence connect with intensity. In this context, cher David, my letter today is trying to find a detachment that might be the interference of a rich reality – in order to analyse the pain.

Do you remember? 1968 was an outstanding point of that circulation of life and death. The customary optical spectrum of light, as ever; but also a new ray coming from the future. Do you remember those initial feelings of being there, at the heart of that huge story, in the first clash with the police, in the first demonstration of liberation? 'Burn, baby, burn.' No, the iconography of those three years, through to 1970, does not sufficiently convey the reality. The *parousia* [presence] cannot be represented simply as rebellion. Consciousness testified that, if there was a god, he had come down to earth – the irrational of the world could then become, and indeed had become, lessened. Life began to have a pleasant taste. Rebellion is the driving power of innovation, but who can say that a child is no more than the

Letter Eleven: Golem 1968–70

pain of childbirth? Who can end a son's love in the face of a mother's death? Rebellion and death are a fecundisation of life and love. With a terrible effort, I am today seeking in myself the truth of this rational assumption. Stop. Stop the tears and the emotion. Stop. Let's get back to us. Let us try. (It's a difficult leap. The general valence of pain has a universality that plucks you out, far away . . .)

Can there be (and, if so, with what modalities and what outcomes) a materialist reflection on 1968? The party's over, they say. The reflection may be bitter. Certainly not for the outcomes that 1968 had produced: those experiences have become seminal essences of our cultural horizon. And not even for the antagonistic development of the movement, as some have hypocritically complained – would it have been possible for the vitality of a historical potential to express itself other than in antagonistic terms? The bitterness is only revealed in my passion, and it comes from the fact of not having been able to enjoy this story. Of course, the relationship between suffering and enjoyment is never linear (we distrust those who, at this juncture, evoke a sweet positiveness and teenage memories) – but common sense has it that the two passions should not accumulate at the ends of a broken arc: in such a case there would be something logically wrong. For me, and for many, 1968 was a contradiction. It was a portentous event – but it was also the trick of Paul on the road to Damascus – it showed us the living god, then pasted him with Hellenistic vices. We were not able to initiate revolutionary will and the potentiality of real processes. There, I told myself ironically, when the subjectivity seemed at its strongest – *La Varsovienne* at the Odéon, and red and black flags against the Springer skyscraper – there we had *un processus sans sujet* [a process without a subject]. This was not in fact the case. But it was the case that often the subject was strutting about, external to the mass movement – as if the colour of Aphrodite could be distinguished from the blue of the Aegean. The spontaneity of mass action and its compactness were torn up and scattered here and there, and out of their rags the media made stereotypes of fashion or provocation. We shall have to be more careful the next time! I really don't find it in me to be ironic today. Lamartine too ended his *1848* with a peroration rather like that: to cite him is not funny, it is actually a bit nasty. And yet . . . (Have you noticed, David, my constant repetition of 'and yet'? This dialectical *aber* . . . as if crying and making mistakes could be assigned, with one little word, to fate. But how else to think?)

And yet 1968 was a big thing. We just needed not to confuse it with 1917 or imagine ourselves to be the Chinese characters who appeared in the writings of Edgar Snow. It was enough to grasp plainly what 1968 showed, the thing it was, the working class that was becoming society – or, better, who was destroying the norms of civil society to show itself as the class of the socialised worker and to reinvent antagonism against the state of mature capitalism. In Italy things had gone more or less the same as in the rest of Europe. The insurrection in the universities and the youth revolt had been a massive fact . . . But underlying all this there was a specificity of the Italian situation – namely a lag in capitalist development and social figures who were less clearly defined, but above all the unitary tradition of the struggles we inherited from the Communist Party and the work of bringing together the different movements we had built up in the preceding years. So here the CGT (Confédération générale du travail) could not take us to Grenelle, nor could the German unions repeat the exploits of Noske. Here the new materiality of the social class struggles of the exploited class – continuous, flowing and absorbent – showed itself to be unstoppable.

There is not much that I can tell you about those years – given the limits of these letters and my tiredness today. I'll just tell you where I was, a few beads of that necklace that I was threading at that time. (My mother used to teach me this game when I was little, as if I were a girl. Thank you, Aldina, for that kindness.) In July 1968, at Porto Marghera, we decided to finish with the trade union and the bosses – we invented that working-class phenomenon that was the general assembly for running the struggle, and we were the first to develop mass action on the basis of the devastating slogan of wage egalitarianism: '5,000 *lire*, equal for all'. The mass pickets, the gigantic roadblocks, the occupation of the railway stations, the marches on Mestre and Venice – when the continuous production cycle stopped in the whole of the Combine and the flame of the last exhaust gas went up to the sky, you could hear from as far as Padua the hymn of joy and the angry power of those 60,000 workers. In October, at Pirelli, on the sidewalks of Viale Sarca – and then an incredible circulation of struggles that assailed the city, gripping it in the same way in which the militant picketing had taken hold in the offices and on the factory floor. From the Cathedral [in Milan] came one of those marches where you have no idea who was in it, down from Cairoli along Portello, then clearing San Babila; and then they take Via Torino, those angry workers from Farmitalia. Behind them came the heavy infantry from Borletti, Siemens, and Pirelli in Via Solari . . . The winter was spent preparing new initiatives – supermarkets at Christmas, night clubs with a populist impulse on New Year's

Letter Eleven: Golem 1968–70

Eve. Comic and sometimes tragic ruminations of a proletariat that was rightly consumerist. But then spring came again. (In the garden of our old house, in Padova, the roses of spring were more beautiful than anyone else's: who knows why? Mother did not look after them at all – her pride had moments of enthusiastic and passive contemplation.) Spring: the movement spread to Turin. In that city I had known loneliness and an indistinct anger: now a huge organisation was being born – on a scale fit to deal with you, you damned bosses! On 3 July 1969, after months of upheaval in the factories, the struggle ran from Mirafiori to the Valentino to Nichelino – a ribbon of Molotov cocktails and thousands upon thousands of militants.

A revenge, a dream. A force that you found everywhere, the composition of the movement, in continuous struggle, in a river of magma. The good old Golem, the all-powerful, whose story Aldina had told me, had been formed. Where are you going? Why not answer him with the truth? It is inscribed on your forehead. Nowhere – we want to be here, with the power that comes to us from our having come together as a class, from our having unified the various branches of the proletariat in a tendential project of power. (Folklore: the ballbrains that were setting up new parties – small parties here, small parties there, small parties all over town. *Grunf, grunf.* Sometimes indeed it all got too much to bear. Get the merchants out of the temple! Come on now, don't get too angry, Toni, the river washes out the garbage.)

In the meantime Marghera was renewing the struggle. The date of 2 August 1970 was perhaps the highest point of the class struggle in those years. After months of clashes and mutual provocations, people came out of the big factories to support the precarious workers in the maintenance and construction sectors – the clash with the police was very violent – the police fled when a large march of workers, coming together after hours of strike action, moved forward singing the 'Internationale'. The industrial zone, the railway, and the motorway interchanges were occupied by barricades for several days. The surrounding region, from Chioggia to Noale, from Venice to Dolo, also experienced barricades and clashes. This was a great victory. August befitted Marghera. (There was a slender fig tree in the garden – my mother was big-built and heavy, but in August she would climb up there anyway, to pick those amazing fruits.) But every town had its season.

Stop. Golem. Psalm 139, lines 14–16:

> I will praise thee; for I am fearfully and wonderfully made: marvellous are thy works; and that my soul knoweth right well. My substance was

not hid from thee, when I was made in secret, and curiously wrought in the lowest parts of the earth. Thine eyes did see my substance, yet being unperfect; and in thy book all my members were written, which in continuance were fashioned, when as yet there was none of them.

Mamma, only today do I understand how the prophetic story and rationality could have been conjoined in the political education that you gave me! Stop.

Let's get back to our story. A massive pivotal moment of workers' struggles was being built, and of mass vanguards. It held solidly the large metropolitan areas of the North, then stretched in an endless variety of experiences and multiple activities, even to the South. At one point it seemed that the directional arrows of Italy's domestic mobility of labour were being reversed – and that they were running in a southerly direction, carrying the struggle with them. So it was that, in addition to the city areas of the Centre South, most affected were the great chemical cathedrals – Porto Torres, Gela and Brindisi – and the steel-producing plants of Bagnoli and Taranto. A pivotal moment of workers' struggles, of mass vanguards that reunited different strata of the proletariat – this was the specific characteristic of that hot season of struggles. What brought about this unity was certainly not the wretched trade union initiatives on harmonisation or on wage stratification or on pensions – it was this incredible circulation of the struggle, of the subjects, and their internal homogeneity on issues of wages and egalitarianism. The pivotal moment of the mass vanguard was now rendered politically effective. Its material and destructuring potentiality now had to be changed into a form of political representation. In both senses, social and political. That is to say, the mass working-class vanguards had to take on the weight of the direct political representation of the entire proletariat, and at the same time had to bring it to life as an effective social counter-power.

(Thinking about my mother again: beyond the mystified forms of the late Risorgimento tradition – Carducci and his Bolognese teachers, Ferrari and Tarozzi – and of the bourgeois emancipation – Rousseau recited from memory – in her teaching she communicated elements of a theory of power that were entirely materialistic. Power was a thing, a force. Money, wellbeing, availability of means. And also hope, desire, and its satisfaction. This hard and realistic conception of power was the other face of false consciousness – of rhetoric enjoyed and of alienation suffered. And yet the self-criticism of the bourgeois generations of the crisis passed on to us a rough but nonetheless effective concept of power. I stripped it bit by bit of its

Letter Eleven: Golem 1968-70

ideological excrescences in order to render it materially. Available for a new use. And all along my old mother had shown it to me, full of the doubts and uncertainty that the self-criticism had brought about.)

It was thus around those social and political objectives that the battle opened within the movement as a whole. The trade union – expelled from factories and reduced to marginality in the first phase – came back in with a clear operation. The assemblies are fine, they said, and the counter-power is fine, but closed within a dimension that is strictly working class. For the time being it was a discourse that was vaguely corporative, and it appealed to some people. We understood it as such then, and we can declare it now. The trade union movement of the factory councils was, first and foremost, an experiment in corporative democracy – first and foremost in the sense that a short while later it became an explicit function of the authoritarian corporativism of the state. In concrete terms, what shedding of tears, what blood, and what seeds of death this operation included, we were to see a little later, when – in the face of the inevitable and expected counterattack by the bosses – the corporative choice, the refusal to socialise the struggles became explicit and repressive and the working class of the big factories found itself compromised as a result.

We, on the other hand, were pushing for a socialisation of the struggles and for the negation of all corporate perspectives according to two broad schemas, which were entirely complementary albeit polemical at the time, as would become clear in the struggles that followed. One proposition was essentially and brutally proletarian – the *Prendiamoci la città* [Take over the city] of the Lotta Continua comrades. A powerful slogan, full of intuitions about the social subject of the struggle. From MacMahon to San Basilio, it would develop its potential for agitation and organisation in struggles over housing and proletarian needs, and above all it would push for an understanding of antagonism to be extended over the whole of the working day, between the production and the reproduction of labour power as a commodity. On the other hand the comrades of Potere Operaio were developing a proposition related to the 'social wage' and founded on an analysis of the social recomposition of the proletariat and of the increase in the quota of tertiary and intellectual labour power as a directly productive component. After so many years, the 'refusal of work' descended from the empyrean realm of theoretical abstraction, looked around and, in a useful first guise, posed the problem of the social valorisarion of the new needs and of the new proletarian subjectivity. So discussion then opened on these themes. In our opinion, the pivotal movement of the struggles of the mass vanguards could have organised itself in the factory, but only – really only – on condition that the two tendencies, towards the representation of the entire proletariat (and in particular of the new quality of labour force in the development of social production) and towards the exercise of counter-power, were firmly established in the councils. Otherwise there was only corporatism. This was our opinion – the form could not be distinct from the new content, and the hymns in praise of renewing the trade unions seemed to us hypocritical. Renewal, innovation? There was nothing to invent, everything was implicit in the movement, and you just had to find a way to let it come out, offer it an appropriate language. In this, however, we did not succeed.

We did not succeed, cher David, in making present what had to happen anyway, because it was there – its being was pregnant, just as the sky is full of light. Just as my spirit today is full of pain. We did not manage to anticipate the decade that we had before us. Of course, the theory was trailing behind. The conception of the mass worker, even though it contained all the social determinations of the development of this subject, was in reality misunderstood as referring to the poor measure of 'working-class centrality'. A measure that repeated Third Internationalist stereotypes and a traditional conception of dictatorship – this betrayal of working-class and proletarian society, this paraphrase of the bourgeois 'general will'. A measure that, within the framework of the social development of productive forces, would soon inevitably yield to the lure of corporativism. At the height of these discussions we met with Bruno Trentin. Someone asked him if he thought that the trade union movement of factory councils could become the basis of a new working-class party, the bearer of the general proletarian interest. He answered evasively. We met Pierre Carniti, the lion of the FIM [Federazione Italiana Metalmeccanici]: in him a very strong sense of the movement was solidly framed in an institutional conception of the trade union. Whereas the former was controlling a future that he feared, the latter, with furtive and skilful little moves, was trying to put back together a jigsaw puzzle that had been broken apart. Meanwhile we were working with the newly created 'Manifesto' group – once again, a busful of left communists of the 1930s, when things were going well, but otherwise former Catholics and Gramscians. On their own, always desperately alone, Rossana and Pintor, a frustrated intellectual generosity that had a taste of the good, of the old style, of hope.

And the struggle goes on, ever onwards. You were overwhelmed by it. I had not been able to tell if the birth of my group Potere Operaio at that stage, had been an explicit policy choice or rather an act that was labour-saving, due to tiredness and therefore the need to make consensual work more profitable. The group as a management structure – as a way of multiplying our intellectual productive forces. Although I had not been able to understand this at first, I soon became convinced of it: the group could not be anything other than this – really just this. Except that some people thought that what they had in their hands was a political organisation – the idiots!

What a mess! How could one reasonably imagine that the world we were all solidly constructing . . . and it was so rich, even too rich – how could one either attempt to represent it in its completeness, or imagine that sectarian differences could cross it and divide it? But this is what happened. Often the dead insinuates itself into forms of life (only the rational defines them and separates them – Aldina, sweet midwifery, strong rational flanks, effectiveness of an intellectual forceps). A cut-price Leninism, built on smug complacency in our intelligence, in our capacity for foresight, a Luciferian intellectual pride – this is what held together the comrades of Potere Operaio. That need not have happened: because they actually were intelligent comrades, good and honest people, perhaps the best people around at that time, and certainly the best of those who are now in prison and in exile. Why, then, overdetermine a style of work that was proving productive? Maybe we were giving the wrong answers to real problems. But the biggest unsolved problem was the organised labour movement, and the temptation was to go for mimesis instead of critical and revolutionary awareness. Which is often a science of pushing to the limit.

However, throughout 1968 and 1969, the contacts with the political parties were continuous. With Luigi Longo, with members of parliament, with the trade union federations. They covered us and procured an amnesty. Gradually, however, the clash became inevitable. Some people, with an opportunistic realism, suggested a sort of mass entrism: let us establish, they said, a dialectic with the official labour movement that engages with all its aspects, leveraging our mass contribution for a renewal of its political line. But how would such a thing be possible, when the movement was prepared to swallow almost nothing of the productivist reformism that was the basis of the ideology of Italian socialism? The break had already happened earlier on. It was recognisable in the impotence of the official labour movement, in its inability to grasp, at one and the same time, the transformations in the social composition of the class and the radical break in communist thought after 1956. Any hypothesis of mass entrism was illusory. We were condemned to an autonomy of the movement, or rather we were preselected for that destiny. 1968 as a refoundation? A lot of people were thinking along such lines. But we were stuck between the opposing tensions of a rebelliousness, which was seeking immediate liberation, and a massive, heavy and continuous displacement of the mass movement. The first wave was short, the second was long. The official labour movement placed itself between the two, proposing the fetish of a mediation, but a mediation that was actually the denial of revolutionary tensions. We were forced to play the awareness of the limit, of dualism. You could not escape this. Any other choice was mystifying. The problem of the party was not immediately resolvable. (Luckily so, we can now say, while we wait to be able to reconstruct both the movement and the liberation.) If you are the prince, you divide: the functionaries of power don't need classical references to grasp the moment of the break and to exploit the fragility of the surface situation. And they were starting a flanking operation against us. But we'll talk more about this later.

What more can I tell you, cher David, about 1968? I have something of an internal resistance, an intellectual diffidence, about talking to you about it. Likewise about talking about my mother, and about the mystery of life and – today – of death that she is for me. However, so far I've only told you about the problems, the hard and contradictory paths that traversed the great green forest in which we found ourselves – but I have not told you much about the forest as a whole. It is difficult to find the right words because you were continuously aware of the gap between the exceptional scale of the phenomenon you were living and the daily reality within which you were struggling – so that either you developed this whole experience in utopian terms (undefined, in your enthusiasm) or you held to the ground of rationality and were ensnared in it. Being a teenager at the time, you probably did not notice the gap. And just as well: only in that way, by ignoring the efforts of the fathers, could awareness become a higher vital complexion, an offer of possibilities, and only in that way could you march further down this path, much further and more surely than we were able to. But I too am trying to do violence to myself, to make me the son of my self (just as is happening today, on the coffin of Aldina) – and to remove the memory from my being, and the nostalgia, albeit powerful. Because this being, I want to press it forward – death and life, my mother and my children – how hard and bitter this discourse is. And then – you see – you have to accept my schizophrenic tension in talking to you about the entire forest – and the fact that I talk to you about it with adjectives that myth merits.

Letter Eleven: Golem 1968–70

The myth of the mother, of birth. 1968 was a golden age, because in that period individual liberation and the revolution of the masses came together. Because love's assault on the heavens destroyed the old figure of power and gave to imagination the mark of potentiality of politics. Because millions of exploited workers and intellectuals, everywhere in the world, felt how freedom and dignity were caressing them. Because the struggle paid – rebelling is right – and desire was concrete. I could go on at length, just as I used to tell these things to my insatiable mother – knowing that my discourse would inevitably remain mythical. But myth is revelation. So if we want, as postmodernists, to tease out its meaning, we elicit it at the point where all the contradictions of the relations of production, material and cultural, came to be realised in 1968. In a revolutionary break. The revolution happened: and it become *le fond mobile de la science humaine* [the moving reserve of human science].* On the surface power was only scratched, but deep down it was delegitimised, unhinged, and dissolved. The class was, on the surface, traversed by a cyclone of hope, then hit by a wave of repression; deep down, though, it was recomposed and rendered, both by hope and by repression, social, autonomous and powerful. From time to time the elements of the transformation came to light. At those points the forest caught fire and everyone was able to see. But we often shut our eyes and shielded them with our arms, because we – old men – might have our sight damaged by it.

1968 continues to do its work. To some it represents a nightmare, to others a hope. It is a new substance, of which we are made, and no one can pluck it from our nature. No, mother, no one will take it away. Since then, how many self-criticisms, how many suicides, how many attempts to tear off, from the skin, that act of rebellion and collective growth. '*Peut-être notre ami Glucksmann a raison, lorsqu'il dit que nous nous devons confronter avec le mal, plutôt que nous bercer dans le rêve impossible d'un bien commun*' [Maybe our friend Glucksmann is right when he says that we should confront evil rather than comfort ourselves in the impossible dream of a common good].† But was not 1968, above all, a confrontation with evil? So why this embargo of hope? But is hope really impossible? Death and pain fecundate life and love. The discourse on the possible overflows that on the necessary. And it is only in relation to the latter that the distinction

---

* Translator's note: unidentified quotation.
† Translator's note: unidentified quotation.

between possible and impossible becomes effectual. I cannot avoid the metaphysical meaning of the Yiddish story: Golem – this artefact of necessity that liberates ever new possibilities. The lower parts of the earth, says the Psalm, are woven and presented to the word that sets in motion the goodness of the body. 'How precious also are thy thoughts unto me . . . how great is the sum of them!' my mother, so dear and beautiful. 'If I should count them, they are more in number than the sand: when I awake, I am still with thee.'* 1968 recomposed in a forward direction the ineradicable frontier of the class struggle – the individual subjects are marked by this necessity and by this possibility. In pain I find again a blessing. I send you a strong hug.

---

* Translator's note: Psalm 139: 17–18.

Letter Twelve
Civill Warre

Rebibbia, 28 January 1982

Cher David,

On 17 August 1971 Nixon de-linked the dollar from gold. From that point on a dollar was a dollar, and that was that. The dollar becomes the phantasm of my will, the capricious harsh reality of my power. Every relative parameter of the certainty of values was thus dissolved. A Schopenhauer for the multinationals. With it the residual and pathetic illusions of socialism disappeared, too – and also the possibility of trade unionism – in other words the project of connecting and reconnecting the wage and the conditions of reproduction to criteria defined by progress, by development and by value – the bosses were smacking you in the face with this truth of theirs, crudely but realistically. They prepared new conditions for controlling the market, in particular the labour market, and they wanted the dissolution of the class composition that had been built by the struggles. In the 1970s we watched the development of all the consequences that necessarily followed from that decision: forced and functional divisions of the labour market, both domestically and internationally, rampant mobility, regressive programmes, monetary policies to match ... That which had been undermined and partly destroyed by the ten-year cycle of struggles, in other words the orderly development of exploitation – was now taken up and theorised by international capital as a possible space for predetermining a new phase of accumulation and rampant restructuring worldwide. Kissinger seemed to us at that moment the romantic genius of reaction, a Metternich lovingly cultivated in the garden of memory and reflowering – Novalis: reaction learns everything from the revolution – the global cycle of struggles had passed its peak, hence reaction could begin to put to good use the lessons learned and, as a result, the articulation of exploitation had to be restored along the lines of defeated struggles – a new dissemination of geographical expressions of imperialist command. Do you remember that, David? We were seized by a strong emotion. From then on everything was clear and had to be so. But it is true that the violent symbol of the transformation of a state of affairs into normative will contains a traumatic effect, when the person taking the action is the enemy and you know that their initiative draws strength from the fact of imposing an overall anticipation, a terrain that the enemy now knows and we no longer know. In any case, we were entering into an age of overdeterminations – physical and savage – a breakdown of development that dislocated every horizon. 'Civill Warre', in the words of good old Hobbes. A company of wolves. And hawks, bulls and pigs. In Italy there had already been attempts to drive the movement into retreat, using the old police methods of Fouché, and Bonaparte the Small – in the bombings of Piazza Fontana. Soon we were to discover that even police and provocations suffer from the structural laws of history and must come to terms with the present level of class composition. Piazza Fontana: a fascist tool, a Turkish deterrent, unworthy of a culture that had renounced the little old world envisioned by Rumor – the scholar of Fogazzaro with the sweaty hands. And anyway it was ineffective in the face of that class of the socialised worker and intellectual operator, which was beginning to develop in Italy too. So it all went wrong. The massacre covered the state in mud and hatred. It took several years for their methods of provocation to reach levels adequate to their purpose. That point was only reached on 7 April 1979: for a new working class, a new repression, social theorems, exacerbation of the mystifying functions of the mass media.

But, while their ability to overdetermine the reaction against the struggles in a terrorist fashion was limited, the initiative of economic and social restructuring was strong. As we saw, between our national political class and the national sections of multinational capital there still existed a divide, altogether in favour of the latter – only in the 1970s did this gap between repression and restructuring begin to be overcome, the one becoming internal to the other. The real counterattack hit directly at the relations of production and at the labour process. For this operation Nixon's August was a blast on the trumpet. From the point of view of analysis there could be no doubt: all the signs indicated that we were entering a phase in which, far from trying to programme – or at least to guarantee – the balance of relations between the classes in development, the capitalist part sought to act politically so as to dismantle the front of the struggles, wielding their sabres wildly in the fray and thereby trying to open lines of penetration and division, of entry into the body of the proletariat. To regain rights over the permeability and porosity of proletarian society. The Keynesian state, the state as planner, which for a certain period (starting at least with the Great Depression of the 1930s) had constituted the regulative idea and the grid of prudent capitalist development, were annulled in their reformist values. Against the independent variability of the economic and political movements of the proletariat, the collective bosses (and with some delay, but also with much good will, also their state) resolutely took the path of capitalist use of the crisis, articulating disequilibrium and repression. This action was intended to break up the combative agglomerations of the mass worker, to destroy their vanguards, and above all to block the circuits of social massification of the struggles.

In fact, cher David, as any humble political scientist knows, this process is normal in the acute phases of class struggle, as soon as the crisis – so much feared by us – comes into the open – the crisis of the relationship between proletarian insurgency and its political expression. 'I have seen in this revolution a circular motion,' as Hobbes noted.* So now we were in the low phase. And yet there was something there, something radical and original, which prevented this operation from being given the epithet of 'classic': this lay in the fact that the operation of restoration and restructuring was not aimed at bringing about a new equilibrium. It did not see itself as an articulation of the movement of the law of value, but rather it rested entirely on the timely validation of political command. Here is Franz Rosenzweig:

> cutting the Gordian knot between past and future that the people itself has not been able to resolve, the state extirpates contradiction from the world and in every moment places it outside the world – to be clear: each time, only for that moment. The state thus holds back, at every moment, the river of the life of the world in order to make it an unmoving water – this river that never ceases to negate itself at every instant, to throw itself into the ocean of eternity, but of which the state makes – in every instant – an eternity.†

---

* Translator's note: *Behemoth or the Long Parliament*, edited by F. Tönnies, London, 1969, p. 204.
† Translator's note: unidentified quotation.

Washington's August smelt of sulphur and war. Absolute and irrational abstraction of the *jetzt Zeit* [present time]. Command took the place of science. We said: the crisis of the state as planner and the production of commodities by means of command; and the rise of the crisis state. Today, at a distance of more than a decade, we understand the theoretical intelligence of the foresight. And what came afterwards simply confirmed it. Both internally and externally, both in national economies and in multinational economies – value/profit is not formed in the orderliness of circulation but it too has become wild, a leopard moving between shrublands and savannas. From that moment political economy went into disarray, like a stuntman, between shades of fiction and simple acrobatic skills. Conversely, the critique of political economy had then to become a critique of command.

And this, cher David, brings us to the list of the hard labours of practice. The critique of capitalist command: what did that mean? There were some, even then, and thereafter repeatedly, who took this theoretical definition as a springboard for a logical step from 'weapons of critique' to 'critique by means of weapons' – to its urgency and its immediacy. '*Ce n'est que du folklore,*' you object, '*glissons, donc.*' Mais ... [This is only folklore, let's pass. But ...] But ... in a movement that was as rich, as complex and powerful as the Italian movement, nothing can be underestimated. Here the kidnappers of [French Renault executive] Robert Nogrette do not transform themselves overnight into *nouveaux philosophes,* nor do the admirers of Mao become allies of Deng – here we had anger, a rootedness, a class pride. Of course, whatever the theoretical–practical dress that the decision for armed struggle wears – and it might also be (essentially it was) derived from the official movement and from its Bibles – what we had was behaviours and connotations that were extremist and anarchic, and one could simply have written them off as extraneous and parasitic. That would not have been very sensible, however, not even in the abstract. And it was certainly not possible *chez nous.* The important thing was to understand its genesis, the lift-off point, which, despite everything, was not purely ideological. Marxism–Leninism, Che Guevarism, whatever soup you like, go ahead and add it; but in the end the origin was practico-theoretical, it is the definition of the impossibility of political action organised around the parameters of the law of value. The perception of the step forward that had been taken in capitalist practice went hand in hand with the political protest, the restlessness, sometimes the fury that, especially in the more politicised layers of the proletarian vanguard of the preceding years, emerged in the light of the relative blockage of struggles and of the blurring of the immediacy of perspectives that had characterised the early 1970s.

I would like to dig a bit deeper in order to arrive at the essence of this somersault of reason – it seems to me that it comes out of a kind of game of mirrors, where the fury and the refusal reflect the image of reality and multiply it a thousand times in a glassy and image-filled *theatrum*, giving to the image virtues that are theurgic, transformative and magical. The armed struggle stems from a natural magic of the frustrated spirit that tries to develop the fury into terror, to potentialise the frustration in a historic orgasm. The armed struggle – the scourge of God – does not remove the reality – it accepts the provocation of capitalist overdetermination as such, with unmoving and paranoid fidelity. With that, however, the reality remains, independent of the fury and of the game of mirrors; and also as the origin of all this. And the crisis of value remains, with its charge of irrationality. The material origin of the decision to take up armed struggle is not therefore cancelled out by the falsity of the game.

It was necessary, however, to avoid being dragged in – into that *theatrum*. Outside of the environment in which 'the flower of the armed struggle blossomed' the debate was harsh and did not centre explicitly on that problem, but, rather more generally, on how to deal with the situation created by an acceleration of capitalist restructuring 'by means of command'. There was a clash between two positions – the 'offensive' option and the 'autonomy' option. That's what they were called in those days – we can laugh at those abstract stereotypes, but not too much, because from each of them there derived very long theoretical and practical trajectories. With false detachment I would say today that the former was a spatial theory, the second a time theory. In the sense that the supporters of the former position were saying as follows: only a forcing, as vanguard, of the spaces of struggle would enable the growth of autonomy; but the second thesis proclaimed that only the times of autonomous mass proletarian self-organisation could trigger the offensive. I don't like to take these little pieces of history and political debate too seriously – and yet, if you take a drop of water, it can reflect the sun. If you break it, you will have two suns. The proposal of the offensive was my nemesis. I have never particularly loved translations, and this was a bad translation. From the German, from the Hungarian, from the defeat of those revolutions of the 1920s. Lukács and Korsch seemed to me, in this context, really mistreated. And even Lenin I felt to be inappropriate in this debate, and the quotations that came thick and fast were completely ineffectual. There were historical and theoretical elements that drove me to polemic, but the reasoning was reduced essentially to this: I did not think that the proletarian subject had, as in the 1920s, an inheritance – the great Russian revolution – to spend (or even to squander), or a model to repeat, or the same subject to exalt, or the same opponent to beat (had we not continually recognised this? were we not born from the identification of this discontinuity?). Rather it seemed to me fundamental to aim at a new accumulation of proletarian strength, beginning from the new conditions of struggle, and especially from the shift in composition that had taken place in the very nature of the proletariat in the preceding years.

It was therefore the path of diffuse autonomy, of rootedness, of an intelligent resistance operating at various levels – that had to be traversed. Certainly a hard path, because it could concede little to the extremist thrusts of many of the revolutionary fractions in the factories – but at the same time it had to keep a strong relationship with them as essential forces for the development of the programme of organisation. In this context new problems began to arise, such as the appropriation of the objective in the factory struggles and the active defence of these processes of appropriation. The same problems that, for at least a decade, American workers had been raising on the objective basis of the transformation of labour processes – the factory was now a 'contested terrain' where the development of the mode of production represented a balance of power negotiated and decided upon day by day. (Philosophers speak of this world as a structure of possibilities – there are endless possibilities in the continuous reconsolidation of the productive forces – their continued openness. It is not true that production is a machine – the cycle is broken by the possibilities – production is, itself, an application of imagination, a time and place of possibilities. Production is the contested terrain of capital, the compacted terrain of imagination, and the area for the subjects' struggles of appropriation.)

Once again at the Petrolchimico plant, that gigantic laboratory of vanguard experiences, there was an attempt at mass struggle on the slogan of an 'appropriation of the reduction of working hours'. In other words people came into the factory and left it according to a pre-arranged programme of shifts that unilaterally reduced the number of working hours from 38 to 35, thus leaving three hours empty of production on each shift. In response to this struggle, the employer would have had to bring in additional workteams, which he did not have, so this would have meant hiring new workers. So the workers were taking back time, and the lack of production was the responsibility of the employer. The struggle was not successful, but it was a significant new step in assembly line practice. Happy are the times when the political confrontation between various positions can be carried out in these big mass experiments! This meant maintaining theory at the level of industry and denying it any artisanal or minoritarian valence – factors that were present in the hysteric repetition of the Bolshevik motifs of the theory of offensive. Things went ahead anyway, between misunderstandings and crafty accommodations, between uncontainable subjectivist impulses and important moments of reflection. But the contradiction could not be contained: first bits of stray shrapnel started firing off, and then gradually the core exploded. The political groups, given that they were born around 1968, were characterised by an enthusiastic and indistinct fusion of offensive and autonomy. The melting of the glue released elements of spontaneous synthesis. So that was how Potere Operaio fell apart, and also Lotta Continua and the other groups – although some of them spent years in the process of disintegration.

However, the core of the thing was not in this dissolving. Certain disenchanted persons frankly wanted this solution. The real problem was that of substance, of innovation, of the liquidation of tradition. No mourning for the death of the small political groups, as mimesis or germination of the official labour movement. Let's rather leave working-class science free in the development of the programme (always re-posed as a problem and, in our case, never resolved), of a nondialectical reversal of the negative, of an affirmation of the positive, of the refusal of the mystifying function of dialectics. Let me explain. With fierce insistence, the theoretical–practical history of the labour movement – although not able to imagine a value that is not the one reclaimed from the masters, although unable to offer an alternative to capitalist development – develops this identity of contents in a homology of organisational forms. In this case, the labour movement links resistance to organisation and identifies phases of internal consolidation in the moments of ebb of the struggle. The labour movement is Hegelian: it recognises itself as a servant; and, as a servant, it organises itself in relation to a master. In terms of both content and form. Will it emerge from this dialectic being worthy of the master? Althusser has always suspected this, and sometimes he has boldly stated as much – before going crazy with it. The function of general representation is determined at this point – a general representation of the interest in development (in times of crisis: we are better capitalists than they are!), and of organisation: in this case too, when the spontaneity decreases, when the crisis of the struggle is a given, organisation takes its place. Organisation is born as a substitutive will, as compensation – as a tension on the negative, of the negative.

Consciousness, *Bewusstsein* = consciousness of the negative. Materialism: my good old Jürgen rebelled against it. Is it not perhaps here that the cynicism and the mystificatory wheeler-dealing of the labour movement have their birthplace? In this claim of the independence of consciousness, of organisation and of the political, which is the breaking of every basic condensation of the *multitudo*? But has it not already become a *contradictio in adiecto* [contradiction between parts of an argument] when someone moves in the social composition of class? And in the face of the explicit drive towards values alternative to capitalist development? Organisation cannot be an exasperation of resistance, the dialectical insurgency of the servant against the master. Organisation and programme cannot be a homology of the positive and the negative. It is clear that the problem resists both moralism and the pathetic: what is in play here is the singular determination of class politics, the tearing that it must operate in relation to the bourgeois theory of command. For me, the clear formulation of this problem was in those years a stormy emotion, like getting a car back on the road after a terrifying skid, after a spin . . . It seemed to me that a rich set of theoretical and practical virtues had been for a while dispersed – stupidly, if not malevolently. It was not so. This masochism of the negative and of the constraint to traditional politics could be, and in part had been, avoided. My comrades and I felt that it was possible to make a new beginning without turning back.

But, we asked ourselves immediately (objectifying the eventual objection), would we not find ourselves paradoxically forced again, precisely by the capitalist breaking of the links of values, by the crisis induced at each articulation of the social, to re-establish the independence of the political and to exclude definitively the hypothesis of the social constitution of communism? We have realistically to grasp the capitalist capacity to dissolve the connections of value – added the critics – the only possibility we have is that of forming the opposite. We have the opportunity – let us arm ourselves with appropriate techniques and deal with the long and dangerous journey through the desert: the assumptions of the 'autonomy of social class' are misplaced, and they are indecent! But no, we retorted: the capitalist breaking of the possible universe of the law of value brings about the accentuation of antagonistic polarities at the social level. As a result, mediations, whether trade unionist or representative, were no longer a given: not because of an overstated Leninism or because of the cynicism of the independence of the political (terrorism was born directly from this), but rather on the terrain of the formation of counter-powers, of a theory of war that would assume its subjects in the new social composition, antagonistic and irreducible, and would develop them constitutionally. Once again, only a paradox represented the real: the explicit and realistic assumption of the theory of war was the only key that made it possible to avoid the blind alleys of armed struggle or of political party depotentialisation of the new and very rich composition of the class.

(Some time ago I reread Hans Kelsen, *Socialism and the State*, written in 1923 if I'm not mistaken. It is useful and fascinating to understand how this apologist of the 'polyhedric practicability' of the state is inclined to read, especially in times of crisis, the contractual relations, relations of force contracted between classes, not in purely quantitative terms, but in a context that is qualitative, juridical in nature, with constitutional potentiality! Only war founds the equilibrium – and also that quantity of the law that makes survival possible. In recent days I have been reading Branko Horvat, *Political Economy of Socialism*, and once again I find, in the crisis of real socialism, the same quest for a dualistic and contractually progressive foundation of law and planning.)

Inside the theoretical practice we had been living, the situation of the class struggle had matured to the point of making possible this determination, which is positive. And finally not dialectical. Hobbes again – or Calhoun: 'not contract but compact' (according to Michele, my cell-mate next door, who is in love with the old reactionary from Carolina and is lucid in constitutional theory as only those who possess the logical parameters of American realism can be).

Cher David, to say that those discussions in the early 1970s showed the diagram of intentions and the lucidity of expression of what I am expressing here would be a lie. Everything was complicated by a confused imaginary, by immediate commitments, by a solidarity that was assumed to be intact, and by even more elementary motives. In reality, all discussion took place in a climate that had the violence of a worn-out marital relationship: the presupposition of love was hypocritical, the atmosphere was vaguely murderous. It is certain, however, that our discussions were not entirely brain-fevered and that our decisions were not idle. A method of work and a mass style of working led us to argue things out in assemblies, in the streets and in the factories. It was impossible to avoid the richness of the undertaking and the effort it involved. It was not the first time that I participated in a mass debate of this magnitude – but it was the first time that the debate was occurring within the new composition of the class, which had emerged in the course of the 1960s: a magma, but one full of plots, tattoos, and codes.

And of absences: that is, the official labour movement. Here the foolish and suicidal presumption of the stabilising effect of the reflux, the arrogant reaffirmation of continuity in the face of the transformation of class composition brought about a bureaucratic politics of small steps for the reabsorption of deviance and for the restoration of tradition. Just as Pantagruel stretches out, hoping that, when the flood waters recede, the frogs will jump into his mouth, so too the party of the Prince! But an error of theory meant that there would be no feast – the new composition was not a swamp with frogs, but living and overflowing water. Cher David, I have to confess: at that time I nurtured hopes of a miracle – namely the conversion of the labour movement! But this was only imputable to my defect of hatred and to the wantonness of my character. And also to another of my shortcomings: I am not able to change my opinions. When things were obvious, why were they not happening? Why are large institutions subject to the evil that Cacania* propagated – the impenetrable confidence of their own reproduction? So, after a while, believing that things had run out of steam and were superficially guaranteed, the bureaucrats lost all hesitation and fiercely began to arm themselves again with arrogance and abuse. Setting up, against the movement, the revenge of the Historic Compromise – which they thought was a small thing, whereas in fact it was unbearable. With deathly determination they prepared to announce the Italic repetition of a Chile-style solution and to preach – as a means of avoiding it – Lenten sacrifices after what they had portrayed as a carnivalesque orgy! Imagination is dead! Mercy, Jesus, have mercy! It ended up with the PCI, far from cynically dominating the situation, as its preceptors thought, becoming itself a twig in the storm that was raised by upsetting the law of value. Kitsch and its rhetoric are amusing when we witness such misadventures – and the opportunities were not lacking. Don't you think, David, that the kitsch of 1977 was in fact cheaply invented precisely by Berlinguer and Co.? By Franco Rodano and his many advisors? The party of councils and councillors, the baroque of the variations on the theme of the Prince, moralism and formalism, a

---

* Translator's note: Reference to Musil's ironical name 'Kakanien' for Austro-Hungary (*kaiserlich–königlich*, 'imperial–royal' = KK, pronounced 'ca-ca', in which the allusion to faeces is immediately and universally recognisable).

fiction. The kitsch of 1977 was an adequate response to the kitsch of the Historic Compromise, the madness of an improvised culture of administration – and then everything came together: that 1977 summer in Rome, dope-smoking, and the politics of the Prince discovered their deep and comical kinship.

But there wasn't much room for comedy for us at that time – the enemy continued to show himself with two faces, a capitalist face representing a power that had exceeded itself and was going wild, and a petty bourgeois face, of a reformism that was timid and intent on avoiding conflict. In those early years of the 1970s the problem was to work on the concrete, following the trail of new subjects who, tired of their old political and trade union representatives, had come out of their lair. The problem was how to follow these subjects like divine hunters – how to recognise in their faces, as soon as they came into view, our grown humanity. Autonomy against offensive, weapons of mass criticism against the critique by means of weapons, a war theory for a proletarian constitution. We had to hold on to our diversity and grasp in the massification of the proletarian movement the concrete emergence of those behaviours of war in which the transition to communism appears as consciousness, both individual and collective – and this happens only there. It was only this consciousness that would make it possible to organise the transition to constitution – the *Civill Warre* – into a process of liberation.

Cher David, you are a Cartesian functionary in the French administration and you have those refined arts of analysis and criticism, of description and belief, which come with an education in the great Parisian schools – but not even you, cher David, would ever be able to explain to the judges of Italian courts, brainwashed as they are by the kitsch of the Historic Compromise, that today, when they sit in judgement over us and over an entire generation on the things of which I have spoken so far, they should enter into and discriminate between these different positions. 1973 – Rosolina, the dissolution of Potere Operaio: such were the conversations. However, a big ironic kiss . . .

PS I have just reread this letter. Forgive me, David, for the highs and lows of my account. Putting side by side the world story of the dollar and the kitsch of the incipient Historic Compromise is some undertaking, and even a poet would be hard put to do it justice. Such a disproportion makes it impossible to write. Yet that was how we lived at that time: like being in a game of sudden accelerations and decelerations, like on a spaceship that was going into orbit – so of course the big story was disproportionate and irreducible to the particular over which it nevertheless loomed. All sense of relation seemed to have collapsed. The traditional theory, the great classical synthesis, allowed the use of modular functions, in both the large and the small. But what was Nixon's 17 August, if not a theoretical and practical event that brought about the breaking of every possible model? So writing should become a self-sufficient parameter – and it is not so. Nor is my writing, as it obscurely tries to seek out what is strong in life and from that point to pursue the various traverses of a world divided. I shed light on my personal theoretical story and on events that affected me, in the hope of arriving at a general set of meanings. How might this be possible? Nothing guarantees it for us. Sometimes it happens. The compasses are going crazy. Let us seek. All that remains is the solid point of support: writing, on the other hand, becomes confused between these difficulties. What remains then as a document is chaos, disproportion, disease, the strain of those contradictions. And the event that all of this brought about. *Civill Warre*: it took a while to understand the dimensions of it. Goodbye for now.

Letter Thirteen
Separation

Rebibbia, 5 February 1982

Cher David,

At this point a new ballad begins. Sad and dramatic in some ways, but exciting in its substance. When desire comes up against a harsh reality, it goes around it, it tries to envelop it and absorb it. As for its internal contradictions, desire tries to solve them by arming itself with a sensuous thought (Peirce: 'hypothesis produces the *sensuous* element of thought, while induction the *habitual* element').* Now, the consideration of the crisis of the functioning of the law of value had brought us to a number of conclusions. Some of these seemed to me frankly reasonable and convincing, and they were the ones that were related to a scaling of revolutionary initiative according to the subjective parameters of a strict dualism. But the road from theoretical determination to concrete determination was a complicated one. When a real problem arises – I told myself continuously – the conditions for its solution must also be given. It will be! But it is true that the transition from the normal science of revolution to a new paradigm, through the puzzles that had ensnared us, that still remains a leap. A leap to be taken in less dangerous conditions – the risk is not free. It became fundamental to grasp and define the new subject. The global antagonism that capital was bringing about, the war that opposed us, *Krieg als fortgesetzte Staatspolitik* [war as permanent state politics] – *bon*, only a subject who possessed appropriate properties for this totality could sustain the confrontation. But disorder and

---

* Translator's note: Charles Sanders Peirce, *Collected Papers*, ii 643.

dispersion announced themselves as the first determinations of that subject. It seemed to reveal itself by diffusing and internalising itself, by distending and separating itself. Moreover, whereas in the classical era subjects were fixed individually, solidly and in party-political terms on surfaces that were translucent and neutral, now the registration of the subject stretched out like a solid shadow and rendered that same surface swollen and pregnant. There was something feminine and powerfully indistinct in the ontology of this new subject. (Are we at the origins of the postmodern? Is the postmodern feminine? For sure, it was Danièle, Grazia, Johanna and Maria, emancipated women that they were, who first showed me the complexity of this problem – in this very first stage of their feminism, the quest for liberation was still oriented towards universal figures – an extraordinary extension of the conceptual horizon emerged from this combination of feminist thought and abstract dynamics.)

In the meantime, in those years – we are around 1973 – all sorts of things were flying around – stories, sounds, experiences, marijuana, LSD, and the fabulous undertakings of alternative culture, both American and German. It was good music. Movement. The processes of liberation were moving ahead on their own singular cultural trajectories, the first sign of which was one of separation. For those who, as Marxists, were trying to relate back that diversity, that separation, to a substrate of subjective identity – to that density of value and of materiality that the traditional definition of the proletarian subject demands – the undertaking might have appeared impossible. And yet, I told myself, if I scrape off the more stupid cultural incrustations, the lighter graffiti of these behaviours, what comes out of it if not the human being, and aggregates of humans rendered poor by the system of exploitation? They, in despair, must recognise – at the social level, in the fabric of that intellectual matter of which they are now made, of that rich second nature out of which they are cut – a deep antagonism and a desire for happiness, a longing for appropriation and liberation, multiplied by the level of contradiction that they are living – and all this inevitably brings me back to the problem of the proletarian, of humans as collective essences who want to break free from their chains and storm the heavens. This is how I was reasoning – but with disenchantment. I did not enjoy this beggarly and generic Protagoras – humanism is not a good aid to revolutionary thought – but because we always found it in the way it must have some kind of meaning. As long as one did not confine oneself to admiration of the generic human essence, I was convinced that this logical operation of defining the essence – and thus its possible articulations – could guide me towards determination. The utopian margins could constitute an elementary introduction to a new physics of the concept. The concept of a determined totality: again, this requirement – and it is evident that the important thing at this point is not so much the requirement as its new quality. My writing must therefore now venture to prove itself on this experiential displacement.

I repeat, cher David – and I am sure that you understand me, because this is now the period in which we did this journey together: the quest for the concept in its new determination was happening *in medias res* [in the middle of things] – because we were active witnesses of that magmatic reality that was traversing the factories, and the schools, and the whole of society – and you were a participant in that enormous cultural *koine* that was being formed. Was it a general displacement of the reality of the very subject of production? Was the so-called superstructural element becoming a so-called structural moment? For those who had never appreciated this bizarre – and philologically incorrect – movement between *Über* [Over] and *Unter* [Under], it was fun to engage in this provocation. Long live the upside-down! In short, we felt that the answer to the question was affirmative, and with theoretical effort we sought the proof. The proof! O happy ingenuousness! Here the proof is given only on the threshold of the infinite movement that the vortex of this transformation produces. It is therefore only through a scientific process of small steps, of loving hypotheses, of cautious anticipations, of enthusiastic intuitions, that we are able to move forward.

(Sometimes, thinking in this way, I have the impression of overturning – but, by this very fact, of taking on board, through some kind of surreptitious homology – the catastrophist thinking that the bourgeoisie lived for itself in the years between the two world wars. Leaving aside Spengler's fascist *Untergang*, I must admit, however, that Pareto and Ortega – especially the latter – but also Toynbee and Borges are present in my culture. But this influence is not linear; the sense of the qualitative threshold of destruction and the sense of construction have always combined in me. It is feminism, and it is Danièle, Grazia, Johanna and Maria that impose on you – through their transformation, which was also mine – the breaking of every catastrophist homology. *Venus, cupiditas* [desire] – and also the *clinamen* [swerve], despite the appearances – are all concepts with something feminine. Materialism is feminine.)

In those years I moved around Europe a lot. I wanted to understand. I was in Paris during the period of the last big demonstrations of the students. *Chaud, chaud, chaud, le printemps sera chaud!* [Hot,

hot, hot, the spring will be hot!] Was this a revival of 1968 or the birth of a new movement, asked the weather forecasters of the class struggle. Neither the one nor the other. You saw at once that these hundreds of thousands of children were not the militants of 1968, and not even something that could have the immediate identity of a resurgent movement. For the most part they were technology students, industrial labour power; immediate intellectuality to be fed into the new machinery of automation and tertiary production. Here you already came up against the Nora–Minc report, against the social dimensions of information technology – it was a precocious adolescence of the subject. It was a new pulse – but nothing more than a pulse – of the new class composition – of that which was forming, accumulating and settling into place.

(A playful interchange with a philosopher of the *Krisis*.* 'What would you say about this? Do you think that the condition is given here for an internal *Vergleichung* [comparison]?' My interlocutor responds gravely: 'The equalisation and the mediation of the different should rest on a *hypokeimenon* [substrate] or should be produced by an *Ursache* [cause].' 'That is not necessarily the case,' I suggest. 'Could the new subject not rather be seen as an *Erzeugung* [creation]?' 'But,' he says, 'this dynamic status would inevitably put itself into tension with an *Urgrund* [source], and would distend itself in vain . . .' And so on. So let's beware of these terrible dangers . . . One thing is certain: beyond any uselessly specialistic language, slipping out, in time and space, I still feel the substantial bodily joy of that movement. A new subject? Yes. And even a figure that is still abstract, indeterminate. But this only means that those who had sought a final instance in the definition of the new subject – and who had seen it almost chiselled out in the mass of the social – would have got rather drunk from it – from its impermeability, its plurality, its irreducibility. Now, in fact, the final instance no longer exists. But does this perhaps mean that the tendency was not real?)

At that time I was in Berlin. In Kreuzberg, around the old hospital that had been transformed into a commune, where von Rauch had been killed, you grasped the full force of this transformation that was under way – intellectual labour power, mass marginalisation – but also the two paradoxes that were gradually becoming central: on the one hand, the identity of interests, within marginalisation, between

---

* Translator's note: reference to Massimo Cacciari, author of *Krisis: Saggio sulla crisi del pensiero negativo* (published by Feltrinelli in 1977).

large sections of the young proletariat and the immigrants, the masses of *Gastarbeiter* [migrant workers], and also the productive proletariat at the lower levels of the social organisation of labour; on the other, within this proletarian assemblage, the identification of needs for the highest levels of culture and enjoyment. Economic poverty, but an enormous richness of claims. Material poverty over and within an extremely intense intellectual composition.

(How everything had changed in Germany, and how strong and creative the crisis of the movement was! I saw the old comrades, Karl Heinz, Dany, Brückner, Gisela, and many others, both men and women – taut, convulsively taut in their understanding – and then Fassbinder, Schlöndorf and many others – strongly committed to expression . . . The battle lines were formed within consciousness, modulated on the exalted chord of the logical passion of the German left – was this again a quest for evidence?)

Outside consciousness strictly defined – in the streets, at each encounter with power – the more the situation was pressurised, the more incentive there was for a unification in separation based on the new values of the latter. Antagonistic separation of two parts of society. And at the same time, in the separation, the first autonomous mechanisms of community organisation, or of directly social organisation and, above all, the first emergence of independent paths, aimed at objectives that were qualitatively irreducible to the values displayed in the shop windows of capitalism. You could appropriate (and indeed they did so) the goods displayed on the Kurfürstendamm – as well as destroying the 'colonial goods' of the colonialist shops of the Madeleine, as anarcho-Maoism did, with worthy theatrics; but you would not reproduce those goods and their circuits. People were taking the goods in order to destroy their symbolism, the temptation of them, the need for them. Instead there were aggregation points such as the self-managed kindergartens, the youth clubs, the communes . . . Life was alternative. You could well comment – as indeed the German comrades commented sarcastically (the sardonic Günter Grass among them): 'what is wrong in us is neither material nor social – rather it is an emergence of the spirit.'

I remember well, cher David, that I told you then about the thrill of the emotionality of that experience. You will also remember how, present at that same time, there were also perversions, both possible and actual, of the discourse on counter-power: perversions that were maturing – in that climate, in that situation – in both Germany and Italy and that tried to overdetermine the situation in the direction of armed struggle and to disempower the novelty of the mass movement that was being constructed. And how many doubts there were, and how many alternative hypotheses that we put forward in the urgency of defining conceptually and putting into practice a correct path for the movement, and of avoiding ill-considered (do you like that word, worthy of Fanfani?), disastrous and unnecessary *détournements*. We produced it with passion, that Enlightenment effort of ours; but also with a bitter irony – knowing well what and how many were the crises that a new subject determines inside itself in the course of its development. The happy idiocy of the individualistic and bourgeois imaginings of a 'nascent state', dull and consumerist, luckily did not affect those proletarian subjects. And it seemed to us, as in some biblical story or gnostic legend, that we had two souls living in one body – the old and the new, battling with each other, and we – in taking sides – could not, however, be unaware of the illness of the whole body. So, once again, the determination of the concept, intellectually fixed, was dissipating itself in practice, and realistically speaking the strength of our political proposition was blocked in the presence (in the fear?) of an insoluble contradiction. It would be some time before we could break this impasse! It would take tragic experiences for these knots to be loosed at the proletarian level. (Danièle, Grace, Johanna and Maria were among those who paid the highest price for this dramatic condition. Plucked too high in the intuition of a synthesis between women's liberation, a transformation of life and a confrontation with the enemy – their violence was matched to the destiny of the liberation of a strength and a desire for so long suppressed – a volcano that was exploding – why are sweetness and nature and the teachings of sweetness forced into this violence?)

Meanwhile on the international stage things were moving fast. *Après 1914 tout a deconné* [After 1914, everything was messed up] – and *après* 1973? The Israeli War brought to the heart of the Mediterranean and to the heart of Europe the subjection of value to the dollar and the subjection of life to the American diktat. The crisis advanced and could be measured by the prices of petroleum products. The level of command went up and up – its irrationality, or rather its rigid autocratic instrumentation, was accentuated with the utmost rigour. It was a moment that justified panic. Between 1971 and 1973 the propulsive power of the collective reaction of capital was entirely rebuilt worldwide, after the defeat it had suffered during the 1960s. It was an electric shock. It was a kind of Congress of Vienna. Kissinger = Metternich? Yes, more or less – a Metternich with a fat wallet, hungry for labour power of whatever colour it might be – Eurocentrism is finished, rejoice you, third-worldists.

Working-class mobility – they won't allow it? So the workers use it against us? So let's have a mobility of capital, and let's break the circulation of struggles. Multinational capital runs wherever there is an opportunity to exploit. A network of multicoloured threads, growing thicker and thicker. 1972–3: we shall never study them enough, those three years. The very idea of power, a bourgeois idea, was changed – it was not a result but a predetermination; it does not accept costs of mediation. Is the theory of vortices a good illustration for our age? Capital too tries to anticipate the thresholds of identity and of transformation, capital wants to predetermine the *clinamen* of the constitutive vortex. An idealistic operation but nonetheless effective for that, in the short term – in the short term, but 'in the long term we are all dead' – effective because it was established on the basis of the dualism of the class relationship and was corroborated by the exasperated desire to win this transition. (As if the *clinamen* and its constitutive power could be reduced to a final cause! Rosenzweig: final cause, or avoidance of the idea of creation.)

No, David, we cannot allow ourselves to be taken by vertigo in the face of the project. But it is certain that many things have changed here – there is a moment of restlessness that dissolves into dirty water our transparency and the good colours of our intellect. Let he who is without sin cast the first stone. What is the body that has survived intact the hammer blow of electricity against its own brain? When has dianoetic *phronesis* [wisdom] withstood violence without itself becoming violence, even if against itself, as in suicide? The 'death persuader'* is a figure of a fierce and defeated rationality. Yet we must fight on, in research, in the continuity of the project. It was not the first time that the storm scattered the traces of a path we needed to follow. All of this was expected and logical, we told ourselves repeatedly – why allow ourselves to be overwhelmed by its unexpected scale? If we are at the point that theory has always confirmed, every step forward in the quality and dimension of the domination has brought about a requalification of the subversive movement of the masses. Equal and opposite – can the reply be defined in those terms? No, this mechanism is improper. It accepts a homology in the conception of power – as if workers and employers were equivalent, as if a stellar distance did not divide the one from the other. The

---

* Translator's note: this is a reference to Peisithanatos, nickname of the Cyrenaic philosopher Hegesias (third century BC), one of the proponents of Hellenistic varieties of hedonism ultimately derived from Aristippus of Cyrene; he advocated the hedonic superiority of death over life.

separation that we experienced as a losing stereotype from the old canons of the class struggle could and should find a new figure and find winning effects in the processes whose dawn we were intuiting. (It is still Danièle and the other women who, particularly on the critique and refusal of any suffocating homology of the idea of power, resisted – but how long can it last, a resistance that is tough, extreme and relentless, without being reduced to suicide? Without realistically seeking, at the same time, partial and new determinations – even when they are promoted by the separation?)

Therefore a working hypothesis that installs itself on this transition and, in the separation, works to construct itself as reality is not improper. From resistance to a new constitutionalism, to an organisation of mass counter-powers that extends over the whole of the social. A revolutionary process completely reappropriated by the masses. The breakdown of the links of value of the planificatory state must therefore be followed by the development of a relationship between proletarians and the state that should take antagonism, in the social totality, as the key to interpretation and to the project. The difficulties experienced in this act of projecting were temporary: the general framework of the relations of production and domination, shifting forward with such an impact, necessarily requalified all relationships. There would be no *Aufhebungen* [abrogations], solution and mediation, transcendence and pacification – no, these would no longer be given. But we had to verify in practice the relationship between hypotheses and subject, between project and subjective forces. How to verify it? Again, I return with my thoughts, cher David, to the strange and varied experience of those years. I remember how much fervour was spent – fervour of theory, fervour of love. We were hostages of our hypothesis, trying frantically to bend to it the totality of a subversive existence. Logical extremism? Overload of subjectivity? Abstractness? Probably we were guilty of all these sins. Nor does the end justify the means. But where was the end and where were the means? Were we not ourselves atom dust, lifted and reshaped by the cosmic wind? Utopia, the burning intellectual hypothesis of a real future, becomes a reality only when one submits oneself to this discipline of perdition. Alienating oneself in being – not in order to identify in one's own negation a new foundation, but in order to grab the immediate positiveness of being. The style of work doesn't correspond to the necessity of the end product? And what else can the style of work be? A state of necessity of theory and of its matching practice, then? I don't know, I have many doubts – nor do I want to succumb to a rational panacea or to an individualistic variant of a dialectical theory of compensation.

In fact this passage – tumultuous as any that has ever been – was a collective enterprise. The new entity was forming itself by measuring within itself a radical constitutive crisis. In all the big cities of Europe there were repeated episodes of struggle, attack, devastation and appropriation that were the counterpart (dark or lucid, who can distinguish?) of the growth of community and of individual and group self-valorisation. We heard an incredible new music, certainly syncopated, sometimes rendered hysterical by a double driving pulse – towards communal togetherness on the one hand, towards a destructive dispersion on the other. (Danièle, Maria, Grazia, Johanna – why were you not up to the game, and also up to its margin of ambiguity? The conceptual richness of your practice of separation could here and now have proposed itself to act as a solid construction of an alternative. Instead, that heroic feminism turned to terrorism. Sometimes I feel cowed before you.)

By contrast, the customary Solons launched an ambiguous denunciation – full of mealy-mouthed commiseration – of the so-called marginalisation. The more intelligent monkeys mocked and mimicked the concept of a 'new proletariat' – which they defined as a combination of exclusion and rejection. The second society. At the same time the concept of 'centrality of the working class' assumed – in this scenario – those definitive moralistic connotations (in Eliseo's discourse, for instance) that are read in obituaries and funeral notices – which is where they belong. Through this rhetorical mediation, then, the centrality of the working class began to moulder into corporatism – in theoretical terms as well.

But things were moving fast. Milan was ahead of other places, as often happens in Italy in periods of major metropolitan transformation. Immediately striking was, above all, the dissolution – under the pressure of the formation of the new subject – of the ancient and traditional divisions of the metropolis. An indistinct swarm was running everywhere – the proletarian reserves were drifting, not towards a Korean destiny but to and within the ring of canals. This was the same trajectory as in Amsterdam, Frankfurt, Berlin and London – and in any number of other places. This is not yet the moment of explosion of the movement, of proletarian youth's ultimatum to the metropolis. Rather it is the moment of internal dissolution of enemy spaces and of reappropriation of a sense of orientation – extended to all the articulations of metropolitan command. And of the construction of the first forms of liberated time, of possibilities to overturn the rhythm of the social working day. The refusal of work began to fill with new opportunities for happiness. A new ballad – a Janis Joplin turning into enthusiasm the low tones of yearning and suffering, a Jim Morrison exalting liberation to the sounds of the California border, a Hendrix screaming revolt and peace – this was the new music that pierced the wall of urban pollution. What is in movement here is not oases in the desert – but a process of reclamation, transformation and cultivation of lands that were otherwise desert-like. (Again, I was about to write 'Israel, the land of the just' – because this was what Israel had been – to me, to you and to many, in terms of education, dreams and experience. But today Israel has turned itself into a Prussia and is a country without charity. Hannah Arendt, in her *Eichmann in Jerusalem*, tells of a prosecutor, a small Galician Jew – of the justice that becomes revenge – the ideology of resentment that blows from the ghetto. Yes, there is always this too, but it must not win. Today, though, it has won. Israel is unrecognisable. Internally, every project of renewal is crushed; externally, you see a fierce drive to expansion and methods of terror against the free nation of our Palestinian brothers.)

But I'm running ahead of myself. I'm sorry, David, and above all please excuse my epic insolence: I'm almost calling myself the master of this attention to the new, when it was you and so many others who taught me this. For me, learning was like an old snake's shedding its skin – the pain of a physical tearing and the cooling effect of fresh air on a skin become newly sensitised. I moved awkwardly. Leaving behind shreds of fatigue and hysteria. Naively I opened myself up. I expressed myself with extreme modesty. But all of you had as much need of the old bespectacled serpent as I had of you. There is a similar story in *Alice in Wonderland*. Because what was happening was not just the birth, recurrent and banal, of a new youth movement, but the formation of a new proletarian subject. Hence a whole cultural baggage had to be brought into question and the paths of producing intellectuality had to be reinvented. Within the massive figure of this subject, which denied itself to capital in order to reinvent production beyond commanded labour. Liberating oneself from capitalist work, liberating human productivity, inventing the future. How they had changed, the old slogans of working-class subversion, while still preserving the same intentions! It was not utopia if it was built into a subject that was making and was making itself. A materialistic *verum ipsum factum* [truth itself is made]! Ha, ha, old idealistic beast, a productive and intellectual proletarian subject possesses you and tames you. A dynamic that is materialistic – production! Gradually the effort to follow the process rationally depended on the results that came out. Results? What strange words still linger in the language of philosophy! The rational miracle of life and the wonder of material production consist in this: that the result is nothing if not innovation. (Hegel messed up innovation, defining it as a reconstruction of historical elements requalified by the synthesis, by the Spirit: a perfect image of the capitalist need to bring everything back to command and to exploitation, to their transcendentalism.) My proletarians, engineers of innovation, finally showed me a world that was potent only if, and all the more so if, it rejected any mediation of exploitation. Every result was exploitation, every generation was a liberation. Of course, I too had to strip myself of my orthodox Marxist influences to absorb this experience. But what could be more Marxist than this identification of the productivity of collective being? In this way utopia was swept into the vortex of the formation of the new world – but, blinking among the ruins of the old, it was always she who was fixing the decisive elements of *choc* and determining the thresholds of change. This physical drama was to be appreciated and lived. *Hominum divomque voluptas, alma Venus* [delight of men and gods, life-giving Venus].* Without fear, and without caution? Have we ourselves, David, perhaps given in to optimism of the will? With circumspect emotion I embrace you . . .

---

* Translator's note: last half of line 1 and beginning of line 2 from the famous opening of Lucretius' Epicurean poem *De rerum natura: Aeneadum genitrix, hominum divumque voluptas,/Alma Venus, coeli subter labentia signa* . . .

Letter Fourteen
A Leap of Joy

Rebibbia, 15 February 1982

Cher David,

> Often one has the impression that an artist, and even more so a philosopher, lives in his own time *by chance* . . . with their appearance, and at their appearance, nature, which does not leap, makes its only leap, which is a leap of joy, because it feels that it has finally reached its goal, in other words there where it forgets that it has a goal and has been in too strong a game of life and of becoming.

Thus Nietzsche, as cited by Deleuze.* In truth, this 'chance', this 'leap of joy' when a genetic transition has been made, is less true in the case of the artist and the philosopher than in the case of the relationship between subjects and historical development: a block defined by chance but which, transforming itself, meets its own desire. So that the determination becomes necessary and productive, after having been ephemeral and even casual – and the leap is that of being, which is, once again, newly and singularly determined. I use the term 'dislocation' to refer to this leap forward of the subject and of nature, of nature and of history – of this block of being that does not deny relations but modifies and requalifies them. *Das Diese nehmen* ['to grasp the This'] – which gathers and pulls them together. In the account I have given you of my life as a researcher and political agitator, I have already told you of other similar experiences – or, rather, of other similar events. We pluck ourselves out of indistinction and emotion, through practice and knowledge – until the world takes

---

* Translator's note: Gilles Deleuze, *Mille plateaux*, citing Friedrich Nietzsche.

a leap forward. But every time – and always in different ways – the sense of the real is determined in such a physically intense manner, releasing within transformation and mobility a kind of frenzy of the new. Then it seems to me that you can be seized by the passion of admiration for the real that has been discovered, and you can be caught as by an ecstatic – or fanatical – drift within the emergence and within the figure of the dislocation. 'Aesthetically, the miracle is that the world exists. That there is what there is':* as usual, the philosopher Wittgenstein sings individually what is a collective perception. It is no less true that there is a miracle – but it is collective. And it is collectively that one is constrained to the admiration of the miracle and overwhelmed by its effects. Here I shall tell you precisely about these movements of the spirit and of the real, which extend over time until the antagonistic subjectivity resumes its free initiative. (Because – let me suggest this in a parenthesis – thought and passion cannot end in admiration, as Nietzsche would have it. The *Übermensch* [superman] – Vattimo correctly reminds us – 'cannot be understood as a conciliated subject, because it cannot be thought of as subject.'† Instead, real thought and passion should be related – as our Spinoza teaches – to the liberating tendency of the collective subject, to ethics deployed.)

So here we are, right now, at the point where we have grasped on the one hand the capitalist passage of the crisis of value and on the other the new potentiality of the social proletariat: the relationship is negative, paralysing. The sphere of communication is tautological. A sort of drift internal to the emerged and magmatic relationship dominated us. They were certainly present, even pressing, the question whether the crisis state and the new historical bloc could be configured differently from how capital wanted, and thus also the question of the necessity of redefining the antagonistic relationship. But every time we tried to get a grip on an antagonistic determination we found ourselves reduced to describing it in a language that harked back to the old world or, if it innovated, it limited the innovation to an insignificant and powerless segment. The prison of ideology allowed only brief instances to come into the light. Infamous ideology. Admired weariness. Maybe it was better to rely on mystification and leave it at that. The historical block of the dislocation imposed itself as unity

---

* Translator's note: Ludwig Wittgenstein, *Notebooks 1914–1916*, 20.10.16. (The *Notebooks* are edited by G. H. von Wright and G. E. M. Anscombe with an English translation by G. E. M. Anscombe, Oxford: Blackwell, 1961.)
† Translator's note: unidentified quotation.

and circulation – the temptation of remaining within the peace of the dialectical correlation was devilishly enticing. In the Macondo forest you can fight to open a space for yourself or you can abandon yourself to the powerful tropical vapours: either way you cancel yourself in nature, whether you go or stay. No. It cannot be so. I do not want it. Infinite stimuli clash against the temptation. So we have to break with Macondo, with admiration – the tension of being enjoys the new only if it liberates the new . . . But how?

1973–1974: how hard it was, having to deal with these problems – and yet how firm was our conviction that we were now definitively in a new historical phase of the class struggle! The crisis had to be seen as a global and collective dislocation of values: this was the content of the admiration – the restlessness that stems from an awareness of the limits of that passion cannot prevent you from grasping the fullness of its importance. The highest level of the crisis was a new figure – and the most mature figure – of the struggle between the classes. Enough of the linear and dialectical view of the 'development–crisis' cycle. Just as in the 1960s we had understood the function of crisis against the tradition of overthrowing, now we had to understand, in its practical specificity, the leap of innovation – of capital and of class struggle – and we had to extract ourselves from that kind of resignation to the eternal return that third-internationalism in all its various guises imposed on us. Crisis and capitalist development, crisis and the raising and deepening of the class struggle: the more capital develops, the more class struggle becomes antagonistic and total.

At this point, David, you wanted to develop a new theory of value – do you remember? Developing admiration into a theoretical discovery, you said: the series of links that production reveals at this level of development, in its social dimension, can be summed up in a pattern of understanding that captures the flow of values, whatever their modified figure, and determines a social measure of them. The dissolution of value in command, the socialisation of the productive force, make it necessary to construct a theory of value as a theory of the administration of social production, as a reweaving of the metropolitan functions of production and of reproduction of value. No sooner said than done: it is an evil little genie, that objectivism, which sets to work here. And how many comrades there were who began to dig in the monetary field, in the administrative field, in the sciences of the territory – the attractions of systems theory and the prestige of the latest transformations in the thinking of the Frankfurt School were naturally very strong – even the teaching of French thinkers of the big reactionary schools was present.

Letter Fourteen: A Leap of Joy

But will it ever be possible, between Offe and Luhmann and Crozier, to reconquer and bite on the real? This new historical bloc, proposed in the narrow centripetal dynamic of its factors, described linearly – an equilibrium of fluids – does it not lead directly to the end of time, to pure ecstasy, to the postmodern and to the world rebuilt on Lyotard's vain circus trapeze? 'Rollerball.' It seemed to me that the presupposition was lost in the unfolding – had we not perhaps taken as our starting point the equation 'deepening of the antagonism – crisis – new capitalist order', where the first term was the principal one – and where, therefore, what became fundamental was the reopening of antagonism against the new order? Conversely, by holding onto objectivistic hypotheses did we not risk a foolish defence of the new order? Prometheus was turning into Narcissus; but, for anyone unwilling to give in either to one or to the other, what was given? We know that the function of understanding is a prerequisite. However, we often acted like cats who, confusing the understanding of the causes with their actuality, preferred the cheese to the mouse that it reminded them of. We should take a better look around ourselves, I told you, David!

In fact we now had the opportunity for this. Never had it been more timely to take the decision to dissolve the 1968-ist political groups – large and small alike. In France and Germany the process took its own course. In Italy, by comparison to the others, we had the advantage of being ahead of the game. Now we were living the pleasure of rediscovering grassroots initiative, a rediscovery of the concrete. In this environment admiration is more difficult and complacency is impossible. The job is that of a weaver – follow the threads, twist them, tie them together with others, give them colour. Thank you, David, for the Velasquez print that you sent me – the *Hilanderas del Prado*. I have hung it in my cell, and it will last there until next time the guards do a search. I look at it and remember the objections – not so much humble as heuristically contrived, as functionally contrived, which I raised against the presumption of any theory of value. We were talking about welfare, about the new nomenclature of production and reproduction, about circulation and the dark pockets of 'underground economy', hypothesising that administration and state accounting might succeed in their control – if this happened, it would undoubtedly give a baseline to dig over and turn into a proposal for a new general theory of the value of social production. The *Kapitalistate* journal team, with O'Connor in the lead, was heading in the same direction in this period, working on the same theoretical hypothesis; vague echoes were reaching us. But the weaver objected that welfare was a mess – thousands and thousands of loose threads, incapable of being resolved into a logic. In this embroidery the ecstasy would have given way to the sword of Damocles. Was this not precisely the conclusion that was being reached by the more astute researchers into welfare? Frances Fox Piven in particular became our friend at this time: at bottom, even the weaver was a radical democrat, as the popular folk tradition attested. Hence welfare not as the basis of an orderly fabric of values, but as a tangle of powers and of needs, like a battlefield. Yet, whatever the objections, the attraction of the model was strong. But even stronger was the tension to demystify its autarchic design in its rigid form.

In 1973 an extraordinary struggle at FIAT broke the relative equilibrium and the social peace, relative to say the least, of that period of transition towards the composition of the social subject. A working-class struggle? Certainly – and a very violent one. Disguising their identities with the help of red kerchiefs, as the criminal courts put it, young workers marched through the factory departments, breaking up assembly lines, showering a hail of nuts and bolts, and neutralising the foremen. In short, they repeated, on an amplified scale, with great strength and en masse, what had always been done, since the late 1960s, in hot periods of contract negotiations. There was undoubtedly an extra element of organisation, precise and rhythmic timings, and an ability to act immediately: an organisational embryo and an invisible, diffuse network of initiatives. But this was not the key element. That was, on the one hand, the social solidarity that aggregated around the struggle – so that strikes had the possibility of going on for a very long time and an incredible level of class cooperation sustained materially the workers on strike. On the other hand – and this was the other key element – the internal marches soon turned into external squads that operated territorially in the community; they patrolled the streets around the Mirafiori and Rivalta plants and blockaded the roads, lighting up the night with the burning tyres of their nomadic style of struggle. The relationship with the workers outside of the factory was seen as central by working-class action in the factory. It was just a foretaste of what was to happen in the years to come: the more young people went into the factories – and the number of new employees in the following years would run into the tens of thousands – the more the factory struggle became social struggle. Turin like Kreuzberg. So that was the element that analysis had to identify – the social totality of working-class action, and thus the end of the specificity of the big factory as the exclusive place of conflict. Every discourse had now to be measured against the

Letter Fourteen: A Leap of Joy

immediately social qualification of the 'party of Mirafiori'. It was on this point that a theoretical initiative capable of lifting itself out of the indifference – however refined – of analysis could rebuild, not a totality to be admired, but an antagonistic social totality – which would be as great and articulated as the capitalist plan of command over social production. So we had to follow the lines, the trajectories through which the red kerchiefs were moving in society. And anyone who felt so inclined could have observed that these productive subjects could materially survive fifty and more days of strike action because each of them could make up for the gaps in the wage packet with a second job or with support from their families – in any case with 'the inventiveness of everyday life'. The reserve army of the unemployed, into which the bosses could once toss you like a useless rag, no longer exerted its controlling function, except in absolutely weakened form. Following the threads of this social network, this everyday inventiveness, you uncovered an incredible network of diffuse production. But there was more: the workers were also participants in the structures of secondary and tertiary education that had been established in the preceding years. This was a workforce that had been sucked into an enormous process of acculturation, which now overflowed out of the factory, even if it subsequently returned there. Paradoxically, through the action of the red kerchiefs, something that was to be an essential characteristic of the coming years began to show itself: the encirclement of the factory by the proletariat. Induction – socialisation – working-class intellectuality, all of them diffuse: a new form of labour power.

But you will say, cher David, that in this case too we are in a theory of value. Because whether value and surplus value find in the factory their place of formation and extraction or they find it in the whole of society, understood and renewed as the overall seat of production – and hence whether the struggle on the segments of value into which the working day is divided happens in a single factory or in the factory-society – this has little effect on the overall unity of the picture. You're right. But, as you know and as our discussion broadly showed, in this explosion of labour force in struggle there was something very different. There was, above all, a new way of understanding life, and this way went beyond the theory of value, no matter how conceived. Because the time and the form of the social reproduction of labour power, the quality of life, the acculturation, the inventivity of the everyday, the community dimensions, became – or rather began to impose themselves as – fundamental problems of the proletariat. Value theory was not capable of quantifying all this.

(Later we would see many attempts to implant techniques of time budgeting, and talk about flexible working hours, and programme(s) of the sequence(s) of 'working time – consumption – style of life – models of culture'. But the worker was by then a savage or a poacher with respect to time.) Thus the practice of liberation was no longer moving simply against the amount of surplus value, but against the quality of the exploitation. In the relationship that the young red kerchiefs had with society, they created a passage that was not just an underground tunnel to escape from the factory-prison – but also the negation of the specificity of the factory as the place of extraction of surplus value, of the determination of exploitation – and therefore as the privileged place of struggle. Factory workers have never seen the factory as an ontological place. They were driven there, amassed there, exploited there. They have never loved it – only ideology, fantastic and vulgar socialism, would claim this. Now, in the transmutation that was occurring, workers had the sense, in the game of exploitation and in the antagonistic apprenticeship of the struggle and of the absenteeism of those years, that their whole life, their whole time and space were involved. The whole of my life is in play. There are no spatial confines. There are no partitions of this totality. The new way of struggle thus had to represent the concrete specificity of the new subject. And theoretical admiration had to be broken – it had to find a logic of struggle on this new dimension.

Doretta and Ruggero were two workers from FIAT-Rivalta. During that period I often used to have discussions with them. They told me what was going on in the factory and during the struggles. The novelty of their behaviour resulted from the fact that, with adventurous confidence, they had built for themselves, with their own hands, a way of life so intelligent, sympathetic and supportive that rarely would you find a similar experience, even among the free-thinking and educated bourgeoisie. Ruggero was studying at university, Doretta was involved in a feminist group. They lived in a house not far from the factory, out in the country. The wine was good, they had good books on their shelves, the music was excellent, the flowers were always fresh: petunias, field poppies, not the eternal geraniums. What did proletarian violence mean for them? It was the effort to live – to live at a level of human dignity and a quality of life that their being factory workers denied them – but now, not so paradoxically, it actually imposed: for their way of living, intellectually and civically, was the quality of the new workforce. A dialectic of capitalist *Zivilisation*? Its contradiction was dynamic – but was it progressive and capable of being transcended? A mug, anyone who still believed in that. In effect, the time of capitalist life was hateful to Doretta and Ruggero. Children of proletarian parents, they had grown up in the appalling rhythms of the working day, which left no time for happiness. The cultural transformation that took place in them could find no expression other than rebellion. The time of liberation, construed as a possibility of happiness, was radically opposed to the capitalist working day. Of the latter time, each of us bore too many scars on his body. Life could – and had to – recompose itself in the social community against the alienation of the factory. I have to confess, cher David: although I have known many famous feminists, it was from Doretta that I understood for the first time what feminism was and its exceptional transformative importance in the composition of the proletariat. Because – as Doretta explained, with an eagerness that made her most beautiful among women – she and her comrades had understood that the factory took away everything from you and did not pay for reproduction and for love – it subjected these too. Or it paid for them through the family wage, very little or nothing, and always in a relationship of domination – the domination of the male and that of the boss. But the problem was that love could not be bought and sold, and she wanted it for herself, for what it meant: the production of life, an exuberance of passion, a richness. A basket of values completely the opposite of capitalist values was what arose directly from this feminism. Marcuse in his later years was in no doubt that postindustrial socialism would either be feminine or would not be at all. But Doretta was far more convincing than Marcuse, and she spoke of communism. Coming out of the factory with her workmates during the strikes, she found the dimensions of a free love and of a radical appropriation. In the struggle she realised her feminism – and she taught it to the liberated 'gals' who were with her on the demonstrations: the battle we are fighting, she would say, is for a restoration of humanity, of freedom, and of love. Working-class struggle is a step in the dance of liberation. A creative 'happening' – as E. P. Thompson put it. (And, once again – excuse me for repeating myself, David – my Spinoza comes to mind: 'Blessedness is not the reward of virtue, but virtue itself; we do not enjoy it because we restrain our lusts; on the contrary, because we enjoy it, we are able to restrain them.'*) In the relationship with society, by occupying the streets around Mirafiori, the red kerchiefs brought violence, yes, but – let us grasp

---

* Translator's note: Baruch Spinoza, *Ethics*, Part IV, Proposition 42; p. 264 in Curley's translation (see note in Letter Ten, p. 116).

the essential – they brought especially the consciousness of a new relationship with a world of alternative values that it was necessary to express – and also the fact that it was idiotic to ask the unions, the bosses or the factory to satisfy that. They moved through the world in leaps of joy – with admiration for what they recognised in themselves. But then admiration is not only a horizon to be demolished, a drift to avoid – perhaps, between Nietzsche and Deleuze, the leap of joy has pushed forward so far that determination can no longer be suffocated in admiration but can grasp its own totality, albeit transformed, and can practise it as innovation. The dislocation is of the subject, within the collective subject.

With Doretta and Roger and other comrades we played long games of cards during rest periods. The conversation ranged from welfare to wages. Between games of *scopone* and *tresette* we discussed the possibility of reading public spending in the same way we had become used to reading the wage packet. Jokingly we often referred to the entries in public spending under the headings of the wage packet, and we complicated the relative simplicity of the former to reduce it to the complexity of the second, and then vice versa. How much humour we injected into the abstractness of the mystifying norms of state and business accounting, and into multiplying the categories of administrative chaos and of the so-called values of the bosses: *Lob des Polytheismus* [In praise of polytheism]!* The traditional sarcasm of the labour movement had become an irony of sophisticated 'radicals'. Then, inevitably, as if following the incline of a slope, the discussion moved from there to the countless things in life that ought to be free – gratis. All the most beautiful things, all those things involved in the movement of desire. 'Nor can a man any more live whose desires are at an end than he whose senses and imaginations are at a stand. Felicity is a continual progress of the desire from one object to another', so said Hobbes, that man of the senses.† In the capitalist world all the most beautiful things are monetised. Free of charge for the satisfaction of desire – this is how things should be. The beautiful is free of charge? But what does that mean? Doing it is not free of charge: only what you do is beautiful. At this point the polemic of poetics against aesthetics returned, with materialistic shades ... Simple talk, teenage discourses ... But the day after everything changed, because you felt and lived those things, and you rebuilt

---

* Translator's note: title of a volume of studies published in 1981 by the philosopher Odo Marquard.
† Thomas Hobbes, *Leviathan*, Ch. 11 ('On the Difference of Manners').

them in the initiative of struggle and in the protest marches. And that subject that had been so abstractly postulated, itself a product of dislocation, and which you had identified at the level of ideas, as an antagonist in the gigantic work of capitalist restructuring, now you saw it growing in concrete terms, en masse, and beautiful, before your eyes. FIAT – a university of proletarian class struggle. Yet again, the best was being taught here. In that continuity of tradition and innovation whose pungent odour only the great metaphysical dimension can offer. Thank you Doretta, thank you Ruggero. My old friend wrote: 'no one knows how much the body is capable of . . .' But here we *do* know. Here we have escaped the possible drift towards admiration and we have grasped it entirely as a potentiality of dislocation in the class struggle. You, too, David, you would soon no longer have doubts. Goodnight . . .

Letter Fifteen
Carnival

Rebibbia, 25 February 1982

Cher David,

If you had happened to be passing through Milan in July 1976, you would have found it hard to avoid Parco Lambro. Indeed I'm sure you'd have rushed straight down there. A huge festival of young people, organised by slightly frivolous alternative groups, but reinvented by the movement. There were so many people there, heaps of them, like sheaves at harvest time in the old days, out in the sunny fields – and, as the days passed, the groups moved around. Even during the day they moved around, looking for shade and coolness. A short-sighted person who, like myself, had taken up a vantage point at the top of the valley inside the park might have imagined being in some technicolour film of generals and pitched battles, set in the period of the absolutist state: a continuous to and fro of masses of people – each group bringing with it carts and tents, musical instruments and basic tools. The dirt was like that described in historical accounts of Albrecht von Wallenstein's campaigns [in the Thirty Years War] – but not more, despite the stories that were going around and despite the fact that the municipal authorities deliberately cut off the water supply. And the movements of these bands of people were accompanied by a halo of dust – so you might have thought that you were watching regiments on the move, until you caught the oriental whiff of that smoke, which went right up to the top of the valley. When you came down from the top, you found yourself immersed in a kind of sinuous, coloured bundle, as full of desires as it was free from taboos. People were smoking, making love, listening to music, spending their time gently coming together and feeling united. Light shadows in search of a collective time and a collective body.

Amazement was the first thing you felt – so it was true that, in those years, resistance and refusal had created this potential for liberation! The emotion was confirmed when you realised that the style was predominantly proletarian. A lot of so-called sociological phenomena were right there, in plain sight, but they didn't have the mercantile characteristics – a bit infamous, a bit eccentric – in which (so-called) scientific descriptions like to dress them. Here there was nothing excessive, nothing that was not fundamentally human. It was actually a carnival of the poor – but, unlike a carnival, it could not resolve itself into ritual, going for excesses and then annulling its behaviours in a state of exception. Rather it was a carnival that consciously sought to be liberation. Maybe it resembled the ancient Greek mysteries more than the Christian carnival. Indeed the second emotion that struck you was one of knowledge. A short circuit between the poverty of the new proletariat and the very high form of its intellectual composition, a game that made up for dire poverty by being played by an intelligent multitude.

But was there really a specific enjoyment of this intellectuality? No. It was and remained a short circuit. The truth of liberation cannot just rest on the particular. The intensity of desire was notable. The naked dancing girl was the image of grace and hope, but the desire did not limit itself to artificiality and convention. The drugs and the music could be an excess. You began to breathe a restlessness. An *Aufstand der Körper* [revolt of bodies], a search for the collective body and at the same time a revolt of the body. You noticed – little by little, but with the rational certainty that filters out from the mass of a thousand sensations and perceptions – that what was happening was the first movements of storm in a clear sky: first you feel in the air and in your nerves and muscles that bad weather is about to arrive, and then you suddenly become aware of the clouds piling up.

The first day of Parco Lambro 1976 was quiet. Then, already on the second day, you had the proletarian expropriation of the organisers' food trucks; then on the third day groups of people headed off out of the park looking for supermarkets to rob – there were sounds of gunshots, and the police turned out in force, albeit at a distance.

> Then it was doubted whether, to meet the greater scourge
> of the crabs that would now come from outside
> like a proud and fast-moving stream,
> it was better to come out halfway and confront them

or rather to retire into the city with good reserves
and close the gates to scorn their wrath.*

It was hellishly hot. All the political firefighters were mobilising their powers of persuasion: don't come out of the park. 'Oh Wallenstein, don't occupy Prussia!' The local Milan newspapers – but we know that the Milanese newspapers build national policy – repeated the threat: stay in the ghetto. Indeed, passing through the fences that bordered the park was like stepping into another world – but it is also true that what was being poured into that funnel was something that had already been fermented, consciousnesses had been transformed, their potentiality was already throbbing, and a multitude was now emerging from the park. *Die Jugendproteste haben den Körper neu entdeckt* [Youth protests have revealed the bodies again]. A refoundation of bodies. A multitude: stoned on hashish, maybe even out of their minds, but new and wild.

> Beautiful virtue, whenever it gets hold of you,
> my spirit is uplifted, as if by a happy event.
> Nor does it believe you to be worthy of contempt,
> even if you were fed and nourished on mice.
> Before your beauty, which surpasses any other,
> it always bows, whether you are known and resplendent
> or you find yourself forgotten; and it is inflamed by you
> even if you are not true and steadfast, but imagined.†

So how could this mass now return to that world of normality, of 'the necessity of sacrifices', of cheap patriotism, on which the Historic Compromise was being built? No; Lent did not come after carnival. Probably only during the Wars of Religion, if you had put yourself at the edges of the two contesting camps, could you have identified so clearly not two armies, but two souls. The trumpeters of sacrifice and emergency played in one camp – strident, low key, ambiguous in the composition of the orchestra. They were promising war.

> You should have heard all the orators
> thundering war in their speeches:
> the likes of Leonidas, Themistocles and Cimon,

---

* Translator's note: quotation from Giacomo Leopardi's satiric poem *I Paralipomeni della Batracomiomachia* (*Notes on the Battle between the Frogs and the Mice*), 5.32.1–6.
† Translator's note: ibid., 47.1–8.

Letter Fifteen: Carnival

Mucius Scaevola, Fabius the dictator
Decus, Aristides, Codrus and Scipio . . .*

How could they have hoped that the mice were going to fall in line? And in the other camp were ingenious and sophisticated animals – the best of music, the best of human passions. And these people were running – young but confident in themselves, anxious but with glimmers of ingenuous hope ready to unfold. *Kraft der Angst und Wut gegen die Zukunft* [power of fear and rage against the future].

If I now think back, cher David, to the non-retractable words, the irreparable actions and the pathways of death that sprang forth from there – from that same Parco Lambro, from that real congress of the social autonomy of the movements – and came flowing down the valley; if I think of this now, I really am not able to convince myself that death is half of life and that there is necessity and a close concatenation in this. Why does it have to be like that? What terrible image of life requires such an insistence on necessity and on death? No, defeat is not a destiny, nor is it even an unknown. *Schicksal inkognito* [unknown destiny], as in Hugo von Hofmannsthal's tedious play? Once again, no. This event was rather woven on the web of the variability of the balance of power, and thus it was a varied and alternating mixture of luck and virtue, of freedom and necessity. Yet, in this restless season, the naive emergence did not enjoy – and did not have sufficient awareness of – its own quota of necessity. It was struggling 'against', and not 'for'. It was fighting against the colonisation of the body, and only intuitively did it sense the new nature of the collective. The initiative was in the hands of the others, it was at home in the vocation of the masters of war; and there they were, outside of Parco Lambro, reciting *novenas* and calling for sacrifice. From within Parco Lambro, on the other hand, struggle, fortune and virtue presented themselves as dance and as hope. Still today it is too early to say who won – the struggle continues. And we have not yet freed ourselves from the pathways of death. And yet . . .

A small aside here. I think back to the front pages and the newspaper headlines of that period. The left was riding high; it had electoral successes. The politics of the Historic Compromise, *aka* national unity, *aka* solidarity, and so on. Big solid headlines on the front pages.

Already through the middle of the shifting dust cloud
you see the solid mass of the crabs

---

* Translator's note: ibid., 29.1–5.

that, quietly and without noise,
was moving gravely forward, with assurance.*

We had given them our votes and they had cheated us. Torpid political bodies, the rustling of robes of cardinals and diplomats, court whisperings: all against us. The monstrous unchangingness of an immobile power. In the face of all this, petty news reportage, small memories. A friend and colleague was watching all this – a Christian democrat, administrator of a few hundred limited companies and expert in today's public law. With the irreverent humour of a Venetian intellectual he thought that the Historic Compromise was like a big net – one day they would pull in the net, and the fish would be trapped. How nice to see them make sacrifices! he added. Then I think back to the communist intellectual whom not even the party whippings had managed to subdue in his nostalgia for the movement. He chuckled bitterly: we shall meet again soon these closet Freemasons who enter into our administrations; they are necessary but they have nothing to do with us. The Communist Party is travelling in heroin. So let's get together for a rethink, he suggested. But, caro Uliano, what do you want to rethink, I answered him – and together! Don't you see the storm that is gathering? Erasmus of Rotterdam, the independent, is no longer in fashion, even if today there are plenty of ships of fools around. Together again? But how? You should come down too, Uliano, come down to Parco Lambro. Here desires are flying high, like kites. But soon the kites will become violence. Beautiful virtue:

> Ah, but where are you? Are you always dreamed of or pretended?
> Does nobody ever see you in your true nature?
> Were you already killed along with the rats, long ago,
> and does your beauty no longer smile among us?
> Oh if you were not painted in vain from then on,
> nor perished with Theseus or with Alcis!
> Certainly since then your smile became more rare
> and less adorned day by day.†

Scandal is useless now; for how many years have we seen the deepening of this division? And now what do you want to add to the situation? *Factum infectum fieri nequit* [what has been done cannot

---

* Translator's note: ibid., 41.1–4.
† Translator's note: ibid., 48.1–8.

Letter Fifteen: Carnival

be undone]. Militant Communist Party members, whatever way you take them, weren't allowed into Parco Lambro. I myself (as I explained to Uliano) was in crisis – the crisis did not affect my ethical consciousness, but its surface, yes. Because here what was directly at issue – perhaps for the first time since this story began – was the very fact of the individual behaviour of the militant – the shape of the wave and not simply the colour of the sea. And there the conversation ended.

But not reflection. When the theoretical enthusiasm of anticipation comes up against experience, then the need for analysis, study and criticism becomes urgent. There was certainly no lack of documentation: it was as rich as daily experience. You found it hard to follow the flow of events. For months now, the expropriation of luxury stores had been followed by expropriations of supermarkets and the self-reduction of phone bills, transportation, electricity bills and tickets for shows; and this went hand in hand with occupations of housing and mobile pickets organised against the small bosses of the black labour market. All this built pathways for a restructuring of the social and political struggle of the new and diffuse proletariat. The squares where fascists and drug dealers operated were cleared out – and in schools there was a renewal of agitation, and factory and neighbourhood communities were beginning to come together in territorial and working-class organising committees – in short, you could no longer keep up with all the ongoing struggles. And this incredible circulation of struggle was accompanied by a leap in people's ways of associating with one another – new types of family were being created and new figures of social aggregation. What the feminist movement had sown as critique and dissolution now reappeared as consciousness and behaviour. Touching the whole of life, the new had a thickness that had a flavour of the old. Of oak, you might have said. It was no accident that the shadow it shed was so dense that parasites and charlatans could hide themselves in it. *Grunf, grunf, grunf.* But more of this later. What we should talk about now is the amazing quality of our life. We were entering a new era, in which there was a paradox: the immediate presented itself as value, and value presented itself as collective, as power, and as hope. Truth was a pre-reflexive essence, a free dissemination of life. From the crisis of the law of value, from the collapse of every objective parameter of value, there leapt forth a tension towards projectuality, which was diffusely and directly interpreted by collective subjects. This transition had a central resonance in the lives of individuals. The personal is political. Intimist and defeatist interpretations, lyrical and miserable interpretations, all followed hard on each other's heels. But there were many, and many disappeared in a flash – lightning without thunder. The personal is political because persons and their immediate values are drawn into a collective function, responsibly collective, and only there is enjoyment given – collective enjoyment of the personal; not representation, not mediation, not institution, but collective immediacy.

But within what figure, within what projection of value? We had already seen all this at the level of analysis, and there the formation of a social force of production appeared clear – enjoyment means producing. But here the problem changes, because, while analysis leaves space for the imagination, life on the other hand constrains it to determination. So here we had to identify that productive thread that turned the new conditions of the collective into a real project. We had to locate ourselves at that discriminating point, without fear of the fierce winds that were striking the crest of the watershed. Towards what was it proceeding: the collective constitution of the subject? In its concrete genesis you found festivity as a creative element – but creative of what? Creation is, first of all, a pleasure in and of itself. Then, later, it has to show itself as an enjoyment of being – but we had certainly not arrived at the seventh day, nor was the day of rest granted to us. The surface should have revealed its own self-formation as a desiring machine, as a war machine, as *potenza* – to put it in the terms that we would be using a while later.

But this was to re-pose the problem, not to solve it – not even to find a route to its solution, the first steps to take. We were installed in a syllogism whose premise was certain – the descent to consequences was a logical tangle and a spasm. All this was clear there, at Parco Lambro, and we discussed it with discretion but with rigour. And with no solution. We insisted hugely on the need to restore the personal as a dimension properly deployed in the collective, and the older comrades – veterans of every kind of battle, perhaps more than others, and certainly less naively so – were prepared for this constructive self-criticism. But at the very moment at which this individual transformation was coming about, precisely the older and more aware comrades were posing the problem of the next stage of the project. Because, if it was not defined, then our living of that moment would only be an episode of abstract seduction. And not *potenza*. And not antagonism.

Hard drugs were banned at Parco Lambro. A number of heroin dealers were beaten up. But drugs were everywhere and you could not curb the flow. Heroin had found itself a position right on the edge of the unresolved problem: it was simultaneously the highest construction of desire and the mark of the absolute negativity of any claim – when the path of desire was not collective, practical and real. Heroin was imagination that, in demanding its due, denied the problem and dissolved the collective. Heroin was our anguish. From the personal to the collective there ran – I said it, I wrote it, I shouted it – a single path; we had to transform our anguish into a higher enjoyment of the project. Shut up you old fool, was the answer that came back – you're running on empty, you've been overtaken by life. There is, in desperation, the same generosity that exists in love: it is on this point that the processes are reversed – this is how I replied in attempting an answer. Shut up you old fool, again. So let's try it ourselves – let's try to discover the link between despair and love on this ontological point that is more powerful than both, because it determines both of them: at the point where there is production. Production of self and production of antagonism. That lessened the force of the 'shut up, idiot'.

Why not try? Is it not basically reasonable to seek to find our reconstruction at the point where our angst has been created? For the angst is not only mine, it is everyone's. It is in our workplace and in our wage; it is within the poor everyday realities of family life; and it is within the rigid measure of the working day. It is the angst of those who are exploited. Exploitation is the opposite of happiness, exploitation is the same as angst. You cannot understand angst without understanding exploitation. But the destruction of exploitation means the liberation of work – realistically, in this condition it is in fact the refusal of work. The refusal of work is a new productivity. But where is there – here, and not tomorrow, here, at this point – a project that can be pursued, a hope of living? A horizon of angst opens. Maybe, maybe . . . But is there a difference between the angst of exploitation and the angst of the unknown to be discovered? On this distinction – on the optimism of an intellect that can affirm its virtue and discover the unknown – is based the whole movement, together, of subversion and transformation. 'No future' is the destiny that they, the bosses, want to impose on us; but the lesson is coming again today – from Zurich, Berlin and Amsterdam – that destiny can be changed by the power of alternative intelligence. The founding of the new revolutionary subject is therefore not generically to remove the angst, but to determine it within the potentiality of a new project. Papageno becomes Ulysses, both of them covered in mud and bird feathers. Instead of waiting for the big clatter of brass and percussion and for Mozart's Enlightenment foregrounding of the chorus, liberation presents itself to Ulysses as nomadism and adventure, as labour and intellectual graft. Parco Lambro opened on the short circuit between poverty and multitude, on the tendency towards recomposing the personal in the collective. It lived its angst when the projectual substance of the new subject found itself unable to arrive at the intellectual and productive enjoyment that it demanded – it closed itself into the self-conscious determination of a task.

Cher David, the 'go forth and multiply' of apostolic memory took place on the morning when those poor returned to their various towns and cities. On that day, the ancient historic body of this Italic nation of madmen must have experienced a certain tingling. And then they soon got used to it, as they always do – or they tried to get used to it. (The so-called 'movement' journalists then began, with a sudden vocation, to launch the most audacious mystifications – they were simultaneously victims and butchers, these homunculi. Their outpourings were worthy of a Pulitzer Prize: Parco Lambro came to be seen as Woodstock. Romulus dug there the walls of the first ghetto. When power gives you its blessing, things start to go awry and you can come a cropper . . . I did not want to get emotional when, after some years, I saw, from the bitter window of my prison, these writers falling prey to despair and suicide . . .)

Parco Lambro was like a melting together – like the start of the production process in the steel industry. The joining together of people's lives with the historical enactment of liberation has never been played as sweetly as in those days. A new steel had been created, tender and very powerful. A new body. Spinoza: 'the more perfection each thing has, the more it acts and the less it is acted upon; and conversely, the more it acts, the more perfect it is.'* It was a challenge for philosophy and a new opportunity for practice. It is strange how the light and the terrible can come together intimately in situations where innovation breathes. But, in the very process of melting together, the diversity of the materials feeds a tension: different diapasons can follow their various veinings with different resonances. In fact, within this coming together, you stand as if trembling after a long embrace. Surges of desire lift you up; moments of sadness depress you. It seems to you that physical tiredness takes the place of theoretical doubt and effort. Did I say 'seems'? No, it really is that way: the interchange between intellect and will is ever present. Perhaps this is the state of birth? Enough, enough of this babble, of these

---

* Translator's note: Baruch Spinoza, *Ethics*, Part V, Proposition 40; p. 263 in Curley's translation (see note in Letter Ten).

Letter Fifteen: Carnival

descriptions that avoid the essence, whereas a poet could describe it in a moment, in a single phrase. Only movement can solve the expectation and render it positive. A new vitalistic presumption? But, by God, if there is an expectation, then there is potentiality. Apollo sows the seed of Dionysus. The ontological inversion of all the terms of the discourse is here the matrix that permits us to define the enormous *potenza* of the waiting as a pressure for transformation. Otherwise we cannot succeed in making connections, in putting together a writing. We find ourselves back with *Métal Hurlant* – continuous flashes – cheapskate postmodernism. Parco Lambro was not an element of this contorted hyper-design. It was a definition of the positive. So let us head down into the streets, into the squares, let us again press forward this explosive *potenza*.

I look back and cannot bring myself to admit, even if we ended up with an abortion, that this act, the sowing of this seed, was stupid. Walter Benjamin:

> The spirituality of Socrates had a character that was entirely sexual. His concept of spiritual conception was that of a pregnancy, his concept of spiritual generation is tantamount to a discharge of desires ... The Socratic question, in the same way as irony, was an erection of knowledge (if I may be allowed this terrible image for an equally terrible thing).'*

So I arrive at the seventh day, and the restlessness finds rest – because the practical turmoil of that subject shows itself to be protected from reality. The future – in that complexion of reality – I saw it as being graspable in terms of the weeks of creation that would follow. You, cher David, you will know how to interpret these, my bits and pieces of the collective hope of those days. So I embrace you. With such sweetness.

PS It often seems to me that what I'm writing is unnecessarily convoluted. Or maybe convoluted is not the right word: overloaded, rather, with content added to the basic theme – baroque, because it seems that I can't avoid alternatives, variants and derivations. Bombastic. This redundancy conceals, it does not clarify. Please forgive this limitation of mine – and also its complement, which is that sometimes I

---

* Translator's note: Walter Benjamin, *Socrates*, translated here from the Italian version published in his *Metafisica di gioventù: Scritti 1910–1918*, Turin: Einaudi, 1982, p. 164.

am clumsy, irritated, inattentive, late, dreamy, writing in shorthand – and this happens each time that some involuntary memory pushes itself forward in me and brings to the surface that other aspect of life that is my ego, my history, my private things, my memories, my loves, and all that. Samuel Pepys, that extraordinary writer of diaries, at a certain point invented a cryptic writing for himself, for when he was writing about indelicate things. Am I creating some kind of convoluted shorthand in order to hide my humanity? Indelicate, shameful? Perhaps – but no more so than anyone else. Often politics has separated the human being from the intellectual. This may be a bad thing, but it's a given. Does it show in writing? Certainly. But how can we overcome this – and other structural limits? By falling back on the private? By pretending and pressing as one's own that which was lived as separate? Or by sailing uncertainly along that coast, which memory gives only as a wild horizon and a dark line? And how can we use a raw material that is so crude? Make the dream, the delusion, talk – they say. I don't dream – or rather I really don't remember my dreams. I cannot undo what has been done, even if it was done badly. And so? Is not this situation of mine entirely commonplace? I think that only a language that is collectively capable of delirium can win back the unity of being as an expression – we cannot go back, we have to go forward. The collective must, of course, reveal the singularity, but how? Small talk, the ontic dimension, the common distribution of signs, customary images – all reveal our interiority, how it is now made; and they carry it forward in an expressive rhythm, to the point of representing a non-disfigured common sense, a non-asphyxial revelation of singularity itself. Otherwise, in private – in this private that is a sign of a past species – love becomes exhibitionism, narcissism rules, and even suffering is told with satisfaction. And this is even uglier than either the baroque or the shorthand – because the private is no longer human.

Letter Sixteen
1977 as a Turning Point

Rebibbia, 3 March 1982

Cher David,

So was this a point where one could get the measure of a new political practice – or perhaps of its defeat? The opportunity was certain – but so too was the defeat. Of course, I worry about presenting the thing in terms that are overstated and somewhat contrived: in fact, when you look at these events from prison, they seem to accelerate the closer you get to the point where the prison gates close and time shuts down. However, the sense of a turning point comes not so much from a posteriori reflections on this historical ephemeral reality that is prison as from the ontological thickness of the class composition.

The period between 1976 and 1977 provided an opportunity to re-establish a mass political method for an independent workers' movement in Italy. Beyond that point, in the medium term, the possibility of relaunching the project and the process remains an unknown. Almost twenty years of preparation and formation of a leadership group, twenty years of penetration among the masses, of correct analysis and correct definition of tactics, and now comes the 'showdown'. In our particular case, the experience has been bitter. All the more bitter as the crisis of the movement's project was due to forces emanating from within – it was due to the explosion of the terrorist variable. An old story: anarchists and communists. Until anarchism is defeated, communism cannot become a party – this was true at the end of in the last century, it was true in the 1920s, and it remained true in the 1970s – all the more so because here the problem did not have a rigid party dimension but was posed within the broader practices of movement. This is the 'American' problem of the organisation of subversion and of communism today: Lenin in New York . . . In short, the unpredictable variable is as modern as the new problem. Terrorism is the anarchism of postmodernism – the old anarchism loses its artisanal quality and its libertarian theatricality, which evoke a kind of *belle époque* nostalgia. Bulletproof vests took the place of dynamite – on the one side Bonnot, on the other Viscardi and Savasta – the propaganda of the deed gave way to the paranoia of a mass-media society. The difference between their respective ethical fantasies is equally violent: efficiency versus utopia, and also the act of informing versus martyrdom. Dostoevsky is really obsolete here. I'll write about this again later. But there is a further element that needs to be borne in mind, not so much to console ourselves and lessen our sense of defeat as to remind ourselves – in spite of everything – of the usefulness of having grasped that opportunity. The fact is that, the movement having been assailed and defeated by a crisis that was internal (and only internal), the conclusion of that season of struggles did not reinforce the existing system – on the contrary, it deepened the structural limits of its possibilities for integration and restoration.

That said, cher David, my thoughts are going back to the period when we were discussing all these things – already with a sharp awareness of being within a process of institutional disintegration that was unstoppable and within an emergence of movement that, albeit intensifying its social composition, was terribly fragile in its political composition. This was the heyday of the Historic Compromise. What was being built was a legislative framework and a feudalisation of offices that, with due efficacy, were supposed to be the means of effecting the dictatorship of the two major parties. A kind of *grosse Koalition* [grand coalition] – the mystified product of a parliamentary centre of gravity supposed to resolve, in a demagogy of unanimity, the problem of the constitutional crisis. This was the crowning moment of the policy, the only policy, that had been pursued by the Communist Party since the end of the Second World War. But all this was so old-fashioned, so tatty! A kind of Prussian reformism, a socialism à la Lassalle, with rhythms that reminded you of the goose step – a strong forward thrust of the leg and then a dragging of the foot: stiffness and slowness intended to give an illusion of motion. A weary expectation that people would go along with it and identify with it, but for whom? Never had the *Critique of the Gotha Programme* been more appropriate than in the face of that orgy of talk of a 'fair wage', of an *equo canone* ['fair rent'], of Jeremy Bentham, and so on. It was an attempt to harness administratively, to castrate

Letter Sixteen: 1977 as a Turning Point

politically, and (ultimate achievement) to activate democratically the great movement of participation that had developed at the end of the 1960s. Rise up, Lazarus! Go back to being what you once were! But the theological reading of the miracle univocally contradicts this exegesis: Lazarus really was dead. If now he has life, it is a new life – so how could they hope to capture this new life through a dead appeal? Reformism had no attraction, the cards were down, the talk of economic development had no bite on the new class composition. The problem of the proletarian subject was that of an alternative set of values and ways of life. The face of the Historic Compromise looked bureaucratic, grotesque, waxy yellow. A reformism of sergeants. *Una risata vi sepellirà* [A laugh will bury you]. But how to get them into line, these workers in sneakers, these 'unpunished' feminists, this young intellectual labour power that projects its mobility on the arc of imagination? Remember the slogans. *Tremate, tremate, le streghe son tornate* [Tremble tremble, the witches are back]; *Zangheri, Zangherà ride tutta la città* [Zangheri, Zangherà, the whole city is laughing at you]. The political establishment structures were ill suited for absorbing the new. Cautious openings were not enough. The division ran deep and the centrifugal forces were multiplying. Aristotelians versus *untorelli* [plague carriers]. Reading the social context as a unified whole and trying to normalise it was impossible. The dominion-sabotage function was the only effectual norm – because the regime's plans appeared immediately as dominion, and the proletarian behaviours, in their immediacy, were sabotage. The social relationship was shot through with antagonism, and the possibility of an equilibrium of participation was halting – difficult, if not impossible: if I ask for a social wage I sabotage the resumption of accumulation; if, on the other hand, accumulation lifts off again, then unemployment and poverty grow – and so the waltz goes on. Easy appeals to sacrifice did not sit well with these people. The immediate, Reaganesque vulgarity of such things offended them from the outset. So, provoked by that vulgar solicitation, by the total inappropriateness of the appeal to virtue, the movement flared up again. *Lama nel Tibet*. ['Lamas belong in Tibet.'] *Lama non l'ama nessuon*. ['Lama, nobody loves him.']* Thereby revealing an incredible social compactness, an impressive extension and uniformity of behaviours, as well as political weakness and a fragmented, jagged multiplicity of objectives and demands. A blast of demands was launched at a leadership that attempted, in fact

---

* Translator's note: reference to Luigi Lama, trade union chief.

demanded, a reduction in complexity and a procedural regulation of social demands. The radicalisation of the conflict was a foregone conclusion. And the 'turbulent environment' of the metropolis was its theatre.

Cher David, I don't want to sing you the praises of this wild situation. But it is certainly the case that this is how it was on both fronts. The economic repression was strong, but so was the revolt. An immediately selective repression began striking at the key groups that were carrying forward the resistance and the counterattack, trying to isolate them socially – taking up corporative demands and crushing generalist demands, introducing a kind of large-scale commodification of command with rewards for political obedience and penalties for disobedience. I don't know how they do these things in the socialist countries, but I have the impression that things there were somewhat analogous. The governance of the metropolitan areas was being modernised urgently and with great effort, and they attempted to control the 'turbulent theatre' in terms of a coercive prefiguring of the labour market, of its various flows and stakes. But all this was beyond its power – because this proletarian subject that had emerged on the one hand dissolved the working day (which production and Power had assumed as a given), and on the other it upset the basket of goods, the set of needs against which capital and government measure their action. The state became the central place of class struggle. Repressive practices and subversive practices crossed all spatial boundaries. Deterritorialisation. The connection between law and order, social control and company profits was immediately grasped and interpreted on the proletarian front as a unitary and hostile schema – hostile because, as the Marxist theoretician says, quoting the texts of the Trilateral Commission that were then all the rage, 'capital tries to limit the transfer of practices of the liberal–democratic state to the sphere of capitalist production, and instead favours the reverse process: the transfer of practices of capitalist production to the liberal–democratic state'. And, insofar as it is the enemy, this connection must be overturned, retraced, and socially sabotaged. If everything has become political, the proletarian subject lays claim to a kind of power of veto over the political arena of the metropolis. In the same way that it is exercised by the organised group of corporative interests? More or less – damned bosses, why not us? – but without any instrument that is not, on the proletarian horizon, pure and simple mass action. In short, the metropolitan theatre is a *chaotische multitudo* [chaotic multitude]. The 'making' of the new proletarian composition disrupts all traditional references, overturns every cognitive parameter. This picture repeats the extraordinary difficulties and the extraordinary adventures of a different period as recounted by E. P. Thompson – that unique British student of Defoe.

But in the cruel underdevelopment of the Italic autonomy of the political, on the Machiavellian terrain of the law – funny or tragic, I'll leave it to you to decide – this is what was unleashed on us, cher David. For example, the journalists and the scholars of social matters battened onto this reality like piranhas – they carved up the movement in accord with the prescriptions of Power, and in this abattoir, like ferocious vultures, they sectioned out the cut that was to be put before the public. Not to be recovered, not to be understood, because in fact – as the art of butchering teaches us – the cut was part of the horse – and here the repression was implicit in the method. A McLuhan-style syllogism of the mass-media. They were propagandising either the ghetto or its alternative – the only alternative that Power left to the process of subjective identification of the new social composition. Great processes of commodification were set in motion, of *having* as opposed to *being*: the market for hard drugs grew, and poison and anxiety insinuated themselves everywhere. 'Slump city.' Why should the commodity initiative not be consistent with state repression? You could even hear minstrels of the regime's high culture adding their bit: lamenting in elevated tones the resurgent *diciannovismo*.* *Sacrifici sacrifici, più lavoro meno salario* [Sacrifices, sacrifices, more work less pay]. Poor idiots! *Sbirro maledetto te l'accendiamo noi la fiamma sul berretto* [You damned cop – we'll put a match to the flame on your cap]. Stop.

It has never surprised me that this cultural insensibility, this tone of provocation, should have come particularly (albeit with some exceptions) from the corporation of historians – a category of academics that, in Italy, deserves to be studied in the unique conditions of its local reproduction and its political provincialism. In love with that shameful past they study, they participate in and are predestined to fall for flattery. Spadolini. Such historians are gravediggers; they do not trust humanity and its unforeseeable trajectories. Evenimential history is pure and simple garbage. Stirring up shit with a juridical rod. Whereas doing, which is forming the world on the unknown

---

* Translator's note: term defined by Hoepli's online dictionary (*La grande libreria online*, http://www.hoepli.it) as denoting the complex of 'political and social phenomena that characterised the period after the First World War, with special reference to the birth of fascism'.

time that has not yet occurred, the metaphysical risk of the existing, of potentiality, only this can be the object of thought.

Well, we were now traversing this new segment of being that was being built. Which masses of men were building. Which the metropolitan proletariat, the social worker, were making. The hiatus between production and history was closing. The metropolitan outings of groups such as the Nights of Fire, as also the strategies of punks and various tribes of skinheads, were first and foremost a reappropriation of knowledge on the part of a collective subject. And the new producer had the same dimension as that on which his action was operating: a whole world – of knowledge, of passion. Here – precisely at the point where these dimensions of the emergence of new proletariat were given – the ultimate paradox was becoming clear: that the maximum of antagonism represented the maximum of positivity. A sameness of opposites? No. Rather, in real terms, a maximum of separation, a liquidation of all homology in a radically alternative mode of existence. In Bologna, Rome and Milan this was a time of big marches – but their violence was not homologous, equal and opposite to the violence set in motion by the forces of repression. It was something else. Of course, those demonstrations were full of militarism and ferocious slogans. But it was a tragic game, a mass catharsis. The symbol of power was taken up in order to be exorcised. The balaclava helmets, the P38s, the raised Winchesters represented a certain liberation of people's thinking. (But, some will object, they were also used to kill. Cynically one could answer by comparing the numbers of the dead on both sides. But it is not the sameness that counts – it is the difference – and this (and only this) does not absolve the killings – indeed, cher David, it only makes you weep all the more.) In the demonstrations, in the struggle, the project was one of peace, of community, of production. A new generation was moving with passion along the road to communism. The word *povertà* [poverty] took on a new connotation – a new real figure among the many that we had materially defined. 'Poverty' perhaps, this time. Poverty at the highest level, as the highest problem.

I do not know whether when these phenomena catch our eye is the only time we can talk of coming close to the going beyond, to being beyond prehistory. It amuses me to take on the paradox of the Nazi professor and of his last adventure in dialectics – when *Dasein*, the determination, the here, the *Da*, the 'this' (and the more the merrier) can only qualify the being-for-death. Well, let us reverse this paradox – it deserves nothing else – why on earth should the meaning of the crisis of being within being, of the collapse of the universal,

Letter Sixteen: 1977 as a Turning Point

have anything to do with the proletarian? Lukács, in his anti-*Sein und Zeit*, had proposed, in the metaphor of Leninism, this reversal – which we now had the chance to see being enacted in the reality of the movement. For the movement, there is no nostalgia for the universal – the determination is therefore not something scandalous but living existence. The determination is posed, here and now, with such fullness and is charged with such imagination and hope that no negativity is given. Determination is to be beyond the negative. So that our task is not the dialectical task of grasping the particularity in order to lead it to the negativity of the universal word – but that of getting ourselves 'taken' by this particular, by its implicit and positive richness. But 'getting taken' is not an operation that involves less intelligence and work than the act of 'taking' – on the contrary, given that it is an action internal to being, it requires adequate techniques, continuous capacities for proposition and invention – it requires a mobilisation of liberty in its contact with being. The processes of self-valorisation that strata of the metropolitan proletariat are beginning to put into action and that are becoming immediately visible are here commensurate with the enormous amount of antagonism in whose form they are constituted – they are simply its paraphrase.

Then we said: the multiplicity of these processes, the plurality of their tensions and of the possible and present contradictions are removed from the superficiality on which they express themselves and brought to an internal *Vergleichung* [comparison], ontological and political – which is an equalising and a concrete idea of the becoming of value. The diversity and richness of the objectives that the communities were beginning to set themselves on the ground, and as a programme of their own social reproduction, had to be grasped within a framework of convergent development. Later we said: let us focus on the problem of production – on the relationship between material production and immaterial production (tertiary, informatics, and so on), which, with all its ambivalences, was becoming central in society at that time. I don't think that these big themes we were addressing then – that of self-valorisation and antagonism, that of the multiplicity of proletarian subjects, that of the complexity of the values pursued, and finally the problem of immaterial production and of its hegemony as a new mode of production – as I say, I don't believe that the emergence of these themes has been undervalued. The effort of a conscious appropriation of this terrain of problems, the destruction of the 'idols' that stood in the way of our perceiving it, were actually pushed to the maximum. So what was there in this force of the social composition of the proletariat, in its impetuous thrust, that blocked the possibility of consolidation?

I don't know the answer. On the other hand I don't think that anyone can set themselves up as teachers in situations where only practice and determination are in command. I can assume things that are out of place or out of balance, structural discrepancies, and so on – but really it seems to me an opportunism of political reason to resort to tired old fables like those of dualism and 'stages' of development at a time when we have signalled – on several occasions, and not accidentally – maximum accelerations towards high points of transformational behaviour. There is something else. It is probably to be found in the continued underlying existence of a disturbed and disturbing sense of totality – and to be identified in the difficulty of filling out the theoretical category materially, to the point of negating the fraudulent nature of all transcendental identity. The subject is now the multitude of the different. Bourgeois civil wars have always expressed themselves in religious wars, for the restoration of orthodoxy: *Bürgerkrieg um den absoluten Text* [bourgeois war against the absolute text]. No, no, the proletarian is very different – the sabotage determines a finiteness, analysis seeks determination. The tension towards the absolute, on the other hand, is a syphilis – a monkey on the shoulder. The refounding of the revolutionary movement fails where theory remains separated from transformative practice, and *potenza* from production, and liberty from liberation. We needed to go deeper, not to rest content with this sudden and premature flowering. But, as we know, when a warm day breaks the chill of winter, few peasants are able to resist: thinking themselves clever, they sow seeds that the frost will destroy. On the other hand it is foolish to grasp in this only subjective errors – the subjective errors are part of the composition. Escher, Magritte and Thom: the overturning is a pattern in geometry, the formless form. Here the thing is serious, because the error is inherent in the figure of being and consists in attributing to it a finality, no matter how understood. Finality of being: or negation of particularity, automatism of compensation, end of responsibility. A philosophy of positivism, on the other hand, affirms the *Dasein*, negating it as the foundation of dialectics, negating it as the base of any being-for-the-other. If thought and action do not bend on this particular fulcrum of being, on its rigid and exclusive determination, on this overthrow, which is being inasmuch as it refers to nothing if not its *potenza* – which is nothing but itself – in short, if all this does not happen, then production and revolution do not arrive at that beginning that both founds and legitimates

Letter Sixteen: 1977 as a Turning Point 181

them. Production set against the revolution, revolution set against production are the last theistic horizon – or rather polytheistic; and anyway barbaric and pagan – that human prehistory knows. In 1977 these stereotypes ended up dominating the scene, the god of production against the god of revolution. Apollo versus Dionysus. Carli, Pandolfi and Cossiga versus the armed groups engaged in social sabotage. Equivalents. A pathetic *batrachomyomachia* [battle of mice and frogs]. God is in fact both production and revolution. This is the only possible terrain for refounding. Yesterday, cher David, we did not succeed; tomorrow we shall.

And today? Today we are experiencing perhaps the height of the tragedy of the ethical, which was introduced into collective existence in those years – a period honoured only by mechanical repetition, and not by the light that difference generates in dazzling form through repetition. However, I do not want to dwell on this any longer: the suffering of rational comprehension is strong. Instead, what might one add to the passion of that time? What did those days mean for us? Perhaps the biggest thing we derived from them was the education of feelings. Because what we were unable to bring about collectively, we often succeeded in achieving in small groups. The chiaroscuro could not be stronger: the concomitant aspect of the struggle was tenderness. But it was an ontological tenderness – a tenderness of being that opens, a dry tenderness, not some romantic mish-mash. And in people's minds the path of revolution was solid, the feelings were as rich as the tension of desire. We were no longer embarrassed to talk about love, because we experienced love as a constitutive potency. And each of us, in that genealogical passage of the collective, selected out being in its positive particularity, in oneself and in others. The revolutionary project became a wellspring. We were for ourselves, not for anything else, and the totality we believed in was the existent – and only that: life against death.

By the time we became aware of the political weakness of this renaissance, when we realised that the time of our liberation would be wiped out by the capitalist measure of the time of death – while, dressed in red, this death call was stalking through the movement – by that time we were too far down that ontological path to draw up a tactic, a defence. There is a tragedy that is linked to life – and it is that of knowing yourself to be so very far from death *per se* that you cast aside the idea of death *in se* and shun with horror the capitalist measure of exploitation. But this has now a logical foundation that derives from the total incommensurability of the 'ours' and 'theirs'. You suffered the tragedy, and the awareness of its enactment was a source of dignity. Thus we found ourselves living and dancing and singing a struggle that was a developing potentiality; we were playing a scene of the great reconstruction of true worldly being. Has the show been cancelled for the time being? I don't think so. Being does not tolerate censorship. Prison is ephemeral, ontology is sacred. And the developments of that time expressed themselves in the unstoppable and age-old passion of the person who walks – still now, and forever – forward. I am thinking of you tonight. I shall continue chatting with you, cher David, about our philosophy and our hope. Goodbye for now . . .

Letter Seventeen
Manhattan

Rebibbia, 10 March 1982

Cher David,

We've already touched on this in our discussions, you remember? For me New York was like . . . it's hard to find the exact words . . . a shock, a revelation, a punch in the stomach, I don't know. Certainly it was a big experience. By 1977 I was becoming a citizen who was less and less pleasing to my government. So in 1977 and 1978 I set out for Europe and America. Was this to meet Carlos and terrorism's Mr Big? Or was it a visit to the world's terror network? That's what the filthy whore Claire Sterling claims. They even claimed to have photographed me with Carlos in Algiers . . . Actually I was neither a fugitive nor a troublemaker for the sake of it. I was driven by something other than the usual desire for escapism or mere intellectual curiosity: it was a practical need for understanding, a journey into a fiction – into a future that the immediate experiences of the struggle did not allow me to grasp intellectually. This was a matter of both urgency and necessity. 'Fiction', precisely – the opportunity to imagine my own future and the future of all of us. Listen to William Blake: 'What is now proved was once only imagined.'* So America, but basically only New Amsterdam, Manhattan. And Asimov's Foundation series. The centre, the motive point of every possible circle. The world of worlds. I felt as if I was standing before Tantor, where all dialectics is removed because the capital accumulated there is so enormous that

---

* Translator's note: famous line from 'Proverbs of Hell' in William Blake's *The Marriage of Heaven and Hell*, composed between 1790 and 1793.

it allows no relationship. Consequently, as in Asimov's story, free and living labour is placed outside of any dialectics and the *doux commerce* takes place on the edge of the worlds. The first sensation was one of being stunned and impotent. You asked yourself – do freedom and life still exist, in some independent universe? It was not by talking with economist friends that you found hope – but Asimov answers in the affirmative, with optimistic determinism: from that liminal world living labour will be able to attempt a refoundation. The shock subsides, you continue to observe, you analyse data and statistics, and you look around: here and there a few bubbles break the surface of the swamp. Then the surface begins to move. Gradually you realise that here in New York the two separate universes intertwine: you begin to grasp it and you smile the smile of a child discovering something for the first time. The massive displacement of power lives alongside an enormous vitality of social labour, which is diffuse and full of potentiality. But in what form? Social labour operates in a scenario of social decomposition and disaggregation – and this makes analysis difficult, because it is 'jeopardised' in the face of the towering, inaccessible heights of power. This is a logical challenge. A puzzle. The obvious normality of this situation strikes both your intellect and your passion. But one could not remain in doubt or try to apply old and suspect stereotypes. Here the proletarian separation was given in the form of disaggregation and was nevertheless both recognisable and alive. 'Loss of animal spirits'? Alienation? 'Desire to die'? Certainly the disintegration contained these elements. But on the other hand in the great social factory a great power of invention was being released – a crazy, multicoloured people was moving frenetically, like toiling ants among the towers of the giant. It expresses itself through symbols of freedom – care for the body, Saturday nights, jogging, lofts . . . – through many, many things that have nothing to do with power. And yet they produce – they produce more than what capital is able, in this wild flowering of initiatives, to organise and to expropriate. The immediate socialisation of the disaggregation valorises the subject. Certainly it also recomposes – simultaneously – the processes of reproduction and the mechanisms of production, because these universes overlap. But who knows any longer on which side stands command and on which side the moment of recomposition? At the top or at the bottom? This tugging, which each does from their own side, is real, and the wealth diffuses itself within the disaggregation, building circuits that nobody any longer knows how to traverse. The crisis of New York, the problem of public spending cuts and the failure of all monetary control . . . The economic crisis is fully prefigured by the social crisis. The rollback of Keynesianism. Where is the top and where is the bottom? The working day has gone crazy – the terms of value bounce between reproduction and production, between immateriality and materiality – the quantity and the quality of value can no longer be separately perceived, and the distinction between necessary labour and counter-power is not perceivable either. Where now is the compelling power of Adam Smith's *Wealth of Nations*, and where is its providential logic? A huge war is in progress at this stellar scale. The strength of the contenders is stretched across all the terms of the relationship; you have to forget about manuals of military strategy because positional warfare and guerrilla warfare become interchangeable. A Thirty Years War that is confused and changeable – which, equally and simultaneously, disrupts and dissolves an old world order and, through mighty travail, reveals a new world – a war that wipes out domestic and international law and all formulae of distribution of wealth – a war that distributes plague and wealth in equal measure.

When you find yourself in this situation, your lazy mental habits set you asking the usual classic questions of the communist militant. But, no matter how keen and diligent you are, you don't find the answer. A poverty of theory. So locating yourself at this point of theoretical imagining, applying critical reason to New York, forces you to deal with the displacement of the logic of capital and to operate an equally vigorous forward shift in revolutionary logic. This in order to understand the relations of class forces within this complexity and to be able to take the independence of the social subjects as your necessary starting point.

One after the other, the images reinforce these arguments – on the one hand, the imaginative presence of the metropolis and its proletarians, people's angry realism in their use of the city, and the attraction and pleasure of its continual renewal, the joy of the streets, the violence, the assault on public spending, the social dimension of the community, and the beauty of its people. On the other hand, yet further images. It comes as something of a shock. Under the attack of this living disaggregation, in the sea of huge towering buildings, the closed, windowless skyscraper emerges – perhaps the most amazing symbol of power 'in the final resort' that human reason can imagine. It is a huge square mass whose internal biology one can only guess at. Social disaggregation has a thousand souls, whereas the skyscraper is power, rigidified and irreversible. Just as the people's reality in this city is disaggregated and all-embracing and ungraspable and dissolved and dissolute, so at the outset you are barely able to imagine the physiology of that other power. I try to imagine it by way of paradox, from the perspective of negativity, of ruin, of death. Herein lies its specificity: it cannot recycle itself into life, it cannot innovate. Unlike the factory of old, the closed skyscraper cannot be rehabilitated, reinhabited, or transformed into lofts. As soon as the physiological pulsations of its arteries deteriorate, as soon as old age hits its facilities and its circulation – once it loses its ability to produce command – it dies. A Mayan ruin? Like some crumbling temple of that great civilisation? Is this the fate ordained by the American god? Pushing the imagination of command to the limits, and thereby overstepping the limits of the reasonable and conjoining itself only negatively, as a symbol of damnation, to the magnitude of the heavens? A new Babel? Maybe. But this Babel is not in the Mesopotamian desert. Instead it is surrounded by a wealth of vegetation, a luxuriance of wild potentialities. The Mayan temples sank into the ancient wilderness of nature. This present temple will sink into second nature, into civil renewal, and into the new wealth of the communism of the masses. But it is a gamble. New York gives you the impulse to gamble, but not the certainty of winning. For the moment, as evening falls, the unseeing skyscraper falls dark, falls silent – and then you see it, this huge beehive, you see it already finished, dried out. In the shadows you find it easy to imagine the falling apart of its powerful décor. No longer does it have that concert of monstrous insects flying around it, the helicopters and the jumbo jets. Now it becomes the habitat of rats and cockroaches. *Shit capital*. In contrast, the local neighbourhoods, which during the day are rendered insignificant by the towering of the skyscraper, light up with renewed vigour and almost forget their wounds. Come on in – we spend the nights arguing with youthful vigour, and the old theories of revolt and freedom find new gestures and expressions. (Reading James Stephens's *The Crock of Gold* this week has brought Manhattan back to my mind, and the idea of how this world of extraordinary lightness – of spirit and of instinct – is the only possible sociological basis of an ethics of radical irreducibility. And perhaps also of a language to match: *Finnegans Wake*.)

What is left of class struggle here? It is life – present – as an alternative to an equally present accumulation of death. Here an enormous wealth is in movement – pores and empty spaces of being are filled with an independent production wherever capitalist command is not able to impose its violence and is obliged to permit the existence of sponge-like and receptive tissues. The story of the closed skyscraper is that of a power that, from the core of its structure, demands to articulate every initiative that might permit the reproduction of its

Letter Seventeen: Manhattan

biological rhythm: autocracy plays out the recurring dream of autarchy. But at each of these articulations power encounters something else – barriers, counter-power. Heterogeneous lines of development. Forces that do not want to enter into the Palace, that indeed hate it. And with this do they cause it to die? Even if only through this active estrangement? Who knows? This is, however, the point: one struggles outside of and against the Palace. This antagonism between death and new life is continuously in process. Capitalist nostalgia for dialectics. (Even for socialism? Reagan, the great reactionary, now wants mass workers of the old kind, Stakhanovites dedicated to the production and reproduction of that baroque arsenal that has become his power. A vain nostalgia!) Master and servant, however, no longer sublimate themselves in solidarity. Thus, in the ostentation of wealth, the imperial palaces weep tears of gold – the ruins of the glory of the conquistadors are always the same. Among these great masses life carries on, disaggregated and harsh. A huge framework and a huge wrapping. *Chaotische.* A thin gas passes through the big aggregates, a deep poison. Is this world so ridiculously weak that a Cortes or Pissarro could destroy it with a mere handful of knights? What is certain is that this world has a fatal disease in the form of power, and powerful antibodies in the form of people and societies: these cannot coexist. Power succeeds, day after day, in stealing this social substance as its foodstuff – but with increasing difficulty, laboriously, poisonously. The linear logic of exploitation has run its course. What we have instead is a frontier practice that traverses the metropolis. Labyrinths, mathematical *réseaux* that have no centre – robbery now replaces the logic of surplus value – discrete or bloodthirsty, the effort and the design of social control are continuously remodelling themselves. The game is over, its theory has become confused. Power has been filibustered out. Can all this be coming to an end? But where's the sense in talking about an end when we have denied all beginning?

Cher, David, you know New York and the rest of the world better than me – many times you have given me intelligent accounts. The fact that I was so fascinated and shocked when I looked into the crystal of New York seemed somehow to have offended you. Maybe you thought that mine was a naive provincialism . . . However, it is difficult to deny that in this crystal is formed the scene of the whole world. I know Americans who see New York as the shitty umbilical cord of the world – and it is! I know Europeans in New York who have fallen for it head over heels! It's true: love and hate, contempt and passion, dislocation and disintegration. Until we learn to call the negative positive immediately, and to understand the shifting of reality – its catastrophic becoming and its settling into *potenza* – we do not understand New York. This is why our senses are thrown when we fail to grasp this *potenza* in theoretical terms – but if, on the other hand, we succeed, then our feelings and spirits can be educated.

My thoughts turn back to Europe, and to Italy. I hear children's cries, and only cries and images of childhood, in the face of this great human beast that is New York. And yet everything that I have lived for and struggled over, all seems to me essential: as indeed it is to have brought up things that are new and freshly come to light – from the prospect of a future that I have already seen lived, *vergangene Zukunft* [past future], and that is antagonistic and open and can therefore be changed. This is the feeling that still brings me to bet on the new generation, that both loves and hates the great American human beast – loves it as a parent and progenitor, and hates it as a beast and as power. *Graecia capta ferum victorem cepit* [Captured by sword, Greece captured its captor]? Nonsense. Slogans from history prevent you from understanding, as well as mystifying the form of events. This is a recurring European illusion: what is the value of it? It is fraudulent, if it seeks to fill in subjectively for an objective *potenza* that is as yet unknown. And if you think, as indeed you sometimes do think, that this formidable reality will produce a revolutionary subject to match its scale – there is no such necessity in this relationship. And yet the lack of necessity in the relationship does not deprive you of the possibility. So you would be doubly fraudulent, which would be totally unacceptable, if you did not think that the revolution is born, and can only be born, at the highest point of development of the beast.

(Carl, my black friend, lives on the edge of the Bronx. His barefoot wife, his two sons, their African clothing – beautiful. He talks to me about the 1960s, and then about the revolt of the New York blackout in July 1977. He tries to explain to me the Afro-American revolution of that whole period. He has an awareness that is incredibly attentive to the limits and the potentiality of the black and proletarian movement. He describes the big attempt that was made: a dynamic centralising of community experiences, organisational mobility and a coalition of class strata, counter-power as a non-delegated expression of political leadership and determination of outcomes, and a 'prophetic' formalising of leadership . . . And on the other hand the reaction – which passes through the corporatism of the middle class and the terrorism of the lumpen elements, through the destructive factionalism of ideologies and the physical extermination of the movement's radical leadership. As I listen to him talking I take notes on what will be my future. But he also throws into the mix the future of the future – and explains defeat as a discontinuity and already sees in the revolt of the blackout (and also in the ever new, variable and stronger institutional intersections of the movement) signs of progress. Moments of mass experimentation and the operation of a revolutionary power – both black and white. Carl has a body more beautiful and better proportioned than Jesse Owens.)

America, America: so no one will ever conquer you. But there, under that huge sky, this new revolution, of a labour power that is intelligent and mobile, full of desires and of civilisation, as destructive and creative as ever man saw, will unleash itself – and already we have progressed a long way on this journey, inside this future history, on both this and that side of the Atlantic.

And what about on this side of the water? The intellectual spectacle in Paris during those years was quite another thing. *Nouveaux philosophes* and other ingredients were seasoning the soup of power. Quantities of self-criticism piled up, and in their ineptitude they deployed an ethical malaise of a kind that subsequently I found only in the Italian phenomenon of *pentitismo* [criminals turning informants]. However, in France there was fortunately no open war, and rediscoveries of Jehovah did not end in confessions at the police station. But, as soon as you broke that mystifying screen, the problem of philosophy – and the problem that revolutionary culture and youth culture were breathing – was the same as that in Greenwich Village. Higelin, Renaud and others were playing a new tune. The fragility and the invincibility of power: this terrible paradox, which no one had the strength to stop. So let's run with it, this paradox, after the defeat of the assault on the heavens, within the desire for renewal that characterised 1968. The world is a totality without foundation. It cannot be destroyed, it does not have a heart that can be ripped out. Only cunningness can permit us – the stratagems of Derrida! – to move. This insistence on strategies and cunning was sweet for me. The Italian movement had moved on this and had articulated a proposal. As the French turned phenomenology in a critical and semiological direction, so the Italians developed phenomenological critique in the direction of ethics and politics. The strategies were moving on the trail of the real. They were on the streets of Manhattan.

Until the point where – and here began the really new – this moving around in bands, on the trail of a truth, revealed itself as production, as desire – as ontological difference and autonomy. Certainly not all that glittered was gold – because, just as had happened in the Italian experience of politics, as a reflection of what had happened in France, a hiatus was gradually created between difference and production; and that which configured itself as the highest theory and the most effective practice of ontological *potenza* was blocked within an unbearable tension and an extreme urgency – a sort of haemorrhaging of subjectivity, a dispersal of intentionality into arabesques of damp spots. 'Shit work.' 'Underground economy.' 'Slump city.' It was what I had seen in Italy in the maturation of the new social subject – and now I was compelled, in this scenario that was open on all sides, to address the problem anew. And I ended up with the conviction that an era had come to an end, that an end of time had been arrived at, an end to the time in which I had lived and within which all my experience had been measured. That time was over because all possible measure of it had been lost, and all my experience – and that of the generations that had grown up with me – inasmuch as it was renewed, had been polluted by that same measure. The very maturation of the new subject, with the enormous scale of its development, could not be understood if we could not change the theoretical framework – radically. The coexistence of opposites, in the theoretical horizon in which most of the comrades lived, had reached the perfection of the ineffable and the insignificant: a before and an after, no longer classifiable, no longer affirmed in their determination – so that, in circulating every different aspect, both the before and the after ended up being ungraspable faces of sameness. I had not yet reached the point where I could think of disaggregation as *potenza*. I was not yet able to bring the discourse to that point of radicalism in which the ideological perspective was no longer there – a recognised nonexistence – and which left space for the actuality of free strategy. But this, my inability to find the words – and particularly this now shouting, now silent haemorrhaging of subjectivity that I was witnessing – were only inscribed in the existent as a residue of a past. My thinking returned to New York, returned to the perceivable representation of a realised antinomy, to the physical and determinate experience of an alternative. The present, in this case, is filled with future.

It was in this situation that I set myself back to working on Marx. Was this a nostalgia for theoretical order? Cher David, how can we be nostalgic for our being? It was not nostalgia. When Spinoza was reading Leone Ebreo, I believe that his remembering fulfilled, for him, the same function that the reading of Marx can have for us today: to seek, among our kind of people, the sense of the most potent utopia of love, and to relate it back to the most potent and effectual subjectivity. With Leone Ebreo, in the Spinozan meaning of *potenza*, and with Marx, beyond Marx. In other words, where we recognise a Marx made actual, a living proletarian *potenza*. We start from being as *potenza*. The *potenza* of the streets of New York, the productivity of the proletarian disaggregation. The revolution is not of tomorrow but of today. The revolution is nothing but ourselves. Those were years, cher David, in which the tumult of our passions perfected our sentimental education. Now I feel old. I cannot even narrate it, this becoming. I risk, like an aged Goethe, refinding it ironically in a classicising epic narrative – or like an aged Malraux, reliving it in intellectual tourism. No, the prison that I am currently enjoying keeps such stereotypes at bay. However, it does not take away the pleasure of having witnessed, at least once in one's life, this formidable ontological drama – the birth of a new revolutionary period, played by a new subject, opening with happiness to hope. The big blocks of nostalgia and of tradition were gradually falling to pieces. *Aus Geschichte lernt man nur eben Geschichte* [From history one learns only history]. From history one learns nothing. A breath of relief. The tenderness you feel, and you feared was going to lead you astray, is guaranteed to you instead in its ontological basis. As in the great pastors of the church, from St Francis to Roncalli. Or in the great feminists, from the great Rosa to the beautiful Rossana. The philosophy of Spinoza and Nietzsche, the revolutionary imagination of Machiavelli and Lenin. The classical is no longer memory – as the world lives the experience of revolution, its intimidating fascination of the classical disappears and you discover its paternity. The tenderness – this opening of a virgin being, of the nights of Manhattan, of the proletarian fires in Italian cities. And now of prison. Was that trip to New York a sign of things to come? Certainly, for the first time since the beginning of this research, the continuity and the indifference do not scare me. Because they cannot be crushed into a single unmoving sameness but rather expand into a revolution in action. To live, to have lived the future. As in Walt Whitman: 'Do I contradict myself? Very well, then, I contradict myself, I am large, I contain multitudes.'*

Cher David, sometimes I fall into the pomposity of baroque imagery – forgive me. I also fear the opposite, to which I am equally prey: the bloodless lyricism of philosophers, their inability to lift themselves out of concepts. Here I have the impression that the poverty of my language and its Po valley shortcomings are reaching some kind of absolute limit. This may be so – it is a language that is still rural, not geared to the functional abstraction of the industrial

---

* Translator's note: Walt Whitman, 'Song of Myself', Part 51.

way of life, presumptuous in seeking to express the metropolis, its problems, and its revolt. I am an immigrant – and I don't look into the means – perhaps even throwing stones, because everyone has anyway realised this miracle that I have understood and lived: the revolution under way. It's rude to throw stones – but not for the immigrant – and for Chaplin's Kid it is innocent. Today I have this great longing. I have a great yearning for this delicate air of spring, which reaches me even in the exercise yard. And a great desire to say the words 'Burn, baby, burn!' Burn the past that binds and deceives you, in order to live the future that you are. To you I write and to you I dedicate, at this moment, my desire. Ciao.

Letter Eighteen
Moro

Rebibbia, 15 March 1982

Do you remember, David? It was a cold day. Windy, with sudden glimpses of sky, as often happens in Paris in March. At our early afternoon rendezvous I saw you from a distance, as you came running and waving that day's edition of *Le Monde*: Moro had been kidnapped. We sat in the café – perplexed. We read the news. We were supposed to be discussing the Rue d'Ulm seminar – but who was in the mood for that? You started off with a blast of questions and hypotheses. An international manoeuvre, a conspiracy, Parliament, counterinsurgency, terrorism, approval of the Historic Compromise, coincidences, counter-intelligence programmes . . .? You went painstakingly through all the possible readings, adding them to the pile or discarding them. 'Why not the Russians?' I added, irritated. The absurdity of the situation – the obviousness of other people's attentive curiosity – I had no problem imagining 'smoking typewriters' everywhere, in press agencies and newsrooms – and also in the corridors of power: how repellent, the inevitable nod-and-wink complicity of the left intellectuals – my attention wandered away and I felt myself losing all motivation. I told myself that it would end up like in Mogadishu the year before, and like the Red Army Fraction after the Ponto and Schleyer affair.* I was wrong. This lack of motivation, however, was to be the main characteristic of my behaviour also in the months to come. The tragedy came slithering in like a snake – you were aware of the danger, but you couldn't measure the

---

* Translator's note: a reference to two RAF kidnappings.

strength of the poison. *Pictures at an Exhibition*. The enormity of the event. He, Moro, with incredible skill and an intelligence born of despair, strove to make the whole story even more far-reaching and enriched it with true substance, through his letters during the two months of his captivity. The disclosure of a politician's humanity, as we know, is a topos of classical tragedy. The pity elicited could be profound.

Anyway, let's get back to us. When the brain can't handle the object in question, the will does not engage. Certainly there were some banal truths that could be stated immediately: these lunatics have raised the stakes beyond all reason; in their lack of rootedness they are running wild with a stubborn arrogance; they are an out-of-control variable within the revolutionary movement. But these were, precisely, banal truths. It would have been easy for me to reconstruct the inner trajectory that had led to all this. Domestic stories. Italian and German. The ragings of ideology and the lack of intelligence in the movement. *Übergang der ersten zur nächsten Etappe der Guerrilla* [Transition from the first to the next step of the guerrilla war]. Paroxystic optimism of the will, and a void of strategic rationality. Between the human condition of the terrorist Chen* and the nihilism of Nechayev there are infinite variations, but their efficacy is always imposed, whether passively or actively, by the movement. Now, in their isolation, the Red Brigades were hurtling towards Nechayev – and soon they would be entirely enmeshed in him. Banal truths. And on the other hand, as the days and weeks passed, you realised how far their madness had infected the people in power – now it was stuck to them like an old tin can tied to the tail of a cat. From that March to the Spanish-style ceremony in Santa Maria Maggiore, the story moved between the grotesque and the macabre – violence and irrationality, geometry and madness. Conjoined? No, simply mixed together. The tears of the politicians, the business at Lago della Duchessa, the hypocrisy, the cold wrath of the bureaucrats, Via Gradoli . . . And what was the result? That funeral mass in Santa Maria Maggiore became, unexpectedly in terms of liturgical practice, the baptismal moment of the emergency, and it contained all the fury that old hags might put into procuring an abortion and a resentment towards oneself that could be placated only by striking at others. There is no sight more obscene than the desire for revenge of an inept

---

* Translator's note: Chen Ta Erh is an assassin in André Malraux's 1933 novel *La Condition humaine*.

political class. Giovanni Montini [Pope Paul VI], tired and humble cleric that he was, did not deserve to be involved in that terrible ceremonial. In Hofmannsthal the great Almoner welcomes the beggar while at the same time he rejects the king – and he laughs at the king. Prophetically. Yet this was not what troubled us so deeply, mon cher David. The fact was that the frame of reference of political initiative had been completely and irrationally dislocated. We had no foothold anywhere. And here, in these conditions, analysis had to be radically renewed. It became increasingly apparent that the kidnapping had not been carried out against Power; this latter had not been soiled by even a drop of that blood, which might have been pumped by the hypothetical heart of the state – the kidnapping had been an expropriation conducted against the initiatives of the new social subjects. It was an expropriation of the movement. The listlessness, the disgust, as we watched and followed the journalistic and institutional progress of the negotiations – we knew that we had to go beyond that and turn our attention rather to analysing the nature of this wild variable and to identifying the position it now occupied in the political life of the country. The problem could not be ignored, just as we could not delude ourselves that the radical mystification of the political framework of the class struggle set in train by the fanatical undertaking in Via Fani could be swiftly moved aside.

You were asking me, David: But who are these Red Brigades, what do they want, by what heaven are they blessed, and what trip is their drug promising them? Everyone knows who they are – I answered. They are the old labour movement, the Carbonari of an impossible revolution – because their revolution is and always will be a revolution of labour – desperate advocates of an eternal 1917, hooked on an ideology that is faithful and reassuring. Terrorism is for them a form of productive labour. Their logistics is a little factory, their organisation is a small and rapacious capitalist firm, their ideology is a project of accumulation, and their clandestinity is a means to reduce business risks. Their consciousnesses are functions of a calculation of profit. At that time, of course, we had not seen the final product of this particular assembly line: the maximisation of murders and then the optimal output of repentance, the weary business of the thirty pieces of silver, the morality and consciousness that were as wasted as people's lives. Nothing they did would have surprised us: what difference is there in fact between those who expropriate delegation rights and rights of control of the masses and those who sell lives to get an insurance bonus? The Red Brigader exists in the realm of production, the repentant terrorist in that of distribution – of death and distress.

The state has only one foul act of intelligence to fulfil in their regard: to treat them as part of itself, to monetise them as equivalents. The Red Brigade recruiting took place in the folds and crevices of that imposing ruin that called itself the official labour movement, and it developed during a period of major uncertainty about that movement's ability to hold on to its corporative power in the factories, in a pervasive and stubborn ignorance about the transformations that were taking place in society, in a nostalgia for an idealised past – the Resistance, the horny-handed sons of toil, and so on – and under the illusion of a possible future restoration. Does the future have roots in the past? Certainly, they tell you – half of them are Stalinists, and the other half are party-line trade unionists – and you see them shed a big tear. The hypocrisy of traditional noble sentiments includes the desire to kill. Just as the small capitalist entrepreneur is a good paterfamilias, so that his exploitation of others goes hand in hand with a concern for the welfare of his children – so the killing of Moro becomes the highest act of a revolutionary morality. It is probably true in this ethic of emotion, or rather in this aesthetics: the only thing that is missing is the sense of the productivity of life and of the responsibility of the masses – which, for a communist, are everything.

(But is there not, within the very culture of the Resistance, a basic defect, a kind of unresolved legacy, as a remote feud that reappears cyclically in different generations? Sometimes I thought this – but Peter Weiss and Peter Bruckner and very many other comrades came to my assistance and explained how the Resistance had been a renewal of life and a struggle against terror. No, what we have here has nothing to do with the Resistance. Here the terror develops not from a lived past, but on the immobile time of ideology – an extreme, physiological function of an ideology that has become absolutised and dead. The Calvinist king-killer is not reducible to the crazed Jesuit who kills King Henri IV de Navarre . . .)

From the Red Brigades' point of view the Moro operation was brilliant. As mountain folks say, if you give a child grappa to drink, you make the child drunk. The outcome of the operation, in itself adventurist and illogical, was to unleash indiscriminately the violence in play, such as exists at the origins of every subject of transformation, in the internal confusion of the new movement, in the laborious business of its growth as an alternative. Cruelty of behaviour and crudeness of ideology were supposed to stand in for the work of communist education that the new proletariat, in its mass form, was pursuing for itself. Did our heroes succeed in this project? In part, yes – for two reasons. First, through the refined intuition – which, by chance, they had – of the crucial moment in the development of the movement; and, second, because Power, with a sudden and ferocious initiative of terror, welcomed this opportunity.

Here, at this conjuncture, we can understand entirely the so-called emergency. This word, by some strange lapsus of the system, still maintains its originary strength and purity: it is a noun conveying the idea of emergence, of the new, of innovation. Power appropriates and distorts its meaning and, out of hatred for the dynamism of transformation and for the sudden happiness of becoming, it blocks it into a concept of *state*: the state of emergency, the state of necessity. To destroy the emergence. *Rechtsputsch*. Emergency becomes exception, a Schmittian essence, for every advocate of the immobility of power and of its metaphysical nature. And then, blackout – the blackout of news and information – another magic watchword of those circumstances – power needs secrecy in order to gather the forces of antidemocratic repression – the dirty character of the state in its most basic essence cannot be allowed to be seen. *Blackout* – there's another paradoxical lapsus, before it becomes a deliberate mystification – we recall the blackout in New York, the carnival of reappropriation that broke out the preceding year – do you remember the incredible beauty of the spectacle, cher David? And now the blood pact between cruelty and stolidity took 'emergency' and 'blackout' as its weapons, gave them (unjustifiably) finalities of constitutional order, and decided on a counterattack. To destroy the new movement. The time had come – the very moment at which the poor body of Moro was found. And the pity of the situation was great. When you can no longer distinguish the face of authority from the sneer of arrogance and revenge, then, as any good interpreter of Corneille knows, the passage to the horrid – to terror, torture and murder – is theatrically justified. Seventeenth-century tragedy is a great repository of these characters. Every aporia must be removed: and what is new is the aporia of the form in which power wishes to be, of its claim to an eternal return. The figure of power has to be restored at any cost. The identification between state and civil society must be coercively guaranteed. From that year of 1978 a new state massacre extended outwards, as a mystified claim over the common good – in heinous laws, in gratuitous and exemplary killings, in thousands of years of prison sentences, in juridical and administrative perversions, in torture, in vindictive propaganda – yes, admittedly in the face of many unspeakable crimes that represented the ever-renewing constancy of the terrorist variable – but above all against the emergence of any innovative behaviours in society and in the factories. With mutual satisfaction, terrorism was being played by the state as an essential moment of legitimation in its repressive action against the emerging social subject. With the addition, when red terrorism was not enough, of railway bombings and crimes against the masses. As for political–economic repression, inflation, unemployment and so on, they continued to operate with their customary efficacy. The reduction of complexity was achieved through the application of state terror. A corrupt and inept leadership accepted this without my evident reluctance, in stupid self-complacency.

How much shame has oozed out since that time! That freedom is indivisible is a sure given of critical intelligence – so the wounding of this indivisibility inevitably has consequences. So the powers of the state began working more and more in terms of emergency, making themselves clandestine, refusing to be open and public, and tending increasingly to merge among themselves and to turn these invisible dynamics into suitable weapons in the pursuit of feuds between one group and another. The dissolution of juridical guarantees for some set the conditions for a ferocious war of all against all. Those who came most exposed into this arena paid the highest price – those who live by the sword die by the sword. The misadventures of the sorcerer's apprentices of the traditional left then went on to brighten our days – even if we were in prison. The policy of no concessions: a rigour of repression that destroyed every certainty of the law, which transformed the guilty into the innocent – after having put the blame on, and having killed, too many innocent people. Parodying a terrible and looming danger, political parties and corporations thus adopted, in their unfriendly relationships, the methods they used to use against their external enemies: internal hostilities in the constitutional parties went into overdrive. In defending his own life, Moro had offered descriptions that now seemed more like curses. His letters, huge in their sudden wisdom, became an unpredictable, powerful, drifting, threatening object: they denounced a lived reality that was a system. Corporatism is to constitutionalism what terrorism is to the movement.

If I pause here for a moment and try to define a general mapping of the meanings offered by that particular set of events, I think we can say that we were witnessing a process, as powerful as it was new for Italy, of a symbolic transfiguration of class conflict. The extraordinary dimensions of the struggle that the development of the new social subject had brought about, and that had imposed themselves – in the globally social figure in which they were represented – were now, through the operations of the state of emergency, traversing the entire institutional context. But this subsumption of the conflict by the state was merely formal – in other words it was closed within the symbolism of terrorism and was charged only with the meanings that the two parties – the terrorists and the state – attributed to it. The true fabric of the class struggle, the true effectual adversary – in other words, the movement of the new social subject – was not recognised. Except in formal terms. The new subject was reduced to a phantasm; its wealth and social autonomy were constrained within the reductive and malevolent figure of terror. But when the real terms of the conflict are mystified to such an extent, only madness and brutality remain: the independent variable of terrorism was matched by a mirror image resulting from the collapse of the system of power. The Italian autumn was tropical – filled not with mists but with destructive cyclones. A state wretchedly poor in democratic traditions underwent a decisive incentive for its own illiberal and administrative overdetermination, with blind and unthinking determination. The emergence of the new subject was blindly attacked and transformed into a legal state of emergency. A Jacobin meteor crossed the Italian sky. Ideas of the compact solidarity of institutions were joined together with notions of public security; the informational blackout appeared as an act of political pedagogy; those who opposed it were hysterically denounced as enemies of the constitution. In reality, we went from a symbolic transformation of reality to a suspension of reality. Not demonstrative facts, but only the indices of violence showed this now. This is exactly what Moro was denouncing in his letters. So had the terrorists won? How could anyone think of this as a victory, the fact that like was accreting upon like? That the blackmail of the Red Brigades could be conjugated with the interests of the ruling parties? This is merely an entropic reaction, a relationship of death.

If you give a child grappa to drink, the child gets drunk, but then remains teetotal for life – that's the completion of the homely proverb. However, between jail and exile, between police repression and trade union repression, the movement now began its new 'long march' – or, if you prefer, a large-scale and solid initiative of maturation and reorganisation. Intent on recapturing reality. (Thank you, David, for the quotation from Origen. The living are saints; the saints are living.) Leave aside the arrival, every once in a while, of the *angelus novus*, symbol and event of sudden transformations – struggle for peace, community struggles for housing, new workers' struggles, freedom struggles in prisons – articulations of one single theme. But more on this later.

So, David, let us return to our reflections of that time and to our conviction of the substantial correctness of the point of view adopted. But – and today we can admit it – how abstract and ineffectual our conviction was! A position that was politically untenable in that transitional phase. And not only that. With a certain masochism, we realised that this position of a double confrontation, with the terrorism of both sides, was not only tactically unsustainable but also strategically immature. But what was to be done? The precipitation of the conflict rendered impossible the proposition of reason – one was reduced to a position of mere witnessing. Hence, again, our lack of motivation. Hence that paralysing sensation that comes from having to transfer the strong ethical insistence of the collective on a terrain of a future proposal and to entrust it to a return of propitious times. But was it possible? This tragedy that we were living, was it not rather a sign of the end of times? Was it not the case that from now on the situation would be blocked around the polarity of war, in a definitive and cruel manner? The temptation of catastrophism is strong when the historic presence configures catastrophe as the immediacy of the *Lebenswelt* [lifeworld]. But does this immediacy not change also the meaning of catastrophe? If the catastrophe is not just a transient and contingent element – but is rather the normal determination, the metaphysical meaning of our living in this time, the epochal and ontological sign of our collective existence – what then? Beyond the groans of power and its desire for revenge, beyond the mad cunning of terrorism, the catastrophe was only an effectual condition. All were products rather than causes of this. Why, then, let oneself be taken by some superficial ambiguous alternative? To avoid a few years in prison?

There were those who did that, with hasty and impromptu demonstrations of obsequiousness to power. But above all there were those who built the pressure, together with us, from within the official labour movement, interceding, through cultural mediation, to help us avoid prison. The blackmail, albeit softened by the refined style, remained what it was. And yet the style and the speech should not be underestimated, in their paradoxical and cynical valency. We pushed toward the dissolution of our double rejection – of the institutions and of terrorism – insisting instead on an alternative: either in the institutions or in terrorism, in other words either within dialectics or against dialectics. What difference does it make, in fact? The important thing, the persuaders added, is to take nihilism as the only present terrain: the nihilism of the institutions that are empty of value, or that devastating nihilism of terrorism. Choose. Yes, they may be equivalent – but the one leaves you free, while the other lands

Letter Eighteen: Moro

you in jail. An honest, practical compromise on the cynical paradox of a pervasive nihilism. Or a mechanicist seventeenth-century temptation! We laughed – a Pascalian response? – we laughed, we, unique among many, at the blandishments of the choices on offer. And that gave Calogero his starting point.

But is there really not a third way? Of course there is, it is present, it is given. Not third but first. It is within the desire for transformation. It is the possibility of the new subject being constitutive, alternative – constitutional. It arises precisely from the fact that the catastrophe constitutes the originary terrain of our existence – a division that can no longer be mediated, that is socially fixed, so that value cannot consist in any relationship with power but exists as autonomy, as separation, as non-homologous and nondialectical construction of a new productive force. If it's war, then let us direct it the way it was commanded by the genius that presided over Brest-Litovsk: neither with the one nor with the other, neither with the Germans nor with the Russian nationalists, but against both of them in terms of class, against the political embrace within which they are qualified. The appeal of the old revolutionary constitutionalism, which is able to give each part of reality its proper place – Calhoun: not contract but compact – enough of the dialectic of the Jacobin general will! – the constitutional position of proletarian autonomy. A revolt and an insurrection, both constitutional; and banish all temptations to Jacobinism and dictatorship.

If only we had been able, mon vieux David, to push this awareness to the limit at that time! But we couldn't. We watched, with despondency and disgust, the fulfilment of that which we lacked the power to block. And the one who lacks strength is often wrong. But what an enormous growth, what a dislocation of the collective consciousness was brought about by this series of unspeakable events! In Moro's grave was a closing of the first republic and its historic opposition. It was not buried by virtue of the terrorists or the ineptitude of the system – or at least they were not the protagonists. The author had been the movement of the 1970s, the development of the struggles of the new proletarian subject. But now the main character was absent. Theatrical masks, contrived characters ran after these events, but all that was present of the protagonist was only disgust for the horrible game played over life. We, who had worked so hard on the workers' and proletarian overcoming of the first republic, were effectively overwhelmed, both by the tragic form in which the event, the long-awaited event, took place, and by the mess of the outcome. As always, in our case the tragedy necessarily had to have a tinge of irony: in this case we had to pay, ironically, the price of the out-of-timeness of our intelligence. Thus, cher David, while you were reading aloud the news of the kidnapping of Moro, I was looking at the clear sky outside the windows of the café and I was smiling: no, these fools have not destroyed the hard and beautiful core of the real, no, they have not constrained us, the struggle goes on. The sky and the transformations of class consciousness will always be able to sustain the long and effectual times of the revolution. If Moro's death marked the end of the first republic, it also marked the entry into the mature phase of the revolutionary project of the new subject. It marked the point at which constitutional transformism, the compromise of the existent, would no longer have been possible. The new constitutional battle of the proletariat had opened – and, sooner or later, once the last corpse-like representatives of the first republic were moved out of the way, it would become effectual. There, one half of me flying with a desire for knowledge, and the other prisoner of a past that I saw uselessly reproducing itself, I was wondering what my future was going to hold. And I saw the difficulties in it. However, hope did not fail. That history is badly made, of this there is no doubt: and even if you anticipate the way in which it renews itself, you find yourself driven into a corner and anyway you risk being covered by the fallout of the event. History laughs at your solitude. But if the solitude is that of a collective desire, it does not stand up and it will be welcomed into a new position of being, into the project of its innovation. With tenderness you hold firm to this principle, even when the violence of events slaps you in the face. And to curses you bring discussion, to bewilderment you bring hope. In short, an ironical Job. On the other hand, the snake of tragedy was crawling close – but it would not succeed in copulating with the earth, as the ancient myth would have it. The land was dry, as dry as the new ontological potentiality of the subject. Everything that was happening would have just slid over it, worthy of beasts and not of human beings. Here a new epoch had begun. With a full sense of the tragedy we lived, I embrace you . . .

Letter Nineteen
Ferocious Alphabets

Rebibbia, 26 March 1982

Really, cher David, if I had to weigh my life – like those Indian gentlemen who are weighed on the scales against bars of gold – I would have to conclude, like Groucho Marx, that I've worked up from nothing to a state of extreme poverty. The strange thing is that I am incapable of taking weights and measures seriously. As the attorney general told me during the questioning after 7 April: 'But don't you understand that you are possibly facing life imprisonment!' – No, I do not understand. Then he added: 'You don't seem to have your feet on the ground.' Ah no, I certainly do have 'my feet on the ground'. I have spent all my life following the spatial indications of the other Marx, the communist, the materialist. It is just that weights and measures, directions and orientations are relative and manifold, and now, as things stand, the systems are neither credible nor unifiable. The paradox of capitalist development consists in this: the most enormous work of unification of the world has definitively split it into two, and master and servant are no longer part of the same family but are two separate races, each with its own civilisation. Jehovah is not the metric yardstick in Sèvres, whatever Bernard-Henri Lévy may think. The bosses feel this truth intermittently. So offensive do they find it that they must distance themselves from a continuous perception of it. No less effective, however, is this intermittent consciousness that they have opted for, and they label deviant and subversive behaviours 'criminal' – simply because these are material from another culture. Then they force you to honour their pantheon: Richelieu, Robespierre and Rothschild – the three Rs of terrorism – protean unifiers of a difference that we maintain intact, of a world that is not ours.

Letter Nineteen: Ferocious Alphabets

Cher David, at midnight on 6 April 1979 we said goodbye to each other – at the Gare de Lyon. By midnight on 7 April I was in Rovigo Prison. While I was fitfully dozing on the train that brought me back to Italy, unaware of the *voyage au bout de la nuit* [voyage to the end of the night] on which I was embarking, they had already turned on the flashing signal of repression against me and my comrades. I was not particularly surprised by the arrest, which followed one of the many searches to which I had been subjected in those years. What did amaze me, however, was the heading on the charge sheet: 'armed insurrection against the powers of the state . . . the armed group known as the Red Brigades . . . the killing of Aldo Moro'. As for what followed, you read it in the papers. Never was a judicial vagary more egregious. Never was a provocation more blind. Subsequently, the sarabande of self-justifications designed to cover the political responsibilities was shameful. To correct the situation, they complexified it – after having set in train a major repressive plan, justice sold itself off to a bunch of utterly implausible repentant terrorists, to filthy rogue killers. Oily legal operators would remove one of the charges, only to replace it with another, so that grotesquely the sum totals of homicides varied between twenty and one – because at least one always had to remain in place, as a kind of sleep-walking guarantee, for the forces of justice, of the possibility of life imprisonment. Yes, life imprisonment, or what the attorney general chose to call being 'down to earth' – or the long journey on the Sentier des chamois in the highest clouds, which in my case meant moving from one special prison to another. (Rebibbia G8, clinical asphalt, only asphalt – sounds and noise reach you in attentuated form – unless it's some prisoner on drugs, screaming out his torture. Fossombrone, wooden . . . everything creaking – an archaic prison, gutted and rebuilt in line with the modernity of new repressive functions, and all the more cruel as a result. Palmi, steel – it screeches in the wind, metallic, and the abstract screeching penetrates into your brain and everything sounds like an out-of-tune violin. Trani, all concrete – a cursed prison – it has a railway running alongside – at night the whistle of the train carries away your hope. Rebibbia, yellow. Fossombrone: the blue of the Umbrian fades into a dirty brown. Palmi, greenish. Trani, grey.) A mad round of prisons, and unbearable tiredness. In the special prisons I was confronted with a past that had been petrified. Anger and desperation that didn't know how to make themselves political. Combatants incessantly restating their vocation of death – Japanese soldiers keeping on fighting for decades after Hiroshima, in honour of the Mikado, in some jungle in the Pacific. I was crushed on this landscape.

In its small way, in its improvised nature, the political–policing operation of 7 April was an action of great design and of overbearing mystifying efficacy, a Schmittian *Entscheidung* [decisionism] by the bosses and their baleful allies and avengers. O you, poor Communist Party, of what dark nemesis did you make yourself the bearer, with your subpatriotic compromises? They had recognised the real enemy, the social enemy, the class enemy, the new subject in his separateness, and with 7 April they had sought to crush him. But this operation took place in the powerful ambiguity of the normative will of the state: in this ambiguous space, crushing is also to recuperate the enemy to oneself, to describe the enemy as part of oneself, to name it as a terrorist face of power. To restore juridical meaning, to reorganise things into categories of crime, to homologate the other race, all in order to relegitimate the unity of a divided power: this is what the symbol of 7 April represented. I understood the operational logic of the accusation; its infamy consisted not in regarding me as an enemy but as an homologous one, in destroying my difference along with my identity. A lightning operation – a reactionary *jetzt-Zeit* [present time] – a reduction of reality and of time to the immobility of destructive legal norms – a cursed blasphemy against the creativity of collective life. On the other hand, the initiative sought to be, and was, a broad underlining, with a big brush, of the end of the 'Italian case' – of that continuity of struggle and proletarian uprisings that the previous twenty years had experienced. The end of the Italian case: this could be a fortunate and 'catastrophic' innovation, I told myself, the beginning of a new history of the new subject: the repression can serve to highlight the dissymmetry of the transition and of the dislocation of the subject . . .

Consolatio philosophiae!* In fact a vague theoretical consciousness cannot always sustain the weary labours of practice. In prison, in the early days, the temptation was to let go of the moorings and set off, to allow my old but secure boat of independence and proletarian autonomy to drift along. It was less wearisome to accept the double diktat to which the state and the terrorists subjected you. It is hard to survive in jail, in the grip of this vice. In prison you become a monk, and you can also become a bad monk – *nec cella ei cella, sed reclusio et carcer est, aut sicut viventi sepoltura* [for him, the cell is not a cell

---

* Translator's note: an allusion to Boethius' *Consolation of Philosophy*.

but a space of reclusion and a prison, or something like a tomb for the living]*: this is how the medieval Cistercian apologist describes the situation. Continuous flashes of death were assailing you from the inside and from the outside: no one who did not live it – that season of ordinary murders – can imagine its abominable cruelty – 'ferocious alphabets' – a war whose parties, according to the attorney general, had their 'feet on the ground' . . . *et tant pis pour l'angélisme* [and so much the worse for angelism]! You have to be either on this side or on that; they tell you so – repeatedly and obsessively. Mars, like Janus, has two faces. Either a repenter or a 'Japanese' combatant, like all those who had their 'feet on the ground'. But the earth goes round, I protested to myself. As far as I was concerned, though, the only thing that was going round was my head, at least for as long as I still had it attached to my body, in this war of fools – but for how much longer would it remain attached? Occasionally, in some special prison somewhere, they did take off people's heads – *grunf, grunf,* with a lump of iron. Prisons that were grade A butcheries. And outside: this was the time of the massacre in via Fracchia. We had to break, break that cage, tear off that hood, fracture that logic. You have to do it, I told myself on the very first day of special prison. But you can't do it. Every movement is mechanically immobilised; it's like being in a big popcorn machine where you are pushed out from the middle to the walls, and wheat and millet and sugar turn into sweet stuff.

What an effort, cher David, to regain a foothold. And what illusions! The movement – you told yourself – or you whispered to the few comrades you had – will regain its identity, and its irreducibility to this insane armada of two sides will become clear again. A movement of liberation that comes forward and looks at you? An illusion of transcendence. Idiot. Pointless. That is where we were, and it was there that we had to settle our accounts and regain our dignity, right there in jail. The movement, if it was to be reborn – and it was likely to be reborn – would find itself beyond the end of the Italian case, and would therefore be supported on the deployed reality of the new subject. It was for this that we had worked, this global dislocation was what we wanted – so the new movement would not have recognised us as fathers because this movement, at its origins, did not want fathers. It was not patricidal but virginal. *Sprachlosigkeit* [speechless-

---

* Translator's note: probably a quotation from memory of a passage from a *Letter* (*Epistola seu Tractatus ad Fratres de Monte Dei*) of Guigo, fifth prior of the Chartreuse monastery: *sic ei cella est quasi carcer aut sicut viventi sepultura* (*Epistolae*, 200–201.5.11).

ness]: do not utter, do not talk, do not repeat, do not remember: that's the meaning of it. But we, yes, we would have been able to recognise it – once again – as a creative sign, and this recognition would have renewed us. The way to recompose oneself within the movement could not therefore be based on brainpower, but had to form itself on the tracks that the movement was signalling, or those warning signs that we intuited. It was a way, a poor but potentially powerful way, an extreme outer edge of a life that was defended, the only one that prison left us: our body, our bodily community. For the good monk the cell is *domicilium pacis, secretum templum, officina pietatis* [the home of peace, a secret temple, a workshop of piety]. It was necessary to work on the body, in the same way that the movement worked on the body. *Aufstand der Körper* [the insurrection of the body]! The opposition is not between life and death but between death and the body – because all the rest of our life had been taken from us.

And yet all one needed was to think a little, and one realised that we had not lost our sense of direction. All the communist theoretical research, around and after 1968, had in fact been going in this direction: from the phantasm of the party as body to the discovery of the collective body. A great classic exploration *De corpore politico*.* It does not matter if explorers fail in an uncharted territory – theoretical research leaves traces and hypotheses. So then, let's pick them up. Let's strip the flesh off the ideology to refind the community, let's articulate the community in order to invent the body. From the body as the last sign of your individuality and existence – as prison would wish it – to the body as a collective substance of communication and of organisation. Let us reappropriate the body through a practice that empties out the meaning of prison, of deprivation and isolation. Cher David, only since the prison struggles took on this dimension was the dreadful pincer grip of state and terrorism broken. On the design of corporeality you rebuilt life. Listen to Spinoza: 'no one has yet determined what the body can do'; 'he who has a body capable of a great many things has a mind whose greatest part is eternal.'† I rediscovered, cher David, what I had desired – in a collective hope that ripped chains off and turned prison into a laboratory of liberty. While the terrorists were killing people and the state was lucky to gamble its legitimacy on piles of corpses, while legal incivility was

---

* Translator's note: *On the Political Body*, the title of Thomas Hobbes's treatise.
† Translator's note: Baruch Spinoza, *Ethics*, Part III, Proposition 2 scholium; Part V, Proposition 39; pp. 155 and 265 in Curley's translation (see Letter Ten).

advancing with Nazi arrogance and betrayal became the exclusive source of truth in our trials, we, in the prisons, joined our resistance to terror to a claiming of a new collective revolutionary body. *In dubio pro libido* – or a will to live, a desire to innovate – collectively. Communism is a race, a way of life. The new prison movements, from San Vittore to Rebibbia, on the right to affectivity and on internal and external solidarity, moved from these early political intuitions. The transformation of the subject, the new cycle of proletarian self-valorisation, the *Vergleichung* [comparison], unity and equalisation of the strata of the socialised worker – all this we remade, *in vitro*, in a prison system that could not contain us because we were too many and too large and beautiful. The belly of the whale could not hold Jonah.

And so it has to vomit him out. On 28 December 1980, in Trani Special Prison, there was a revolt against conditions in Asinara Special Prison. Like Japanese soldiers from a war long since over. In a *coup de main* the Red Brigades kidnapped warders from the political prisoners' wing. They connected their action to the D'Urso kidnap, which was underway at that time, and they started sending out hallucinatory messages. The state decided to fight fire with fire. On 30 December, as the revolt was running out of steam, the state shows its infinite power as apocalypse – special forces landed from helicopters onto the prison roof, using explosives to break through the gates and walls, and firing wildly. They took us all into captivity and subjected us to a fearsome lynching. It was the body – the extreme poverty and extreme richness of your body – that had to be suppressed. A massacre ensues. They destroy and devastate everything in sight. The few means of reproduction of your body, your books and notebooks, letters from loved ones and postcards from your children: they tear them up, destroy them and drown them in piss. They throw you down the stairs; they split heads; they hammer you with lumps of wood, on your knuckles and your knees; they lash your ribs. The state unleashes the lumpen. When you have run the last gauntlet of the murderous thugs, you finally end up in an open space where you can rest. Your head is bleeding. You put your bloodstained hands on the concrete walls, making meaningless arabesques. But it's not over yet. During the night the lumpen return to the attack: 'Kneel, son of a bitch'; 'Beg for forgiveness'; 'Your wife sucks cock'; 'Communist shit' . . . The winter night is wet, God has spat out this thick dew. A huddle of men embraced, holding each other close to resist the wounds, the cold, the fatigue. There can be no stars on a night like this. Like whiplashes in the

Letter Nineteen: Ferocious Alphabets

dark, like freezing rays, the spotlights of those killers search you out. And the body just resists. Then, the next day and the days after that, huddles of men again, dozens at a time, in a big barn of a dormitory, like wagonloads of Jews on their way to Poland – to sleep at last, at least to sleep.

But you have to survive – and only struggle allows you to survive; the reaffirmation of your body and of the community of these bodies together. 31 December 1980: a New Year's Eve that is at once desperate and very sweet. The world is far away. You no longer know where you are. There has been a news blackout on what is happening to you. You have to regain a relationship of communication with the outside, at all costs. Drumming sounds from everywhere. People banging on the bars, on the doors, on the gates and the ironwork that close you in. A huge drumming noise, like the rumble of a subway tunnel, a sound that overwhelms you until your whole body is shaking. An incredible unity develops; the sound waves carry the pollen of solidarity. Proletarian unity is a high unity of the new social and intellectual labour power. What we have here is a low-level unity, abysmal but entirely human – the unity of poverty, of the body, of the wretched of the earth. Here you understand the metaphysical substratum of slavery: the negative limit of the human productive essence that is configured in it. The new body resists. Besieged in the cells, for one week, two, three, four . . . Masked individuals enter, fearsome and ferocious beasts. They beat, they search, they terrorise, they kidnap your comrades. 'You're going into solitary!' Sudden transfers. *Jetzt-Zeiten*, blitzes of death, and again there follows the stark capitalist negation of the time of life. You spend sleepless nights barricaded in. You defend yourself by collecting up garbage and throwing it into the corridors to prevent the incursions of the guards. Metres and kilograms of filth, mixed and muddy, all piled up. You're a rat now, caught in a deadly trap. But you must resist. I have never felt so much the need to cry, and never has my body so vigorously refused it.

Cher David, death is the enemy and the body is the friend. We lived a whole story, and it was neither more nor less than the parabola of the incarnation of the proletariat. The historical tragedy of the capitalist mode of production is the fullness of time. The end of time, the crisis, is a great renaissance. A great new body. Had it not been for this thought, which I had permanently stuck in my brain, I would have given in to the temptation of suicide, which often crept up on me. Rosenzweig: 'The terrible capacity to commit suicide distinguishes man from all other beings that we know and that we do not know.'* A shame of the spirit. I had my support from the body, from its hope. If there is spirit, then killing oneself is stupid – one does not die. You live again, petrified and unmoving, in the memory of other spirits. The body, on the other hand, does not want to die, because it is life – not something that comforts but something that produces. The body is a proposition of life. In the cells at Trani, where this extraordinary spectacle of resistance was running wild, you saw the body die in the misery of individuality and restructure itself into community. 'Against the destruction and colonisation of the body.' A gentleness, playing cards, doing tarot, delicate homosexual approaches, and then discussions, political polemics, rebuildings of the project, clashes, thoughts, feelings, reason, and a mutual and fraternal *Aufklärung* [enlightenment]. A transformation taking place in hell. *Freaklich in die Katastrophe* [Freaklike in the catastrophe].† Is this not the fate of the new subject? Is it not in this absolute misery that you recognise yourself to be part of the movement? And with you it grows to maturity? Is it not in this internal mediation that multiplicity becomes responsibility and community becomes tendency? Our animal spirits need all this, and there is no more than a pinch of utopia in this experience.

In fact this matter of the bodily community is a productive discourse – it is the *ens realissimum* [most real being], on which takes place the clash between the classes, to decide who will appropriate the effects of productivity and who will organise this collective productivity. In the cells of Trani we experienced at first hand a story of the modes of production. On the one hand, the custodians, the guards – enemy lumpen – in cahoots with the boss. On the other, the transformation and upwards equalisation of intellectual labour power, of the various class experiences. A division that was a diachronic section. Thus we experienced, and not just occasionally, a theoretical history of the working class and of its political transformation: from the composition of the party, universal and abstract, to this warm body of the communist community.

You come now, you policemen of high culture, you indecent Arbasini, you diplomats in pink, you angelic sewer rats, and you laugh at our warm community, sometimes wearing face masks, sometimes raggedy-arsed, but always, in the factories and in society, building and producing a condition that is denied to your position

---

* Translator's note: unidentified quotation.
† Translator's note: title of a 1979 article by Hartmut Schulze.

of nonproductive privilege, of whores, judges and voyeurs! But let's leave the dead to bury the dead.

The long journey into the underground world of imprisonment still continues. The '7 April case' is still here, cher David, refusing both the terrorist blackmail and the blackmail of the state, both of which are intent on the regulated homologisation of the body with the soul. Whereas our project is to destroy the soul, in whatever way it proposes itself. And to recognise the place of the body in the collective constitution of the proletariat. So I was living in prison the first concrete dimensions of a long-term project, the realisation of the new dislocation of proletarian composition. A major effort that nevertheless enabled us, within the continuing struggle, to be participants again, but now transformed, in the resumption of the movement. The whale gets shipwrecked, and Jonah finds himself on the beach again. Jonah, Ulysses – and then us; a shipwreck that repeats this eternal myth of renewal. Not an eternal return, but an eternal renewal: only jailers of thought can think of reducing the second to the first. A renewal that carries me continuously beyond 7 April, beyond the trial, beyond the countless skirmishes that this case entails. Outside of any possibility of rendering my memories homologous to the procedure and to the substance of the trial and to its logical circularity and unmoving sameness. Far from the 'ferocious alphabets' of this age of repression. The project of breaking the resistance of the body fails, the body testifies only to its corporeal nature, to what it is and what it becomes – it recognises no form of transcendence, not even judicial. It is irreducible to soul, to spirit, to an equivalence with justice. *Principium individuationis. Quantitate signatum* [The principle of individuation. Signed by quantity]. But then it is a body of higher qualities of expression and of communication.

Now, I don't know what more to add, cher David, except that in this I feel justified, both responsibly and morally, in the face of a story that is body – both mine and that of the collective, together. At bottom, if you think about it a bit, it is precisely by insisting like this on ourselves that we avoid the continuous frustration of a philosophical reduction of problems: we are fighting a life battle, solving the unattainable universal in the proposition of the collective – and, faced with nothingness and negation, we lessen them in the positivity of the body. Of course, the body is fragile. But it is capable of many things. It reproduces life and produces the world. The body is frail, but extreme poverty is an extraordinary force. For my part, I imagine communism as a great collective body that takes on board, transforms and enhances the productivity of the single individual. And don't start talking to me about Menenius Agrippa and organicism! This body is a surface of liberty. This body is made up of singularities from within, and they build and rebuild it indefinitely. It is for this reason that the only memory is of this collective subject – I do not know how much longer it will take to see it mature, but it is certain that this is the way I have lived it, and it is on this that my memory is hooked. I don't understand reasons that are not the strategies that this body has seeded and brought to life. So this is how I see the past, and I proceed to the next stages of my life as a prisoner – with pride in having participated in this. And with a great longing to see you all. Goodbye.

Letter Twenty
Renaissance

Rebibbia, 7 April 1982

Cher David,

I've been inside for three years now. I ask myself what has changed outside of prison – this helps to focus my restlessness. Once again, I have the sensation of being – in the parabola described both by the story of subjective liberation and by that of human emancipation – in a situation that is initiatory, propaedeutic. These conversations that I'm having with myself are elemental, even in the strong sense – rather than having the fragmented rhythm of philosophy, they are more like music in their flowingness. Pipeline. Here, in describing this structural morphology of the passions and the ways in which it affects me, in the confrontation with the violence of the other, my solitude finds a moment of reflection. I have completed one, two, three innumerable experiences. So, once again, a breaking point. A desire for a projectuality. New *Wanderjahre* [years of wandering]. (It is as if each time a transition has been accomplished and one has liberated oneself from the indistinction – in practical terms, by constructing a displaced composition – there arises a new scenario with new demands. This moving from one threshold to another is the form of my joy – and it is a creative overthrow of life.) On this new margin of being, freedom and knowing seek to turn themselves into potency – into collective organisation and into struggle for transformation. Freely, having burnt all memories and preconceptions. It would be worth the effort to collect these transition points within theoretical frameworks, if we were capable of the kind of powerful imagination that characterises the approaches of originary or very early ages – life's fables, morphologies in the manner of Propp's fables. Would that we were not ashamed of the sensual ideas of classical times – love, violence, knowledge! (And then – why not? – organisation and revolution. Are they not classical themes?) The reality is that we are faced with weaker and more adulterated narratives: emotionality, cynicism, utopia, set to the rhythm of admiration and determination – along these lines I recognise alternatives and motivations expressed in these letters – but there ought to be other ways of expressing this process of passions and overthrows. Relocating itself at ever higher levels of composition, being determines the productive power and the constitutive potency of the subject. Thus far I have considered these dynamics by following the track of my own lived experience. Now, on this edge of being, I would like to succeed – how eager I am about this! – to build a bridge over the void, to take a grip on the tendency. Being in prison both blocks and refines this possibility – it blocks the project of the body and locks it within experimentation, albeit a passionate one – but it also sharpens the bodily imagination, the first and most fundamental among the faculties of the collective experience. It lives by experimenting, and, in experimenting with the time that is not yet, it constitutes it. The horizon of the imagination is narrow when viewed from prison. Escape is difficult. And yet, between the contradictions, difficulties and small experimentations, the adventure of constitutive imagination has to be embarked upon.

Now, the transcendental is practical. I have found myself in recent years rereading its foundation, in Machiavelli, Spinoza and Marx – the three authors of the modern, anomalous and savage struggle against spiritualist metaphysics and its historical figure: the absolutist state of nascent capitalism. I took to it as to a beloved body. On the opposite face: the declaration of the formal nature of the transcendental lies at the base of concepts of representation and sovereignty and of the abstraction of the market and the political – and all this fits like a glove the boss's hand. There is no longer any room for these ideograms of exploitation. And yet, whether conscious or unconscious, they frequently emerge where you would least expect them, both in the refusal of the practical character of truth and in a creeping loyalty to spiritualist definitions. So I find myself alone and facing a certain hostility from the comrades when I reject the old communist aphorism 'pessimism of the intellect, optimism of the will'. But I ask: when a task out of symmetry with reason is entrusted to will – is it not the case that the transcendental, the collective and the tendency become a spiritual and independent presupposition rather than a practice? A presupposition that is as prudent and cautious as the will can be terroristic and crazy? It seems to me, instinctively, that 'pessimism of the intellect' is an ideology of economic determinism and 'optimism of the will' is a statement of Jacobinism. And so what, then? So imagination and the desire of doing, the desire for project, for a transcendental that is absolutely practical reverse the aphorism, so that it becomes 'optimism of the intellect and pessimism of the will'. In order to establish an ethics rationally and to take it as a horizon of the bodily imagination and thus as a project of constitutive liberty. Rationality cannot be either determinism or valuelessness if it is capable, before all else, of grounding itself in practice. (And so we shall also erase the word 'transcendental').

Rationality is a passion in the strong sense. The prohibition of the possibility of passion, which prison's regime of isolation and deprivation imposes, is thus a ban on reason and a limitation of it. And this, cher David, is the cause of my great tiredness. But I am resisting – imagination has resisted and has helped us not to be expelled from the realities of the political movement. Indeed, precisely in this solitude, with this angst in our bodies – 'pessimism of the will' – albeit with a head that is not capable of giving up the pleasure of reason and of modulating its sensual systems in imagination – 'optimism of reason' – I find that I am there too, there with the movement in the whole of Europe, between the end of time and new hope. With that same attentiveness with which, in 1981 and also before, we followed what was happening in Amsterdam, Zurich and Berlin – *die grosse Bruch* [the big break]. 'No future', the comrades said – but actually they were putting their future into practice, occupying houses and transforming them into community. And they were fighting – they had resumed the struggle – against the danger of nuclear war, against the proliferation of the nuclear industry, against the increasing militarisation of the territory and of the cities, against the destruction of the human biosphere, against the slavery of family relationships and the slavery of production, against unemployment and welfare cuts, against prison and torture. They had restarted the struggle. Where previous generations had wanted to build a future, this generation was asking: do we still have a future? And the anguished reply was followed by a new, very powerful and rational 'here and now'. *Hier-und-jetzt-Denken* [thinking in the here and now]. What could be more constructive than this pragmatic and combative rationalism? If the whole of being can be unmade and destroyed, then being can also be constructed and made whole. It is a new radical Calvinism, a practice of predestination. A labouring *Beruf* [vocation] on the infinite distance and liberty of grace. Optimism of the intellect and pessimism of the will. There is nothing more important than this. One single condition: that this generation really is the product of the development of the struggles and of the long travail of theory, a Renaissance, the potency of all that desire for transformation – built, imagined and tested – in the preceding decades. For sure, *es ist nicht alles rot, was grünt*. Not everything that grows green is red. But, whereas for us, in many instances, the negative was preponderant and overbearing and the need to destroy had engaged people's consciousnesses in contradictory ways, now the constitutive content of negativity has revealed itself. What we have here is not transcendental sublimation, nor is it the old dialectical solution. The sublime is left only to the *grunfs*. For us there is instead a revolution that has already taken place, in bodies. 'Funny, wise and true' is the nature of this genetic appearance – an eternal happening of the ethical happiness of birth.

You see, cher David, this is precisely what the optimism of the intellect is based on: the fact that the fundamental determinations of the revolutionising, of radical transformation, are given in this situation. Otherwise we would not be able, with such irrevocable assuredness, to conceive only of what is dead as being our adversary and to see it irremediably depicted on enemy faces. Nor could we, without such a certainty, recuperate everything to our desire – the divisions would pass also into our own bodies, whereas in fact they do not affect the generative processes except by separating them from the old and the inert. This revolution is aggressive – it dissolves the separations that the tradition of exploitation had piled up. Being seeks to conquer the ontic. Being is whole within the positive pole of an antagonism whose other pole is the entirety of negativity. So let us work towards a constitutive hermeneutic, to an expressed genealogy of the future. Only death is placed there, at the front, as an enemy. And that is why bastards, reactionaries and bosses want us dead. The nuclear is the symbol of their state. Exterminism. Robert Oppenheimer says: 'the world is moving in the direction of hell with a high velocity, and perhaps a positive acceleration and probably a positive rate of increase of acceleration.'* With a degree of black humour E. P. Thompson adds: 'I don't think of the extermination of all forms of life. I just think of the extermination of our civilisation. That is no small matter.'†

The angst is reborn on this extreme limit – which is precisely that of the arrogance of power. The angst that is born, however, becomes

---

* Translator's note: unidentified quotation.
† Translator's note: unidentified quotation.

immediately struggle for peace and revolt for life, construction of community, a concrete utopia in the relationship of collectivity. The dry images of my Veneto come to mind and, as if in a delirium, a parade of people and experiences, and all our attempts to think things in concrete terms, and the determinations of the struggle – the Petrolchimico plant, the faces of a thousand comrades, the courage, the hopes, the defeats, the sweetness, the love, the Golem – the gentle giant of my renewed adolescence, Torino-FIAT, Berlin, Manhattan, the turning points, the carnival, the ferocious alphabets of despair, of repression and of resistance – and always going beyond, moving from threshold to threshold, and living reason. I would say that the centuries have never seen such an extraordinarily massified Renaissance. It was a fullness of time. From around us disappeared all sense of guilt – guilt is only the stuff of Power, inherent to its existence, incarnated in its project of destruction. Power is *Schuldfrage* [the problem of guilt]. Revolution, on the other hand, is possible in peace, because people's consciousnesses are revolutionised. Power is despotism – revolution is freedom.

(Sometimes, talking about the world as we see it from prison, it amuses us to oppose two *Idealtypen*: the 'oriental despotism' of the tendency of capitalist power – be it bourgeois or socialist – and 'gothic government', that is, the appearance of castles, of communes, and, why not, of bishoprics – which represents the diffusion and the wealth of the new subjectivity and materiality of constitutional desires. Of course, all this happens on the basis of the enormous displacement that the computerised unification of the universe has brought about, on the deployed horizon of communication – so we should beware of the foolish image of craft solutions to problems, or of spending our time on Proudhonian utopias of the 'small is beautiful' variety or on the Camorristic institutionalism of our professors of law – the landscape of gothic government is universal and computerised – it is not the landscape of Neapolitan nativity scenes!)

It is here, then, on this displacement, that we measure the effectuality of the Renaissance. And the arrogance of the repressive anomalies that we are suffering. Cher David, with dark irony I sometimes think that this same prison that I am enduring is the effect of a nightmare Stalinism, taking place within a revolution in progress. A revolution has already happened – it is now being suppressed, just as it was in Russia in 1917, while it is still in its cocoon. But it nevertheless continues to expand its presence. We wait for it to give birth to a large multiformed butterfly. Remember Yalta? That solid sign of the counterrevolution, that syndrome from which we have suffered so much? For sure, it is not a worn-out old tool – but it is equally true that the status quo is unsustainable in the face of the new composition of the proletariat. Time resolves the past and its fatigues. Whereas the Soviet dissident movement, even in its most decidedly workerist aspect, still had a value that could be used in the eternal game of mirrors that was distorting reality – and it was indeed so used – Solidarnosc did not permit it any longer. It is a revolutionary movement that mediates the great means of the insurgency of the industrial worker with the complexity of popular culture and of the new layers of the intellectual and tertiary proletariat. This recognition, which traverses both the West and the East, of the necessity of a radical transformation, this maturing of the 'revolution in the two Germanys', very probably represents the true trend within which we are called to define our liberation. Poland, a continuing exception in European history in modern times, has now become, in a strong sense, its structural cypher. It goes without saying that the need for war and destruction turns entirely on this symbol – like on the *clinamen* [swerve] that innovates the vortices of physics. Stopping war and affirming peace is therefore revolution. Developing that constitutional dimension where the radical independence of the proletariat resides in the effectual possibility of consolidating itself and proceeding forward.

For this reason, cher David, it's so important to hold firmly to the extra-parliamentary and anti-constitutional character of the movements – not to exorcise eventual integrations or to avoid old and by now impossible compromises, not to exclude opportunist movements through institutions (which may be necessary expressions of the pessimism of the will) – but to guarantee the objective of reason, in other words the dynamism of the liberation of the subject. We are not gambling on opportunity, but on necessity. The point of view is not deterministic – and thus prey to an astute rationalising logic, illusorily stretched between adversities and defeats – rather it is necessary because it is given and must therefore unfold, and in the practice of its unfolding it becomes real. The point of view is not historicist – a ball of wool whose thread extends endlessly and without interruption. Break it, Ariadne, so that the legend does not repeat itself and life becomes new! – albeit constitutive and constitutional; it commits itself solely to the truth of the autonomy and independence of the subject. I am struck by the ontological radicalism of this configuration of the tendency – the fact that the refusal of work has become irreversible and insistent on the destruction of the working day and on the construction of community; that the concept of productivity is now being joined with that of knowledge; that social crisis is not the result but the premise of economic crisis; and that a completely new basket of goods of proletarian valorisation has affirmed itself, ruining the market and its blandishments. The real abstraction of exchange as a form of social synthesis is failing. (From within our societies, those selfsame obscene corporativisms that govern them are the proof of this.)

So a new constitutional form has to appear. But a new constitutional form is, first of all, a new way of being responsible. So what was this political responsibility of the bourgeois – then, in development, and today, in the crisis of developed capitalism? If such a concept ever existed, what is now left of it? Responsibility: it was, in origin, flight from the determination of the existent, and trust in a kind of weakened theodicy, such as the one personified by the market. It is now, of course, rejection of humanity – justified by the crisis and resolved in a universal and mystified projection of its necessity. There is no longer even faith in destiny – there is only a kind of expression of the will to potency, a sign of selfish misery, of an inner moral tearing, which in the lack of logical reference and determination becomes simulation. (The discussion on the life of Moro, and the negotiation, and the holding firm . . .) This world of a bureaucratic bourgeoisie has become an Aztec kingdom, David – our Castoriadis refers to this; for he recognises again, speaking of the USSR, the figure of world bourgeoisie: *de te fabula narratur* [the story is about you], as he already taught us. An Aztec kingdom, hierarchical and cruel. Thus a simulation of the universal, of the economic plan, of the emergency, of the common good. But is it not possible to have responsibility without simulation? Is it not possible to have responsibility in terms of tendency and of the collective? As a project? Is it not possible to have responsibility as revolution, intersubjectivity and community? And to make it materially real and juridically effective, this living concept? It is possible – in a constitutional process in which the functions of communication do not become determinations of Power and the potentialities of the subjects are recognised in their ontological force. If there is an ethical call, and therefore responsibility, they can today live only as the destruction of every mechanism of neutralisation of subjectivity and as sabotage of every process of alienation. *Aufstandsforschung* [study of revolt], as the sociologists put it. The concept of responsibility becomes constitutional only through the analysis of the insurgence of the subjects.

Cher David, do you remember Harrington's *Oceana*? I'm rereading it. In our situation we could repeat that very real, Machiavellian utopia. Harrington sees a monarchy or a republic as being based on the capacity of landed appropriation of the gentry or of the small peasantry: it is the amount of land appropriated by individual classes that determines the figure of the political regime. Now, for the criteria of land ownership that he uses to define the classes, let us substitute the themes of the appropriation of time and of the liberation of innovative needs that now characterise the proletarian strata. In this context, political responsibility is reborn as a concept, in the construction of free time – and the proletarian republic wins over the capitalist monarchy to the extent that the determination of time is actually in the hands of, and under the responsibility of, the *multitudo*. Liberated time is appropriation of the world of communication, insofar as it ties communication to production and to freedom – it is a republican reappropriation of being, a mass construction of freedom. A liberation of free projectuality.

It is on this terrain that the traditional labour movement – but also the mass Catholic movement, here as in Poland – has to be constrained. They are constrained. To the extent that works do not follow the historical felicity of the tendency, consciousnesses become a source of simulation and the political forces are delegitimated. I am not interested in the daily news – particularly when it's read from prison. What interests me is the tendency of this epochal transformation we are living. I am interested in this utopia that is becoming so real as to be domestic. I am interested in Solidarnosc – in other words, in the possibility of feeling the new *potenza* of this proletariat, which has become the sole source of the knowledge and of the development of this people of emancipated poor – and in how the *potenza* becomes liberation. Never as much as today did the urgency of cancelling the memory of the single articulations of the crisis of spiritual and political life – *consummatum est* – go hand in hand with the necessity of uncovering the accumulated potentiality.

For this reason it has been useful for me to write these letters to you, cher David – to review the past no longer as a past, but more like a future. (It's like when, here in prison, I remember a very sweet conjunction of love; and the perception is immediately a future, a desire that I live.) Gradually, one story has come to its end and another is beginning – and that transformation, which each of us has lived in oneself, each one has rediscovered as operating in reality . . . I call this the 'Niccolò da Cusa effect': the macrocosm is contained in the microcosm. Historical–social reality is commanded by a law of displacements produced by the collective consciousness of liberation.

From the point where the revolutionary workers' movement set out to oppose itself to the social organisation of capital, this law has become fundamental. And the process has finally reached this high level of *potenza*. A degree of potentiality that, in me, reproduces the indifference of the situation that I took as my starting point in this story, in the experience that is the plot of it – but only formally. What I mean is that we are all just as poor as when we were born, and in the indifference of a maternal womb we felt ourselves mixed up – but now we are immersed in a new indistinction and in a new love – the benefic Queen of the Night in Mozart's revolutionary story – and we recognise ourselves. A story of emancipation has begun again. The fact is that we do not have a politics, but we do not even have preconceptions and predeterminations. A projectuality: this reconstruction of ours is a rebirth, and our having removed all links with the history and the leftovers of the traditional labour movement gives us an enormous strength. In short, today the rebuilding of a revolutionary politics on a human scale is once again possible. This is why the indistinction in which we are living is only formal – actually it interferes on a surface that is transparent and powerful. A surface that is solid, a stronger and more sensitive skin, as happens to all animals after the winter and after moulting. The revolutionary class presents itself on the stage of today's society as the only force capable of dominating it. The proletarian class – the poor, the abstract labour power (intellectual, male and female) – is a law of society well before it is empowered to enact this law. Really we do not need to invent anything – but only to express, to build, to lay out positive proposals, to reveal what science and consciousness already possess. Here we can also reconcile ourselves with memory. In fact, today this emergence may turn out not to be simple rebellion, but the maturity of an effectual dominion. Without ever losing the restlessness of its subject. When this maturity of being proposes itself to us, we can decently call the passion of admiration our own – and here the production that we are capable of, and admiring, can and must develop itself into a practice of collective organisation and into the reconstruction of a theory of value on, and of, the complexity of the social fabric. But admiration, production, and consequent revolutionary organisation of value will always be synchronously traversed by new displacements and by processes of the collective consciousness moving towards even higher configurations. Solitude, violence, knowledge – love, suffering and freedom will renew once again the story of life. We are in the future – our present reflects some features of that future. Kojève, '*l'identité de la satisfaction et de l'insatisfaction devient sensible*' [the identity of satisfaction and insatisfaction becomes sensible]* – any abstract and transcendent premise, any dialectic are removed on the sinuous, ambiguous front of the human – on the horizon of transformative practice. The future has a relationship of reciprocity with the past – but it is ontologically prior to the past, even though in logical terms it comes after. And this is how I think of our friendship, cher David: projected forward, together. And I embrace you . . .

---

* Translator's note: Kojève's original words can be found in his lectures on Hegel's phenomenology (*Introduction à la lecture de Hegel*, Paris: Gallimard, 1947). For an English translation, see Alexandre Kojève, *Introduction to the Reading of Hegel: Lectures on the* Phenomenology of the Spirit *Assembled by Raymond Queneau*, edited by Allan Bloom, translated by James H. Nichols, Jr. Ithaca, NY: Cornell University Press, 1969.

Index

Adorno, T. 62
Afro-American revolution 188–9
Agamben, Giorgio 8
Algeria 52, 78, 84
Alquati, Romano 88
Alquié, Ferdinand 24
Althusser, Louis 59, 135
Amin, Samir 37
Amnesty International 52
anarchism
    and communism 173–4
Arendt, Hannah
    Eichmann in Jerusalem 150
Aristippus of Cyrene 147
Armed Proletarian Nuclei 2
Asimov, Isaac 7, 183–4
Auschwitz 47
autonomy of workers 97–106

Bachelard, Gaston 24
Bacon, Francis 101
Bataille, Georges 101
Benjamin, Walter
    Metaphysics of Youth 16
    Socrates 171
    'The Religious Position of the New Youth' 17
Bentham, Jeremy 174
Beolco, Angelo 15
Berlin 144–5
Berlinguer, Enrico 138
Bernanos, Georges 18
biographical materialism 6

Blake, William 183
Bloch, Ernst 31, 36, 60
Bloiy, Léon 26
Bobbio, Noberto 59–60
bodies and death 207–12
Boethius
    Consolation of Philosophy 205
Bollack, Jean 14
Borges, Jorge Luis 143
Bortignon, Girolamo, bishop of Padua 20, 22
Brecht, Bertolt 7, 41, 65
Brest-Litovsk, Treaty of 201
Brückner, Peter 60, 196
Bruno, Giordano 102

Cacciari, Massimo 144
Caiani, Matteo 59–60
Calhoun, John C. 137, 201
Calvinism 215
Calvino, Italo 8
capitalist development 32
    and the class struggle 154
    critique of 132
    and Judaism 65–6
    multinational 129, 130
    in the Veneto 17
    and the workers' movement 81–2, 87, 88
Capograssi, Giuseppe 59–60
Carducci, Giosuè 122
Carniti, Pierre 124
Castoriadis, Cornelius 219

Catholic church
  GIAC (Gioventù Italiana di Azione Cattolica) 24
  and historicism 47
  and the labour movement 25–6, 27, 29–30, 33
  priesthood 16, 20, 21, 22
  and utopianism 40
  in the Veneto 15–17, 19, 20–1, 30, 68
Chabod, Federico 46
Chesterton, G. K. 21
Christian democracy 16, 18
  and the Historic Compromise 138–9, 166
class struggle
  and capitalist development 154
  and historicism 47–8
  July 1960 movement 76–86
  and New York 186–7
  in Sicily 26
  and the state 176–7
  and terrorism 199
  in the Veneto 67–9
Classe operaia 101
Cohen, Albert 37
Commonwealth (Hardt and Negri) 1
communism
  and the body 211–12
  in Germany 61
  and humanism 59
  in Israel 36–40
  prison movements 208
  and the revolutionary movement 173–82
  and the transcendental 214
  in the Veneto 17, 73–4
  and worker autonomy 100, 101
  and the workers' movement in Italy 77, 83, 84, 88, 93
  see also Marxism; PCI (Italian Communist Party)
constitutional concept of responsibility 219–20
Contropiano 101
Corneille, Pierre 197
corporatism
  and terrorism 198
Cossiga, Francesco 181
Croce, Benedetto 32
Crozier, Michel 155
Curiel, Henry 37
Cusa, Niccolò da 220

death and the body 207–12
Declaration (Hardt and Negri) 1
Defoe, Daniel 177
Deleuze, Giles 10, 53, 54, 152, 160
democracy
  and the workers' movement 83
Democritus 39
Derrida, Jacques 101, 189
Descartes, René 6, 44
dialectical materialism 29, 30, 71
Dialektik der Aufklärung (Horkheimer and Adorno) 56
difference, affirmation of 10
dislocation 152–4, 160
Dolci, Danilo 25, 26

Ebreo, Leone 190
economic crisis
  and worker autonomy 99
Egypt 36
Einaudi, Giulio 1, 8
Empire (Hardt and Negri) 1
Epicurus 39
Erasmus of Rotterdam 166
Eratosthenes 95
Escher, M. C. 180

factory workers 2, 19, 20, 72, 82, 89, 90
  autonomy of 97–106
  and the events of 1968 121–2
  FIAT 156–61
  Petrolchimico plant 20, 98, 102–6, 107
  Porto Marghera 73–4, 98, 98–9, 108–10
  and the refusal of work 92–5, 149–50, 169, 218–19
fascism 32, 41
  and the Resistance 48
feminism 142, 143, 146, 149, 158–9, 167, 191
FIAT 88, 90, 94
  1973 strike 156–61
Fichte, J. G. 46
Finley, Moses 111

Forma stato 101
formalism 73
Fortini, Franco
  Argomenti 51
Fossombrone Prison 3, 4
Foucault, Michel 10, 39, 101
France
  Catholic protest in 24
  Negri in Paris 24–6
  Negri's exile in 9
Frankfurt School 57, 62, 64, 65, 154
future–past relationships 10, 221–2

GAP (Gruppi di Azione Patriottica) 78
Garin, Eugenio 47, 52
Gemeinschaft (communitarian spirit) 19
Genet, Jean 27
German philosophy 56–9, 65, 101
Germany
  anarchism in 107
  Berlin 144–5
  'revolution in the two Germanys' 218
Geschichte und Klassenbewusstsein (Lukács) 56
GIAC (Gioventù Italiana di Azione Cattolica) 24
Gioberti, Vincenzo 31
Giolitti, Giovanni 72
Golem 121–2, 128, 217
Gonzaga, Luigi 21
Gracián, Baltasar 27
Gramsci, Antonio 7, 18, 29, 47
  Gramscian hegemony 30–1
  Letters from Prison 8
  and the Piazza Statuto 89
Gramscianism 80
Grass, Günter 145
Great Depression (1930s) 131
Greece, classical 111
guns 78
Gurland, H. J. 61
Gurvitch, Georges 24
Guttuso, Renato 97

Habermas, Jürgen 64
Hardt, Michael 1, 9

Harrington, James
  Oceana 219–20
Hegel, Georg 25, 30, 35, 48–9, 50–2, 53, 151
  on imagination 34
  Phenomenology of the Spirit 49, 53
Hegelianism 50–2, 56–7, 65
Hegesias, Cyrenaic philosopher 147
Heidegger, Martin 36, 50, 57
Hercules 111, 112
hermeneutics 46
heroin 168–9
Higelin, Jacques 189
Historic Compromise 138–8, 164, 165–6, 174–5, 193
historical materialism 29, 63
  and sociology 32
historicism 45–9, 50, 51, 52
Hobbes, Thomas 130, 131, 160, 207
Hofmannsthal, Hugo von 165
Hölderlin, Friedrich 36
Homer
  Iliad 40
  Odyssey 44
Horkheimer, Max 62
Horvat, Brankom *Political Economy of Socialism* 137
humanism 48–9, 50–1, 54, 57–9, 63, 142–3
Husserl, Edmund 50, 57, 58
Hyppolite, Jean 24, 25, 30, 49, 51

idealism 32
Il Gatto Selvaggio (*The Wild Cat*) 91
Il Manifesto newspaper 8
imagination 14, 25, 34–5
  and the transcendental 214–15
Israel 35–40, 42–3, 64, 66, 150
  War (1973) 146
Italian parliament
  Negri's election to the Chamber of Deputies 3, 9

Jackson, George 7
Jacobinism 201, 215
Jewish communism 36–8
Joyce, James 7, 21
  Finnegans Wake 186
  Ulysses 24
Judaism 65–6

July 1960 movement (Italy) 76–86
Jürgen (sociologist in Tübingen)
    60–4, 136

Kapitalistate (journal) 155
Kelsen, Hans
    Socialism and the State 137
Keynesian economic policies
    ending of 131, 185
Khrushchev, N. 71
Kirchheimer, Otto 61
Kissinger, Henry 129, 146
Kojève, Alexandre 52, 221–2
Kołakowski, Leszek 62
Korsch, Karl 133
Koselleck, Reinhart 32
Kosik, Karel 62
Krahl, Hans Jürgen 16
Kuron, Jacek 109

Labor of Dionysus (Hardt and Negri) 9
labour movement 24–33, 114–15, 135–8
    and the autonomy of workers 97–106
    and the events of 1968 125–6
    and historicism 47
    July 1960 movement 76–86
    and liberation 220–1
    and the Red Brigades 196
    in Sicily 25, 26–7
    in Turin 69–75, 87–96
    in the Veneto 67–9, 70, 71, 72, 73–4
Labriola, Antonio 83
Lama, Luigi 175
Lamartine, Alphonse de
    1848 119
Le Bon, Gustave 116
Lenin, V. I. 7, 133, 191
    State and Revolution 32, 83
Leninism 39–40, 47, 88, 137, 179
Leonardi, Claudio 72
Leopardi, Giacomo 7, 115, 164
Lévi-Strauss, Claude 14
Lévy, Bernard-Henri 203
liberation
    and the revolutionary workers' movement 220–1

Locke, John 47
Longo, Luigi 125
Lotta Continua 135
Lubac, Henri de 24–5
Lucretius 14, 38–9, 151
Luhmann, Niklas 32, 88, 155
Lukács, Georg 62, 133, 179
    Defence of History and Class Consciousness 6
L'Unità newspaper 8

Macchina tempo (Negri) 4
Machiavelli, N. 7, 191, 214
Machiavellianism 33
Magic Flute (Mozart) 56
Magritte, René 180
Malraux, André 191
    La Condition Humaine 194
Manifesto group 124
Mannheim, Karl 42
Mao Zedong 38
Marchesi, Concetto 38–9
Marcuse, Herbert 56–7, 115, 159
Maritain, Jacques 18
Marquard, Odo 160
Marx, Groucho 203
Marx, Karl 7, 29, 31, 39, 61, 65, 190–1, 214
    Capital 26, 73, 82, 93
    and Hegel 49, 50
Marxism 29–30, 31–2, 65, 151
    critique of 61–4
    and the July 1960 movement (Italy) 80–4, 85
    and Porto Marghera factories 73–4
    and Turin 71–2
    see also communism
Meinecke, Friedrich 46
memory 13–14, 221
Mendès-France, Pierre 24
Merleau-Ponty, Maurice 24, 49
Merton, Robert K. 32
Metropolitan Indians 2
Michel, K. M. 35
Milan
    Parco Lambro 162–72
    Piazza Fontana bombing 130
    youth movement 149–50
Mirafiori factories 88, 89, 94, 121
Mogrette, Robert 132

Index

Moldenhauer, E. 35
Momigliano, Arnaldo 72
Moro, Aldo 3, 5, 7–8, 193–202, 204, 219
Mounier, Emmanuel 18, 26
Mozart, Wolfgang 221
Multitude (Hardt and Negri) 1, 9
Murri, Romolo 26
music 142, 149–50
Musil, Robert 15, 30, 138

Naguib, Muhammad 36
Nazism 41
Nechayev, Sergey 194
Negri, Aldina (Negri's mother) 22, 118–19, 120, 121–2, 123, 125, 126, 127
Negri, Anna (Negri's daughter) 74
Negri, Enea (Negri's grandfather) 28
Nenni, Pietro 71, 77
Neoplatonism 46
Neumann, Johann von 61
New York 183–92
  blackout (1077) 188–9
Newman, Cardinal 47
newspapers 20
Nietzsche, Friedrich 152, 160, 191
Nights of Fire 178
1968 events 16, 118–28, 144
  in Italy 59
Nixon, Richard M. 129, 130, 140
Nora–Minc report 144
Notarnicola, Sante 90
nuclear weapons 215, 216

O'Connor, James 155
Offe, Claus 155
Ohnesorg, Benno 107
Olivetti factory, Ivrea 88
Opocher, Enrico 59–60
Oppenheimer, Robert 216
optimism of the intellect 215–16
optimism of the will 214–15
Origen 199
Ortega, José 143

Paci, Enzo 49, 51
Padovani (Padua University professor) 27–8

Padua 13, 21, 120, 121
  Socialist Party 25
Padua University 27, 38–9, 41
  activist committees 110–11
  Institute of the Philosophy of Law 59–60
  Institute for Political Science 2
Palmi Prison 3, 4, 107
Pandolfi, Filippo 181
Panella, Marco 9
Panzieri, Negri 6
Panzieri, Raniero 79–86, 87–8, 95–6
Parco Lambro, Milan 162–72
Pareto, Vilfredo 143
Paris 24–6, 189
parliamentary voting law (1953) 25
Parsons, Talcott 32, 46
Paul VI, Pope 195
Pavese, Cesare 8
PCI (Italian Communist Party) 2, 3, 8, 59, 205
  and the Historic Compromise 138, 174–5
  in Turin 69
Péguy, Charles 25–6
Peirce, C. S. 141
Pepys, Samuel 172
pessimism of the intellect 214–15
pessimism of the will 215–16, 218
Petrolchimico plant 20, 98, 107, 134–5, 217
  and worker autonomy 102–6
Piazza Fontana bombing 130
Piovesan (trade union official at Petrolchimico) 20
Pipeline, use of the term 1
Pius XII, Pope 24
Piven, Francis Fox 156
Plato
  Sophist 57
  Symposium 53, 62
Poland 218, 220
political responsibility 219–20
Ponto, Jürgen 193
Porto Marghera
  events of 1968 120, 121–2
  factory workers 73–4, 98–9, 108–10
  Petrolchimico plant 20, 98, 102–6, 107, 134–5, 139

Porto Marghera (*cont.*)
  Potere Operaio 98, 123, 124–5, 135
postmodernism 69, 127, 142, 171
Potere Operaio 98, 123, 124–5, 135, 139
poverty
  and communism 178
  identification with 16, 18, 19–20, 22–3
  and the labour movement 26, 27, 28
  and utopianism 40, 42
power
  and liberation 220–1
  and revolution 217
Prigogine, Ilya 88
prison movements 208
Propp, Vladimir 213
Proudhon, Pierre-Joseph 217
Proust, Marcel 54
PSI (Italian Socialist Party) 2, 8, 25, 29

Quaderni Rossi 82, 87, 89–90, 101

racism in Israel 43
Radical Party 9
Ranke, Leopold von 30, 46
rationality
  and the transcendental 215
Rauch, Georg von 144
Ravà, Adolfo 59–60
Reagan, Ronald 187
Rebibbia Prison 3, 4
Red Brigades 2
  kidnapping and murder of Moro 3, 5, 193–202, 204
  prison revolt 4–5, 208–10
Renaud 188
responsibility, political 219–20
revolution
  and power 217
Revolution Retrieved (Negri) 5
Rilke, Rainer Maria 15
Risorgimento 17
Rodano, Franco 138
Rosenzweig, Franz 131, 147
  on suicide 209–10
  The Star of Redemption 36, 57

Rossi, Pietro 46
Rovighi, Vanni 30
Rovigo Prison 3, 4, 204
Russell, Bertrand 37
Russia
  October Revolution (1917) 22, 39, 41, 42, 134, 217
  see also Soviet Union

Sartre, Jean-Paul 49
The Savage Anomaly (Negri) 4
Scheler, Max 42
Schelling, Friedrich 46
Schleyer, Hanns-Martin 193
Schopenhauer, A. 57, 129
Schulze, Harmut 210
Serres, Michel 88
Sertillanges, A. G. 47
Sicily, labour movement in 25, 26–7
Simmel, G. 19, 57
Smith, Adam
  Wealth of Nations 185
Snow, Edgar 120
the social question 17–18
socialism
  and the July 1960 workers' movement 77, 80–1, 85
  and the labour movement 114
  see also PSI (Italian Socialist Party)
Socialisme ou Barbarie 80
sociology 32
Socrates 83, 171
Solidarność 112, 218, 220
Sorokin, Pitirim 32
Southern Italy
  and the Veneto 17–18
Souzy (Egyptian communist in Israel) 36–40, 42, 43, 64, 65
Soviet Union 38, 39, 80, 219
  dissident movement 218
  and Hegelianism 51–2
  and historicism 45–6
  and radical humanism 50–1
  see also Russia
SPA-Stura 89
Spadolini, Giovanni 177
Spanish Civil War 41
Spengler, Oswald 143

Index

Spinoza, Baruch 4, 6, 7, 49–50, 153, 190, 191, 214
  Ethics 116, 159, 170, 207
Stalin, Joseph 27, 29
Stalinism 27–8, 31, 40, 47, 112, 217
  collapse of 62
  and the July 1960 workers' movement 83
  and the Red Brigades 196
Stephens, James
  The Crock of Gold 186
Sterling, Claire 183
strikes
  FIAT (1973) 156–61
  and the July 1960 workers' movement 77, 84
  Porto Marghera 108
  Vetrocoke plant 98
structuralism 51, 53, 101
Sturzo, Luigi 26
suicide 209–10
systems theory 154

Tambroni, Fernando 76, 77, 78
terrorism 174, 183, 193–202
  nihilism of 200–1
  and the state 197–8
  three Rs of 203
  see also Red Brigades
Thirty Years War 162
Thomas, Dylan 103
Thompson, E. P. 159, 177, 216
time
  and political responsibility 220
Togliatti, Palmiro 30–1, 33, 71, 77, 99
  death of 97–8
Tönnies, F. 19
Toynbee, Arnold J. 143
trade unions 47, 79
  and the events of 1968 120, 122, 123, 124
  leaders 27
  Porto Marghera 108
  and the Red Brigades 196
  in Turin 69, 72, 89, 90, 92, 94
  in the Veneto 68, 69, 73
  and worker autonomy 99, 103–4
Trani Prison 3, 204
  revolt 4–5, 107, 208–10

Trentin, Bruno 124
Trilogy of Critique (Negri) 7, 8
Trilogy of Difference (Negri) 7
Trilogy of Love (Negri) 7
Troelsch, Ernst 46
Tronti, Mario 35
  Operai e capitale 101
Turin
  Piazza Statuto revolt 87–96
  workers' movement 69–75, 84, 121

United States
  American sociology 32
  American workers 134
  and communism 173–4
  economic policies (1973) 129, 130, 140, 146
  New York 183–92
USSR *see* Soviet Union
utopianism 25, 34, 40–1, 42, 53, 151
  and the dialectic 44
  and historicism 45
  and worker autonomy 100

value theory 157–8
Vattimo, Giani 153
Velasquez, Diego
  Hilanderas del Prado 155
Veneto 14–15
  Catholic church 15–17, 19, 20–1, 30, 68
  dialect 104
  dry images of 14–15, 217
  emigration 68
  labour movement 67–9, 70, 71, 72, 73–4
  Rosolina 139
  and the South 17–18
  see also Porto Marghera
Venice University 110
Verantwortung (responsibility), philosophers of 113
Vesce, Emilio 5
Vetrocoke plant (Porto Marghera) 98
Vetter, Father (SJ) 29
Vietnam War 105
Virgil
  Aeneid 102

wages
    social wage concept 123, 175
    wage egalitarianism 120
    wage labour and the Piazza Statuto
        92–3
Wallenstein, Albrecht von 162
war, theory of 137
Weber, Max 19, 57
Weil, Simone 18, 21
Weiss, Peter 196
Whitman, Walt 191
witnessing 15–16, 21, 25, 200
Wittgenstein, Ludwig 57, 58
    Notebooks 153

work
    attitudes to 21
    refusal of 92–5, 149–50, 169,
        218–19
Workers' Autonomy (Autonomia
    Operaia) 2, 4
Workers' Power (Potop) 2, 3,
    4

youth movement 149–51
Yugoslavia (former)
    workers' councils 41

Zancanaro, Tono 21